LITERARY S
WELL-BEIN

Books by Ronald Schleifer

Modernist Poetics in China: Consumerist Economics and Chinese Literary Modernism (with Tiao Wang)

Literature and Medicine: A Practical and Pedagogical Guide (with Dr. Jerry Vannatta)

A Political Economy of Modernism: Literature, Post-Classical Economics, and the Lower Middle-Class

Pain and Suffering

The Chief Concern of Medicine: The Integration of the Medical Humanities and Narrative Knowledge into Medical Practices (with Dr. Jerry Vannatta)

Modernism and Popular Music

Intangible Materialism: The Body, Scientific Knowledge, and the Power of Language

Medicine and Humanistic Understanding: The Significance of Narrative in Medical Practice (with Dr. Jerry Vannatta and Sheila Crow)

A Postmodern Bible Reader (edited with David Jobling and Tina Pippin)

Modernism and Time: The Logic of Abundance in Literature, Science, and Culture, 1880–1930

Analogical Thinking: Post-Enlightenment Understanding in Language, Collaboration, and Interpretation

Culture and Cognition: The Boundaries of Literary and Scientific Inquiry (with Robert Con Davis and Nancy Mergler)

Criticism and Culture: The Role of Critique in Modern Literary Theory (with Robert Con Davis)

Contemporary Literary Criticism: Literary and Cultural Studies (edited with Robert Con Davis)

Rhetoric and Death: The Language of Modernism and Postmodern Discourse Theory

A, J. Greimas and the Nature of Meaning: Linguistics, Semiotics, and Discourse Theory

Rhetoric and Form: Deconstruction at Yale (edited with Robert Con Davis)

Kierkegaard and Literature: Irony, Repetition, and Criticism (edited with Robert Markley)

The Genres of the Irish Literary Revival (edited by Ronald Schleifer)

LITERARY STUDIES AND WELL-BEING

STRUCTURES OF EXPERIENCE IN THE WORLDLY WORK OF LITERATURE AND HEALTHCARE

Ronald Schleifer

BLOOMSBURY ACADEMIC
LONDON • NEW YORK • OXFORD • NEW DELHI • SYDNEY

BLOOMSBURY ACADEMIC
Bloomsbury Publishing Plc
50 Bedford Square, London, WC1B 3DP, UK
1385 Broadway, New York, NY 10018, USA
29 Earlsfort Terrace, Dublin 2, Ireland

BLOOMSBURY, BLOOMSBURY ACADEMIC and the Diana logo
are trademarks of Bloomsbury Publishing Plc

First published in Great Britain 2023

Cover design by Gita Kowlessur
Cover image: *Starburst Sunshine*, origami tessellation, produced by Cyrus Schleifer

Open access was funded by the University of Oklahoma.

Bloomsbury Publishing Plc does not have any control over, or responsibility for,
any third-party websites referred to or in this book. All internet addresses
given in this book were correct at the time of going to press. The author and
publisher regret any inconvenience caused if addresses have changed or sites
have ceased to exist, but can accept no responsibility for any such changes.

A catalogue record for this book is available from the British Library.

A catalog record for this book is available from the Library of Congress.

ISBN: HB: 978-1-3503-3568-4
        PB: 978-1-3503-3567-7
        ePDF: 978-1-3503-3569-1
        eBook: 978-1-3503-3570-7

Typeset by Integra Software Services Pvt. Ltd.
Printed and bound in Great Britain

To find out more about our authors and books visit www.bloomsbury.com
and sign up for our newsletters.

For all my teachers

including

My parents, my grandparents, my uncle George, my brother Robert, my second-grade teacher Mrs. Fairchild (PS 40, NYC), my junior high school teacher Mr. Austin (PS 104), my high school English teacher Mr. Marks (Stuyvesant High School), my first-year humanities college teacher Karen Klein (Brandeis University), my graduate school teachers Earl Wasserman, Hillis Miller, Hugh Kenner, Avrom Fleishman (Johns Hopkins University), my wife Nancy Mergler, my physician teachers Jerry Vannatta (internal medicine, OU Health Sciences), Mark Allee (internal medicine), Casey Hester (pediatrics), Eddie LeClaire (gynecology), Aneesh Pakala (cardiology), and Rita Charon (internal medicine, Columbia University College of Surgeons and Physicians), Abraham Verghese (internal medicine, Stanford University College of Medicine), John Stone (cardiology, Emory University School of Medicine), my editors Ray Ryan (Cambridge University Press), Doug Armato (University of Minnesota Press), Thomas Dwyer (University of Michigan Press), Allie Troyanos (Palgrave Macmillan), Ben Doyle (Bloomsbury), and my many many students.

You will hardly know who I am or what I mean,
But I shall be good health to you nevertheless,
And filter and fibre your blood.

– Walt Whitman, *Song of Myself*

CONTENTS

Acknowledgments   x

1   Thesis and Contexts: The Real and the Construed; or,
    the Double-Take of Literature   1

2   Introduction: On the Discipline of Literary Studies   41

3   Disciplined Knowledge and the Experience of Meaning   65

4   The Nature of Value and the Nature of Language   117

5   The Discipline of Death: Primary Emotions, Aesthetics,
    and the Neurological Basis of Genre   155

6   Disciplined Vicarious Experience: Action and Ethics in
    Literary Studies   193

Works Cited   251
Index   259

ACKNOWLEDGMENTS

Besides the lifetime of teachers to whom I dedicate this book, there are many others from whom this book has benefited and many institutions, the support from which has made this book possible. First of all, I want to thank Russell Reising for reading through a later version of this book as a whole and offering useful suggestions and clarifications throughout that helped me do my best work. In addition, Patricia Waugh read through the whole of my work more than once, and her sympathetic intelligence has helped me more carefully articulate my argument. Parts were read by David Levy and Sotirios Barber, who also made my argument and writing better. In addition, in Chapter 3 I mention the patient help I received from Peter Juul Nielsen in allowing me to more fully understand the Danish vocabulary in Louis Hjelmslev's *Prolegomena to a Theory of Language*. And long conversations with James Zeigler—my long-time friend and now editor of *Genre*—Joshua Nelson, Justin Sider, Rilla Askew, Paul Austin, Tiao Wang, Courtney Jacobs, James Hawthorne, Bridget Parmenter, Regina Martin, Robert Con Davis-Undiano, and Stephen Regan inform much of what follows. Boris Vejdovsky kindly invited me to develop the lecture that became Chapter 5; and a shorter version of that lecture "Death, Literary Form, and Affective Comprehension: Primary Emotions and the Neurological Basis of Genre," appeared in *The Routledge Companion to Death and Literature*, ed. Neil Murphy, Daniel Jernigan, and Michelle Wang (New York: Routledge, 2021), pp. 140–53. Finally, in the Introduction (Chapter 2) I take up several pages from my essay "The Aesthetics of Pain: Semiotics and Affective Comprehension in Music, Literature, and Sensate Experience," *Configurations* 26 (2018): 471–91. But the whole of this book warrants particular thanks as well. The anonymous readers for Bloomsbury reinforced my sense that one of the finest aspects of our profession is the care and attention that is taken for the work of strangers. My editor at Bloomsbury, Ben Doyle, made it all happen. Finally, I gratefully acknowledge financial support provided by the Office of the Vice President for Research and Partnerships, the Office of the Provost, the University Libraries, and the Dodge Family College of Arts and Sciences, University of Oklahoma. In addition, I want to thank the Dean of Arts and Sciences,

David Wrobel, and Chair of English, Roxanne Mountford, for helping me rearrange my pandemic schedule that allowed me time to focus on this book. At the end of Chapter 2 (pp. 63–4), I add further acknowledgments for many friends in China, whose advice and welcoming engagements in 2020 and over many years occasioned this book altogether.

Finally, the cover image of *Literary Studies and Well-Being* is an origami tessellation, "Starburst Sunshine," produced by Cyrus Schleifer based upon design instructions for the "Childhood Evolved" tessellation in *Origami Tessellations for Everyone* by Ilan Garibi (Self Publishing [December 12, 2018]; available on Amazon) (photographed by Joshua Nelson). The author gratefully acknowledges permission to use this image by its producer, designer, and photographer. The pattern and precision of delicately folded paper, through which sunshine gleams—a structure of experience—create a promise of comfort, well-being, and Walt Whitman's "good health" in a version of the materialist and intergenerational aesthetics described throughout this book. An image in a poem by Derek Mahon discussed at the end of Chapter 5—"Everything Is Going to Be All Right"—figures well-being in terms of "a riot of sunshine."

CHAPTER 1
THESIS AND CONTEXTS: THE REAL AND THE CONSTRUED; OR, THE DOUBLE-TAKE OF LITERATURE

Did she put on his knowledge with his power
Before the indifferent beak could let her drop?

—Yeats, "Leda and the Swan"

I have chosen to call this book *Literary Studies and Well-Being* because "well-being" is a concept and a word that brings together imagined fulfillments of life experiences and also a more mundane sense of simple good health; it's a term that joins together what I am calling the "worldly work" of literature and healthcare. A good part of the sense of *well-being* I pursue in this book is encompassed by Aristotle in his ancient deployment of the Greek notion of *eudaimonia*. *Eudaimonia* is usually translated into English as "happiness," but it can, as Ian Johnson argues, plausibly be translated as the flowering forth or realization of human potential, which he explicitly describes as human "well being" or "living well." The English rendering of *eudaimonia* as "happiness," he writes,

> causes some difficulties if we do not remind ourselves that by the term Aristotle means something much wider than the word happiness might suggest to us. *Eudaimonia* carries the notion of objective success, the proper conditions of a person's life, what we might more properly call "well being" or "living well." Thus, *eudaimonia* includes a sense of material, psychological, and physical well being over time, for the fully happy life will include success for oneself, for one's immediate family, and for one's descendants. This notion links the *Ethics* directly with the Greek traditions, especially the *Iliad*, in which the happiness of life includes a sense of posthumous fame and the success of one's children as vital components. We may better get a sense of what

> Aristotle means by the term if we take the advice of one interpreter
> and see *eudaimonia* as the answer to the question "What sort of a life
> would we most wish for our children?"
>
> (cited in Schleifer and Vannatta *Chief Concern* 62–3)

This unpacking of the meaning of *eudaimonia*—it is an example of philological philosophy I describe throughout this book—is of great importance because it allows me to articulate the worldly work of both literature and healthcare in relation to one another. Both literature and healthcare, I argue here, promote "living well" insofar as they promote what the novelist Stendhal describes, in defining aesthetic beauty, as "the promise of happiness" (66). This is also the promise Derek Mahon articulates in a wonderful hospital poem I discuss at the end of Chapter 5, that "everything is going to be all right" (Mahon 240).

One of the most striking features of the American *Declaration of Independence* is the phrase "the pursuit of Happiness." Many historians—but not all—suggest that Thomas Jefferson and then The Committee of Five, who wrote and edited the *Declaration*, were influenced by John Locke's late seventeenth-century writings about civil life. Thus, in *A Letter Concerning Toleration*, Locke describes "civil interest" as "life, liberty, health, and indolency of body; and the possession of outward things" (*Letter* 26); and in the *Essay Concerning Human Understanding* he asserts that "the highest perfection of intellectual nature lies in the careful and constant pursuit of true and solid happiness" (*Essay* 2.21.51). I should note, as I do at the end of this book discussing the concept of "philosophical physician," that Locke himself was a physician. I also suggest that Jefferson's term *Happiness* is related to Aristotle's notion of *eudaimonia*. And I further suggest the idea, most likely outside Jefferson's understanding, that a strong working definition of *Happiness* is related to the even more ancient Chinese concept *le* (乐), a word-concept carrying several different meanings in Chinese, including "the feeling of joy, happiness, optimism and well-being … [so that] it can describe the melody of music, the sound in harmony. Moreover," as Defeng Yang and Zhou Han note, "the original meaning of 'Le' in ancient times, is basically the well-being gained when recovering from illness and when finally healing" (82). I begin, then, by "unpacking" Aristotle's notion of *eudaimonia*—along with Jefferson's term *Happiness*—to make clear my contention in *Literary Studies and Well-Being* that part of the salutary work of literature in general is to create Stendhal's "promise of happiness" (66) in his larger description of the nature of beauty. Such "work" makes clear, I believe, how much our understanding of literature can benefit from thinking of literature in relation to what I call throughout this book the work—the "worldly work"—of healthcare: its pursuits of healing, well-being, and reflective everyday care that contribute to the betterment of all our lives. In my argument I contend that the pursuit of *eudaimonia* contributes to the worldly work of literary studies as well.

Let me spell this out in more historical terms—in a "double-take," so to speak, on the purposes of this book as a whole. During the past twenty years, much admirable work in the "health humanities" has focused upon what studies of literature contribute to the understandings and the practical work—the "worldly work"—of healthcare. Such a project aims at developing healthcare practitioners who bring greater care to those who come to them ailing or in fear or faced with terrible suffering. The overall goal of *Literary Studies and Well-Being* turns this inside out by noting the intergenerational caretaking of healthcare in a manner which allows us to comprehend the nature and discipline of literary studies in new ways. The literary arts represent and provoke experiences of understanding and emotion—what I call "the experience of meaning"—and in this study I examine how the practical pursuit of well-being in healthcare reveals purposes at the core of our engagements with and understanding of literature itself: its deployment of aesthetic experiences to shape action in the world, its ability to clarify "habits of thought" that define our cultural lives (structures of experience beyond individualist psychology), its ability to occasion moral education—and perhaps most of all its capacity to articulate and deepen shared senses of human well-being.

The Thesis in Short

In pursuit of this end, *Literary Studies in Well-Being: Structures of Experience in the Worldly Work of Literature and Healthcare* examines the discipline of literary studies by defining and justifying its object of study, namely "literature"; by articulating the goals and purposes of its study; and by setting forth the methods the discipline has developed in order to achieve those goals and purposes. It defines "literature" as verbal and narrative discourses, which present and provoke "experience," and it spends some time examining the nature of "experience," particularly in relation to the matters-of-fact studied by the physical and social sciences (see Exhibit 1.1).

Exhibit 1.1: The Experience of Meaning

When I contend that literature provokes as well as presents "experience," I am agreeing with Ludwig Wittgenstein's observation, examined in Chapter 4, that we *experience* as well as (cognitively) comprehend meaningfulness and that the experience of meaning is characterized by the feeling or "force" of understanding such as the feeling we have when we figure something out or, perhaps more vividly as a feeling, the sense of bewilderment we experience when we cannot figure something out. Michael Clune describes one understanding of literary art as "not the transmission of experience but the communication of meaning," which gives "voice to truth" (45). Such an understanding, which he traces in relation to the work of Henri Bergson, assumes that "the infiltration of our experience by language pollutes that experience" (45). Clune also suggests an alternative to this stark understanding of literature as "communication of truth," namely the understanding of literary art as involved with the experience of readers rather than with the renown/knowledge of authors. This is Wittgenstein's "experience of meaning," which is close to what Clune describes as "the desire to preserve and intensify sensation" as opposed to "the desire to preserve a person's name and image." The two conceptions of literature Clune sets forth characterize the opposition—or the "double-take"—between Classicism and Romanticism (16). This is the "double-take" of knowledge and power in language and discourse I describe in this chapter. (It is also the "double-take of Heisenberg's uncertainty principle [see Schleifer *Modernism and Time*, Ch. 5 "Analogy and Example" which maps Heisenberg's uncertainty principle in relation to the "coupling" of propositional and performative language in J. L. Austin's speech–act theory.] For a fascinating unfolding of Heisenberg's principle, see Benjamín Labatut's description of "Heisenberg's discovery" [161]: namely, that "certain properties of a quantum object, such as its position and quantity of motion, were coupled, and the relationship between them evinced strange properties. The more precisely the one was identified, the more uncertain the other became" [159]. Labatut calls his book "a work of fiction based on real events" [190]. I might call the present chapter—and the present complex book of chapters and chapter-lectures—the "gathering" of many-voiced apprehensions of literature, which combines fiction and reality, construed value and the reality of knowledge.) Moreover, when Clune describes "semantic richness" (in relation to Nabokov) as "the fact that in it we find new meanings, and new relations between old meanings" (69)—and when, more forcefully, he argues that "what science misses, and what literature supplies, is a way of understanding the special role of experience" (80)—he is suggesting that one aspect of "the special role" that literature fills is to emphasize the "experience of meaning," which Wittgenstein apprehends in language more generally. For further elaboration of the experience of meaning, see Chapter 3 and Exhibit 3.7: Religious Experience.

The goal and purpose of literary studies—like the goals and purposes of intellectual disciplines more generally—are to focus on its object of study, "literature," in order to allow us to engage with and comprehend more fully the complex set of features and relationships its object of study entails. Disciplines in general pursue this goal: to develop a vocabulary, particular procedures, and strategies of attendance, which encounter—and perhaps even define—particular features of the world on a particular level of engagement. Finally, *Literary Studies and Well-Being* contends—here is the thesis in short—that such purposeful engagements with literature, particularly in relation to the human activities of caretaking pursued in healthcare and in the health humanities, allow us to see more fully structures of experience by means of a "double-take" of engagements provoked by verbal and narrative discourses. Such structures of experience, I contend, govern the sense of meaningful value that inhabits much—if not all—of human experience altogether, and certainly the human project of caretaking. The term *meaningful value*, I suggest in a kind of philological unpacking I talk about in a moment, is an instance of saying the same thing twice in a manner that calls upon a double-take of language: to be meaningful *is* to be valuable. (See Exhibit 1.2.)

Exhibit 1.2: The Worldly Work of Literature and Healthcare

The special vantage of analyzing the discipline of literary studies in this book is the engagement with—really the particular starting point from—the health humanities. The taking up of the practical work of healthcare—which involves the cure, care, and compassion for human suffering—allows one to isolate the features of "literature" in the context of the thorough-going materialism of what Aristotle described as "practical wisdom" or *phronesis*. In his history of the term "experience"—which offers an extended version of the philological philosophy discussed later in Chapter 1—Martin Jay explicitly understands the "sedimented meanings" of what Aristotle defines as *phronesis* to include "experience" (12, 15–16). The work of philology, I note, is to "unpack" such semantic sedimentation. Towards the end of his study, Jay examines Michel Foucault's inspiration occasioned by "non-philosophers in the traditional sense: 'What struck me and fascinated me about them,' Foucault asserts, 'is the fact that [such non-traditional philosophers] didn't have the problem of constructing systems, but of having direct, personal experiences'" (cited in Jay 391). In fact, *Literary Studies and Well-Being* aims to comprehend together the work of literature and healthcare under a category with which I end this book, that of the "philosophical physician"—who inhabits, actually or vicariously, a disciplinary position between a strict empiricism and a self-contained idealism. Such a disciplinary position is found in practical literary studies and worldly, materialist philosophy. These disciplines—literary studies, healthcare, even "materialist" philosophy (which I describe as "philological philosophy")—are, as Joel Whitebook notes, "simultaneously scientific and philosophical .... They [are] philosophical in that they [reject] scientism—that is, the claim that empirical science exhausts the domain of legitimate knowledge .... And they [are] scientific in that they [reject] philosophy's pretensions at self-sufficiency" (100). These disciplines do so, as I note in my conclusion—but also throughout this book as a whole—in pursuit of the worldly work of human well-being.

The Exposition in Short

As is already noticeable, the exposition of *Literary Studies and Well-Being* is somewhat complex: it offers an argument punctuated by "exhibits" and, after this "thesis" chapter and an introductory chapter, a series of chapter-lectures—also punctuated by exhibits—based upon a lecture series presented to Chinese scholars who teach English language and literature to Chinese engineering students at the Harbin Institute of Technology. In this way, the style of this book—like the explicit work of healthcare and, I argue, our implicit engagements with literature—is actively collaborative and actively improvised. What I have learned in many years of engaging people committed to careers in healthcare with the literary humanities—of learning from people pursuing the practical work of health and well-being even as I share with them the well-being promoted by literary studies—is that the complexity of different frameworks and agendas is, very often, the starting situation of serious healthcare problems and problems of well-being more generally: patients and healthcare workers aren't quite sure what is going on or what is relevant or irrelevant in the narratives they encounter and re-narrate. In short, in serious or complex medical situations often it is not clear whether particular instances of information are "distractions" from a proper focus on the matter at hand or matters that require the "active absorption" of what I am describing as the "double-take" demanded by literature as well as healthcare in order to grasp a fuller understanding of what is going on. This, as we shall see, is the problem of the necessary "double-take" of literature: the "agendas" of literature as the articulation and shaping of the mores of a particular cultural moment and its simultaneous—and seeming contradictory—provocation of aesthetic "experience"; its knowledge and its power; its confusion of categories of fact and fiction.

Both healthcare and literature, moreover, call upon and emphasize the "practical wisdom" of *phronesis*, which aims to discover what, Martha Nussbaum argues, "is to count as the end" of action (61, n15). Thus, in Chapter 6 I note that the goal of *phronesis* is to be able to discern what *counts* as the "ends" or goals that practical wisdom pursues such that a full awareness of the work of practical wisdom is precisely what the study of literature adds to the learning and practices of healthcare even as the worldly practical results of healthcare widen our sense of the "work" of literature. That is, practical procedures do not simply find the best strategies to pursue the end of an action by some form of instrumental reason, but rather "entwine" or "entangle" wisdom and worldliness, knowledge and power. Thus, in short the complicated and not-altogether linear exposition of *Literary Studies and Well-Being* aims to promote—as literature does and the practical reasoning of healthcare often requires—the "active absorption" of experience by replacing or supplementing the authority of argument with the experience of engagement. Like the close reading of literary texts, it aims at widening experience along with accumulating knowledge: it *entangles* in its very exposition, so to speak, construed value and the reality of knowledge.

To accomplish this, *Literary Studies and Well-Being* pursues an exposition that mimics a particular *experiential fact*, namely the manner in which, as Dr. Rita Charon and Maura Spiegel argue,

> narratives that emerge from suffering differ from those born elsewhere .... Not restricted to the linear, the orderly, the emplotted, or the clean, these narratives that come from the ill contain unruly fragments, silences, bodily processes rendered in code[, which include] ... shameful, painful, prelingual limitations, absences, breath-taking fears.
>
> (vi)

Needless to say, I am not suggesting that the complicated exposition of *Literary Studies and Well-Being* is a discourse of illness. Rather, the patient-provider interchange in the clinic participates in the same organizational structure of the "double-take of literature" I am describing in this chapter: at once it encourages the informed *pronouncement* of the healthcare professional (e.g., "everything is going to be all right: you simply have a low-hydration headache") and at the same time it encourages a worldly ongoing *conversation* revolving around sharing the values that both the patient and the provider bring to the clinic. In a similar fashion—which takes its place among the many similitudes, analogies, homologies, etc. which this book focuses upon and pursues—literature both offers and provokes the "communication of meaning" and "the transmission of experience" Clune mentions (45): experience to be understood and undergone, the real and the construed. Thus, later in this chapter, when I discuss the lecture format of this book—which I designate by the odd phrase *lectures-book* and also set forth the further oddity of referring to its last four chapters as *chapter-lectures*—it is my hope that these somewhat awkward gestures of defamiliarization, like the *punctum* Roland Barthes experiences in relation to photographs discussed (along with defamiliarization) in Chapter 5, remind readers of the idea/experience of double-take and, perhaps more importantly, what I am calling the *experiential fact* of discourse in the clinic and in literature.

Such an *experiential fact*, like the phenomenal experience Charon and Spiegel describe as they characterize the language of the clinic, can be understood to be "artefactual." In analyzing the projects of Thomas Kuhn and Bruno Latour, Patricia Waugh argues that

> scientific facts are artefacts: but that does not mean they are fictions. When Latour talks of ["building … arenas and new spaces, shelters 'in which to gather,'"] it sounds hospitable and welcoming, … but he is actually calling for more understanding across the humanities and sciences. For the assemblage is not simply a 'gathering' in the sense of a hospitable coming together of groups of people, it is a concept resonant with the new systems of thinking in the biological environmental and molecular sciences that model complex systems which are entangled, unpredictable at different scalar levels, emergent and uncertain.
>
> (108)

Latour's "gatherings" are worldly: one such gathering, I am arguing, takes place in the clinic; another in our engagements with literary texts. In this, I am suggesting that the discourses of illness can help us understand the discipline of literary studies in an experiential rediscovery of "things as we know them to be, yet reordered and redescribed, shimmering in a transformed light" (Felski 102). That is, my focus on vicarious experience throughout this book and these lectures—throughout this *lectures-book*—examines how literary texts situate us alternatively inside and outside experience itself; how they situate us alternatively in both the power and knowledge of experience itself, in the double-take I am describing here. The pursuit of such an examination, I believe, needs to call upon experience in its very exposition—the "new systems of thinking" Waugh describes—in the manner in which the face-to-face (or imagined) collaborative interchange of lectures supplements the disciplined "constructed systems" (to quote Foucault [cited in Jay 391]), which the systematic exposition of "traditional" philosophical thinking sets forth. (For a more extended discussions of the book's exposition—which follows Martin Jay's understanding how Montaigne's essay "On Experience" "performatively instantiates what it substantively argues" [25]—see Exhibit 1.9: Montaigne's Many-Voiced Style and the section on the "discipline" of improvisation in Chapter 3, which examines Stanley Cavell's analysis of how "a passionate utterance is an invitation to improvisation in the disorders of desire" [185]; also, in a more thematic vein touching on the overall purport of the book as a whole, see Exhibit 5.6: A Well-Being Theory of Value.) In Chapter 3, in analyzing the discipline of improvisation, I note that Stanley Cavell argues that the transformations of lectures into books in Austin's *How to Do Things with Words* and Aristotle's texts themselves entail the disciplined attention to the engagements of interlocutors and to particular discursive situations (perlocutionary persuasion embedded in what he calls "the scene of instruction" [204]); in this, Cavell might be suggesting some of the improvised expository strategies that a "lectures-book," such as *Literary Studies and Well-Being*, might pursue (see Exhibit 1.3).

Exhibit 1.3: Exhibitive Form

As I mention in a moment, the subtitle of this book was inspired by Raymond Williams's articulation of "structures of feeling" in 1977, when he notes that "structures of experience" might have been a "better and wider" description of the phenomena he is trying to articulate (132). Still, half a dozen years before Williams discusses "structures of feeling," the philosopher Richard Kuhns published a book entitled *Structures of Experience*. In that book he contrasts the discursive practices of philosophy and literature—he focuses, in part, on classical tragedy—and offers a more-or-less metaphorical description of the kind of exposition I set forth in this book in relation to the "dramatic" situation—the *performance*—of a series of lectures. "Drama," he writes, "is philosophical in the sense that it reveals a truth in the totality of its exhibitive form, not in the individual statements which make it up. It matters not that poets may be dreamers and 'possessed' as Plato depicts them …. But [drama] is, if it has any merit, poetical, and poetry is a different mode of statement from history and from philosophy. It is, however, like philosophy in that it aims at general statements of a theoretical kind, even though it is unlike philosophy in rejecting argument. But if it lacks argument, what is its structure?" (7–8). Kuhns answers his question by thinking of Artistotle (and the *Poetics*): "Aristotle's answer," he avers, "is that [drama] has a motion and a progress of its own peculiar to itself: the progress of what I shall call *affective rhythm*" (8). It seems to me that the "affective rhythm" Kuhns describes might be better set forth as a strategy of defamiliarization described by the Russian Formalists (see Chapters 4 and 6 below). In any case, it is my argument here that this lectures-book pursues the counterpoint and harmonies of the affective rhythm of a many-voiced exposition.

The Argument

Literary Studies and Well-Being grows out of a series of lectures presented in Harbin China in 2020. But those lectures themselves grow out of the author's long-time practical work in the health humanities teaching and writing with people trained in the biomedical sciences. My colleagues had been accustomed to understand the humanities as not susceptible to the discipline of the exact and generalizing treatment pursued by the nomological ("law-like") sciences such as mathematical physics and chemistry and by the retrospective and often statistical discipline of the social sciences. Such sciences focus on facts and events that are "commensurable," which describes phenomena that allow investigators to conceive of similar facts and events to be identical, at least for purposes of analysis. In the "Polemical Introduction" to *Anatomy of Criticism*, which calls for a disciplined program for literary studies—an essay that first appeared entitled "The Function of Criticism at the Present Time," a title he borrowed from Matthew Arnold—Northrop Frye describes how physics transformed itself when, instead of "taking the immediate sensations of experience, classified as hot, cold, moist, and dry, as fundamental principles," it discovered that "its real function was to explain what heat and moisture were" (44).

The issue of the "commensurability" and "incommensurability" of worldly phenomena is of central importance in understanding the nature of disciplinary knowledge. The abstract commensurability of different phenomena—which allows for quantified mathematical models of phenomena—claims to focus on what is "real" about the world as opposed to the manner in which human beings interact with or construe the world. In this opposition set forth by nomological or "positive" science, the interactions of human "experience"—and human "meanings" connected with experience—are taken to be "constructed" on the bases of changing (and ephemeral) social systems of meaning rather a solid pre-existing "reality" independent of human meanings. Such "constructed" engaged understanding, many have argued, somehow "denies" reality. In this, however, "reality" is understood to be curiously beyond worldly experience, such as the immediate sensations of hot, cold, moist, and dry.

Still, the strategy of "constructed" understanding might better be understood as the practical reasoning of inferential understanding—what philosophers call "inference to the best explanation"—in making sense of the world, and particularly it might be better understood, as I note in Chapter 3, in relation to the semiotic category of *purport*. (I should point out that we *construe* the purport of statements, which might be described as their "insinuations." The term *purport*, articulated by the linguist Louis Hjelmslev, is, I suggest in Exhibit 3.4: Hjelmslev's Purport, closely related the Charles Sanders Peirce's semiotic notion of "interpretant.") Francis Steen, whose work I discuss in Chapters 3 and 5, describes such inferential understanding as the activity in social creatures under the category of *construal*: his example is the playfights of rhesus monkeys, in which older monkeys engage with younger monkeys in play designed to teach the younger cohort what to expect in real combat, to create inferences about the world. As we will see, anthropologists call such playing acts of "keying" experience, which is to say acts of marking "features" in experience as worthy of attention for actual members of a cohort, which Steen describes as adaptive intergenerational lessons design to teach younger members of a social cohort how to "construe" the future. Such "keyings"—and literature itself, in my argument—constitute *the scene of instruction*.

It is my contention that the term "construe" is better than "social construction" because it describes species activities whose purpose is to make living (and survival) easier in a practical worldly fashion rather than engaging in arguments about the metaphysical or ontological "nature" of reality itself. It is also my contention throughout this book that *construing* present and future engagements with the world—engagements of feeling and affect as well as understanding—is the work of literature and the goal of the discipline of literary studies. It is a contention borne of my engagements with intergeneration caring in the work of healthcare. Thus, when a scholar like Joseph North in his thoughtful and passionate history of literary criticism in the twentieth century somewhat casually dismisses the "therapeutic" work of the health humanities and more specifically the "directly therapeutic ... field of 'narrative medicine'" (188) as simply "marginal" to literary studies, he couldn't be more wrong. The intergenerational caring of healthcare is positioned to teach us—to allow us to *construe*—the worldly work of literature and the discipline of literary studies.

The Scene of Instruction. Such intergenerational caring constitutes the scene of instruction I mentioned a moment ago. In his essay "The Wittgensteinian Event," Stanley Cavell meditates on intergenerational caring when he describes "the scene and consequences of inheritance and instruction and fascination [the child observing his elders]" (202: Cavell's bracketed emendation), and he goes on to say "how the child is imagined to be treated is a fateful matter, bearing, for example, on nothing less than Wittgenstein's response to skepticism" (203). He sums up these observations as "the scene of instruction," which takes its place along with

Charles Taylor's "dos and don'ts[—the cultural 'pattern' for behavior and belief—]that people accept and mutually enforce, without there being (yet) an explicit rationale. And as children, we learn some of the most fundamental patterns at first just as such" (271; see Exhibit 1.12: A Note on "Habits of Thought"). Cavell ends his discussion of instruction with an observation that might apply to North's political history of literary criticism: in "emphasizing society's resemblance to a prison rather than to a schoolroom, [philosophical thinking] may push too hard to *fix* the power between generations" (207). In addition, in his analysis of Wittgenstein Cavell addresses North's denigration of therapy. "Has not philosophy itself, at least since Plato, claimed for itself the task of therapy, or say liberation from bonds of illusion, superstition, bewitchment, fanaticism, self-distortion? ... I hope I have never denied that the process of acquiring genuine knowledge may itself be therapeutic" (211).

Commensurability and "Reality." Errol Morris offers a detailed—and often a wonderfully fascinating—account of the debate between "commensurability" and "constructedness" in *The Ashtray (Or the Man Who Denied Reality)* (especially Ch. 5). Morris's text is a sustained critique of Thomas Kuhn's notion of "paradigms" insofar as "Kuhn's defence of science as a *paradeigmatic* process fundamentally weakened science's claims to epistemological distinctiveness and authority" (Waugh 94). (Morris's title comes from the fact that when he was a student, in a moment of pique Professor Kuhn hurled a cut-glass ashtray at him.) This concept of "paradigm" in Kuhn governs what can be taken to be or construed as "reality" within a particular scientific community; Morris associates it with Ludwig Wittgenstein's notion of "forms of life" or "life forms" (*Lebensform*) (92–4). In *Literary Studies and Well-Being* I take up the term of Thorstein Veblen (borrowed from his teacher Charles Sanders Peirce), "habits of thought" and, in passing, a term of Owen Flanagan, "space of meaning" to describe something like this conception of Kuhn's notion of "paradigm." (Joseph North nicely sets forth a description of "aesthetics," a description which unpacks Veblen's and Peirce's notion, in his gloss of Lauren Berlant's "tracking affect" in literary studies: Berlant's "aesthetics," he argues, is "the structured/creative ... and heuristic ... activity by which subjects encounter and remake elements of their experience as sources of value, using the common experiential resources of the culture at large" [177; see Berlant *Cruel* 15–16].) I say habits of thought are "something like" this notion of Kuhn's "paradigm" because Morris argues quite vociferously that Kuhn is an "antirealist," by which he means that Kuhn is a full-blown "social constructionist," who believes that all accounts of the "real" world are constructed from systems of meaning rather than being discoveries of or encounters with what exists—facts and events—separate from systems of meaning (see Exhibit 1.4). I contend, at the end of this chapter, that Veblen's/ Peirce's notion of "habits of thought" does not present itself as an alternative to realism but rather as a particular species of material realism (see Exhibit 1.12: A Note on "Habits of Thought" for a discussion of this contention).

Exhibit 1.4: Scientific Realism

Here is Morris's account of the "real" world separate from systems— and "habits"—of meaning. "Arithmetical operations have an objective existence. As such, the concept of addition stands apart from us (and our minds), much as does the Andromeda galaxy. Ask yourself, What was the concept of addition in Cambrian times—600 million years ago? I'm not asking, What would a trilobite think about addition? Or about the *Lebensform* [Wittgenstein's "life form"] of trilobites 'scuttling across silent seas.' The question has nothing to do with their biology or ours. Doesn't the concept of addition precede *us*? And *them*? Is *life* needed for addition? Or does addition stand apart from all living things?" (100–1). This is a version of "positive science" and the *Wikipedia* definition of "fact," with which I begin Chapter 4. Morris also emphasizes the *discoveries* of science: "in a world inhabited by somewhat sentient creatures, like ourselves, it is likely that someone (or something) would eventually discover [DNA]. Why? Because it exists. It is a discovery, *not an invention*. A discovery, *not a social construction*. The sharp distinction between *created* and *discovered* is crucial to an understanding of science, a distinction that Kuhn muddies" (146).

Note, however, in his exposition Morris quotes (or slightly misquotes) a line from T. S. Eliot's "The Love Song of J. Alfred Prufrock": "I should have been a pair of ragged claws / Scuttling across the floors of silent seas." The *allusiveness* of reality—or at least the allusiveness of the experience of reality—complicates Morris's assertion that "the concept of addition stands apart from us," and, by implication, that such "natural" or "brute" facts are the foundation upon which the "secondary" disciplines of the humanities are based.

That is, the possible allusiveness of meaning, which suggests the existence of families of meaning (see Wittgenstein §77) rather than the absolute commensurability of "facts" that transcend their historical occurrences, is always a possible aspect of our experience of the world. As the linguist Emile Benveniste argues in distinguishing the human sciences from the natural sciences, "phenomena belonging to the interhuman milieu ... have the characteristic that they can never be taken as simple data or defined in the order of their own nature but must always be understood as double from the fact that they are connected to something else, wherever their 'referent' may be. A fact of culture is such only insofar as it refers to something else" (38–9). Rather than the *identity* of commensurability, then, the always-possible *similarity* of allusion—or *analogy* or *evolutionary homology*, to mention terms that recur in this book—isolates a different object and level of analysis and explanation in the discipline of literary studies, the "double-take" of experience I describe here in Chapter 1. To put it succinctly, there is not a hierarchy of intellectual disciplines, in which, as Morris suggests, somehow "the concept of addition" is more basic and more "real" than semantic families of meaning because it is "separate" from human experience: for Morris addition is not an "invention" but an existing organizing principle of reality. As Jonathan Kramnick contends, in what is an implicit answer to Morris's privileging addition or DNA, "one discipline fails to reduce to another because the world explained by the disciplines is plural in kind, containing many varieties of things, from millipedes to minuets" (22).

What I call in a moment Morris's "naïve realism," which forms the basis of his critique of Kuhn, describes a critique focused upon, in the words of Patricia Waugh, Kuhn's "departure from the ideal of scientific reasoning formalized by logical positivism." "Positivism's stated purpose since the 1920s," she notes, "... has been to build an absolutely certain logical and empiricist foundation for science in order to strengthen its claim to be exclusively the domain of knowledge and truth" (100). Waugh nicely argues that Kuhn's anti-positivist stance—which Morris takes to be the essence of Kuhn's analyses of the history of science—takes its place with two other impulses in Kuhn's work. The first is a "double-coded and paradoxical account of the intellectual history of science" (102)—akin to the "double-take" of literary studies

I outline here focused upon the power as well as the knowledge occasioned by the "political" aspects of literary studies conceived as critique. And the second is a "return," so to speak, "to the ideas and vocabularies of the later Wittgenstein; of pragmatists such as Dewey, Cavell, Goodman and Quine; and of ordinary language philosophers such as J. L. Austin who *provided the original intellectual scaffolding for Kuhn's concept of the paradigm*" (Waugh 107). This second impulse focuses closely (as Morris does not) on the *worldly work* of disciplined understanding pursued throughout this book.

My understanding is different from both Kuhn's extreme constructionism in Morris's argument and Morris's own somewhat naïve realism. It is my contention throughout this book that the *qualities* of the real—which is to say, the experiences of the world—are a function of systems of meanings because meaning itself is tied up with value, which in turn is tied up with horizons of possible worldly engagements governed by inherited and learned ways of engaging with the world—of *construing* the world—whether they be mathematics or semantics and what Wittgenstein calls "the paradigm of our grammar" (cited in Waugh 95).

For Kuhn, however, Morris argues, systems of meaning are "incommensurable" with one another; because there is no base of the "real," they cannot be translated into one another. It is my argument that we can, indeed, translate the discipline of literary studies in relation to other disciplines, that there are what I call "homological" bases of comparison among intellectual disciplines: it has been part of my work in sharing the humanities with colleagues in biomedicine. More specifically, it is my argument that analyses of experience—which is to say, the "qualities" of the world—lend themselves to "constructivism," which is a term Waugh contrasts with "constructionism" (108), even while the world itself, its facts and events, are not necessarily simply or arbitrarily "constructed." (Waugh nicely distinguishes "constructionism" —the seemingly simple and arbitrary attributions of "antirealism" Morris discerns in Thomas Kuhn's paradigms— from "constructivism," which is a form of "realism: the epistemic objects that emerge from the new sciences[, which] are real but distributed, fragile, unstable and in complex agential relationships with their instruments of discovery" [108].) For this reason, such "constructivism," to which analyses of qualities lend themselves, is not simply arbitrarily "subjective"—some kind of arbitrary trilobite experience—but related to the complex entanglements of the feedback of information theory I touch upon in my last two chapters, "the new systems of thinking in the biological environmental and molecular sciences that model complex systems," which Waugh nicely describes (108). My examples in later chapters of facts and events of "the world itself," which are not "constructed," are the wavelength of the color blue, between about 450 and 495 nanometers, and the audio frequency of the note "e-natural," 165 hertz (HZ). Such mathematical ("measured") accountings of color and sound are the work of the nomological sciences. Still, the description of the wavelength of the color blue calls for a range of (mathematical) measurements, and this range of measurement implies that "blue," even when measured by quantitative scientists, is, as I note in Chapter 4, a qualitative and experiential designation that one learns to "construe." On the other hand, "e-natural" on the scale of Western music lends itself to strict scientific measurement, even while the quality of an oboe's "e-natural" is another matter, which I also take up in Chapter 4 (see Exhibit 4.5: The Quality of Overtones).

Thesis. This is a complicated opening exposition, which counterpoints the seeming ahistorical ("mathematical") precision of the nomological sciences with the occasioned ("semantic") meanings/future-oriented construals of the humanities (or "human sciences"). In arguing for the distinctive nature of the intellectual discipline of literary studies, Jonathan Kramnick argues that the "goal" of literary studies is not to solve problems—as is often the goal in the nomological and social sciences—but to raise and complicate questions: "one distinctive feature of [the 'literary critical method']," he writes, "is that it scales up the level of complication while remaining internally coherent, coordinating features of syntax and tone with dimensions of historical and narrative situation" (34). Kramnick nicely sums up his thought by noting, in a gesture of philological unpacking, that "the word for this kind of scaling and this kind of explanation is of course reading" (34; see Exhibit 1.5).

Exhibit 1.5: Reading

The term "reading" repeatedly is part of the discussion of the discipline of literary studies, as well it should be. In the course of these chapter-lectures and exhibits, I bring up Nietzsche's notion of "slow reading," I. A. Richard's notion of "close reading," Rita Felski's notion of reading "literature as 'literature,'" among many others, and I repeatedly use the term "reading" in my own exposition. But I should say something here by way of setting forth the thesis of this book about the *disciplinary* use of the term (and, implicitly, of "terms of art" more generally that shape disciplinary understanding). In his philosophical, psychological, and neurological survey of "mindreading" entitled *Simulating Minds*, Alvin Goldman argues that we can usefully define "imagination"—or what he calls "making believe"—in terms of the opposition between endogenous and exogenous processes. (Note that the work of "making believe" is that of construal.) "'Making' believe," he writes, "is the activity of *endogenously* producing token states that resemble beliefs, that is, states that are normally produced in an *exogenous*, nonpretend fashion .... What simulationists call 'pretend states' are states like make-believe, make-desire, and so forth. They are states produced by an operation of mental pretense, or E-imagination [enactment-imagination]" (48). Reading, however, erases the distinction between endogenous and exogenous: we "take in" an "outside" text, but that very "taking in" confuses the inside and outside in ways I examine in the final chapter. Goldman's use of the term "resembles" takes its place among the "likenesses"—or "analogies," or Wittgenstein's "aspects," or "homologies," etc.—that recur explicitly and implicitly in engagements with the discipline of literary studies. Such analogical likenesses constitute a distinctive feature of the human sciences, an analogy (if I may say so) to the formulaic necessary and sufficient conditions of the nomological sciences and the retrospective and often statistical explanations of the social sciences (whether they be individualistic or holistic). Michael Clune, following Georges Poulet's "Phenomenology of Reading," argues (backed by cognitive psychology), that literary "works invite us to imaginatively occupy another person's thoughts, feelings, and sensations" (29)—that is to say to situate ourselves in "exogenous" states. But the use of cliché in literary texts—as in Gustav Flaubert, James Joyce, and Flannery O'Connor, great masters of the cliché, but also great masters of free indirect discourse more generally, of which cliché is an extreme example—offers an instance when cliché-texts, seemingly coercively rather than imaginatively, occupy a reader's or a speaker's thoughts, feelings, and sensations. Jonathan Culler nicely analyzes these phenomena under the philosophic category of "use/mention" (342 n.11). See Exhibit 3.6: A Note on Necessity and Sufficiency for a further discussion of "reading."

In focusing on complications, Kramnick offers a version of what Gaston Bachelard describes in his study of twentieth-century literature and twentieth-century physics as "the *complexification* of what appeared to be simple" (45). Still, my experience with the health humanities has taught me that "complexification" in the work of healthcare does, in fact, "solve problems" in the interhuman milieus of caretaking, reading, and human institutions more generally. In any case, as the word "complexification" suggests, one need not choose, once and for all (as Morris argues Kuhn does as an "antirealist," and Morris himself does as a "realist"), between meaningful engagements with the world—paradigmatic *experience* of the world—and the matters-of-fact of the "real" world itself.

Philological Philosophy. My focus on the term-"word" *complexification* in the preceding sentences suggests the opposition, which Fredric Jameson makes, between "analysis, not so much of a concept, as of a word" (12). The focus on words rather than concepts—and, in Kramnick's discussion, on "finely wrought sentences[, which] do the work that neuroscience fails to accomplish by detaching the experiential from the personal so it may reappear as the matter of narration" (127)—is the work and discipline of philology, which is, like "reading," an important part of the discipline of literary studies altogether. In his history of literary criticism, Joseph North describes what I am describing as this "philological" practice as "close reading" and "practical criticism" as they were articulated by I. A. Richards and William Empson (see 26–8). But the "close reading" he describes in Richards and Empson—and more emphatically in the American New Criticism he also describes—does not fully take up the history and culture that is also encompassed by philological philosophy, particularly as practiced by Nietzsche and others. (I should add that North's point is that history and culture were "incipient" in "the materialist practice" of Richards and Empson [27] as distinct from the conservative "idealism" of American New Criticism of the mid-twentieth century.) Edward Said succinctly defines philology as the "abiding basis for all humanistic practice," and he goes on to specify that philology is "a detailed, patient scrutiny of and a lifelong attentiveness to the words and rhetorics by which language is used by human beings who exist in history: hence the word 'secular,' as I use it, as well as the word 'worldliness'" (*Humanism* 61).

Kramnick further spells out my sense of philology when he describes the pursuit in literary studies of the "teasing out of the meaning of words in their very particular contexts of use or pausing over the mode of experience in specific literary forms" (3). By way of example he further notes that the fact that the complex word "form," which "appears sometimes as shape, sometimes as pattern, sometimes as habit, line structure, model, design, trope, and so on[,] suggests not that formalism is incoherent but that 'form,' like 'cause'— perhaps like any useful and compelling term—is not a word without content but a notion bound pragmatically to its instances" (47). J. L. Austin makes a similar argument about the word "free": "like 'real,'" he writes, "'free' is only used to rule out the suggestion of some or all of its recognized antitheses. As 'truth' is not a name for a characteristic of assertions, so 'freedom' is not a name for a characteristic of actions, but the name of a dimension in which actions are assessed" (*Papers* 180; see Exhibit 1.6).

Exhibit 1.6: Philological Philosophy

My colleague Tiao Wang and I have variously designated such a focus on word-instances (including those instances in finely wrought sentences) in our study of Chinese and English literary modernism as "entwinement, semantic overlap, imbrication, montage-meaning, configuration, analogical thinking" (65), and, as in Morris's allusion to T. S. Eliot, in relation to Walter Benjamin's famous discursive tactic of "the art of citing without quotation marks" (*Arcades* 458). We focus on what we call (and what I am calling here) "philological philosophy"—found in Nietzsche, Wittgenstein, Benjamin, Ordinary Language Philosophy, Shoshana Felman, Martha Nussbaum, Stanley Cavell, among others, and in certain strains of semiotics—whose task is the unpacking of assumptions inherent in particular word-usages. Jameson describes the work of what we are designating as "philological philosophy": it aims to focus on the entwinements of semantic phenomena (manifest in "words and language") as "an explanatory feature rather than an object of study in its own right" (Jameson 33). Hence the scare-quotes around particular words—e.g., "experience," "reality," "imbrication," etc.—provoke the "double-take" I talk about by reminding us of the "worldliness" (and the "wordiness") of signifiers, signification, and meaningful value in human interactions. (Here again is the allusive: *worldly/wordy*.) Cavell describes "the philosophical questioning of the use of a word [in Wittgenstein, which] epitomizes, in its apparent triviality and in our resistance to the apparent triviality, a chronic sense that our lives are in mortal question." (200)

Here then the Thesis: instead of choosing either "reality" or "experience"— the Real or the Construed—as the starting point of inquiry "once and for all," in these chapter-lectures I call for a repeated "double-take" on phenomena (conceived as fact or experience): the grasping of phenomena as "twice told," as in the duck and the rabbit in the optical illusion Wittgenstein notes, which I examine in Chapter 4, or as in Morris' own allusive gesture in describing prehistoric trilobites scurrying—or is it "scuttling"?—about. Hence, as I said, the scare-quotes around "experience" and "reality" are the call to look twice. The development of the *activity* of picking out features of the world of indefinite complexity in order to apprehend and understand more of that world than we did before—the activity of *disciplined science* examined throughout these chapters—is promoted by the disciplined engagement with literature and the humanities (see Exhibit 1.7).

Exhibit 1.7: Deliberate Discipline

In his account of the discipline of literary studies, Kramnick focuses on the quality of deliberateness, which in its deliberate re-considerations is, to my mind, a version of the double-take I discuss. (For a thorough philological-philosophical analysis of "deliberate," see Austin *Papers* 272–88.) Kramnick describes "norms" which characterize and distinguish intellectual disciplines. "With respect to the humanities," he writes, "the first that one might observe is a norm of deliberativeness much heralded in recent attempts to value the 'slow' nature of what we do or to define the literary disciplines in particular around an ideal of attention. At ostensible odds with corporate values of efficiency, speed, and responsiveness[—one might describes these "values" as the values of corporate healthcare as well (RS)—]the humanities on this view value a contrary pause over what might otherwise get passed over or assimilated, what might require linguistic or historical or formal training of one or another kind. I would draw attention also," Kramnick continues, "to a related norm that is perhaps less easy to see .... This is the norm of the open question, a tolerance for letting some difficulties stand once they are articulated" (26–7). I should add that philology is built upon the combination of linguistic, historical, and formal training. Listen to Nietzsche: "philology is that venerable art which exacts from its followers one thing above all—to step to one side, to leave themselves spare moments, to grow silent, to become slow—the leisurely art of the goldsmith applied to language: an art which must carry out slow, fine work, and attains nothing if not *lento*. For this very reason philology is now more desirable than ever before; for this very reason it is the highest attraction and incitement in an age of 'work': that is to say, of haste, of unseemly and immoderate hurry-skurry" (cited in Harpham 37).

Interdisciplinarity: The Argument Again

Still, it is my hope that the complicated exposition, replete with these "exhibits," with which I begin this thesis chapter, will settle down to an exposition that doesn't erase complexities, but nevertheless offers itself up to an audience like my colleagues in China or my biomedical colleagues—both of whom are not fully immersed in the particular words constituting the specialized language of the discipline of literary studies, the "terms of art" which Kramnick persuasively argues are the backbone of all intellectual disciplines. In his argument, Kramnick questions the degree to which interdisciplinary studies are practicable insofar as each discipline responds to one set of features about the world and develops a working intellectual vocabulary, particular procedures, and strategies of attendance, which encounter—and perhaps even define—those features on a particular level of engagement. My job in the chapter-lectures of this book—as it is my job in working with students and practitioners of healthcare—is somewhat different from this, though I contend it is similarly *disciplined* as the work Kramnick describes. It is to offer to Chinese friends inhabiting a culture and tradition very different from my own a sense of the goals and function of criticism at the present time in the United States and to offer to friends committed to careers in healthcare service to fellow citizens the ways in which the function and "purport" of literary studies can offer them a "double-take" on their work—more often these days in America their *intergenerational* work—of cure, care, and consolation.

I begin my argument concerning the discipline of literary studies, then, by assuming that the objects of investigation in the humanities—and in the discipline of literary studies more specifically—are facts and events understood as imbricated in human experience. "Imbricate," I point out in

Chapter 4, is a technical term describing the "overlapping" of scales on an animal, of tiles on a roof, of layers of tissue organized in surgery. It nicely spans the natural world of things, the social world of work, and the creation of artifice in human affairs, which is to say it spans the nomological, the social-scientific, and the humanistic disciplines. Experience, the book argues—following work in the philosophy of science, neuroscience, semiotics, speech-act theory, and the aesthetics of literary studies—is not simply "immediate" or the "immediate sensations," which Frye describes, but rather is mediated through structures or schemas that condition "experience." The book also contends that such "experience" is not simple self-evident sensations ("qualia") but rather organized around what aesthetics, linguistics, and economics describe as "value"—and what speech-act theory describes as "force" and evolutionary biology describes as "purpose" or "function" (see Ngai 195 for a catalogue of moral, aesthetic, and economic value; elsewhere she adds the mathematical "value" of set theory—something I mention in relation to Bertrand Russell in Chapter 5—as an example of the expanding focus on "value" as opposed to "the realm of fact" in the nineteenth century, "especially in Germany" [226–7]). That I employ scare quotes around "experience" in this exposition, as I have already suggested, aims at indicating a "double-take" on experience itself, which feels to be unmediated—this might be the defining quality of experience altogether—even while it is conditioned by structures. Frye's formulation is an important starting point: it describes the efforts, in physics, biology, and even history, to abandon self-evident sensational experience for atemporal formulaic and statistical truth—truths that are particularly free of "immediate sensations of experience." Frye himself is interested, among other things, in atemporal archetypal truths. But it is the contention of *Literary Studies and Well-Being* that the humanities are particularly interested, not in abandoning sensational experience in favor of "once and for all" truth, but scrutinizing, in an exact and systematic way, the nature, power, and value of experience itself (see Exhibit 1.8).

Exhibit 1.8: Reluctant Realism

In *The Ashtray*, Morris describes Noam Chomsky as a "reluctant realist," in a manner that clarifies a significant distinction I follow in this book between atemporal truth and the experience of qualities. A "reluctant realist," Morris says in explaining his judgment of Chomsky, is "a realist about scientific terms but not about terms in ordinary language" (112). When Morris asks Chomsky whether the vague or ambiguous nature of a proper name such as "the Charles River" means "there are *no* entities out there," Chomsky replies: "Oh, there are. But I'm talking about ordinary language and ordinary thought here. In the sciences, you depart from that and you start trying to develop systems in which there really *is* reference. Take the question—is water H_2O? Scientists will say water is H_2O. But they're not using the word 'water' with its meaning in natural language." A term like "water," he goes on to say, might describe the constituent part of tea, even though the tannic acid in the solution that is called "tea" complicates the nomenclature (i.e., the "words") "water" and "H_2O." In ordinary language, tea is still thought of as a species of thirst-quenching "water." Chomsky goes on to note "that's the way [ordinary] language and thought work. Scientists, of course, don't want that. They want their terms to really pick out some mentally independent entity in the outside world" (116). Throughout this book, I repeatedly return to the manner in which intellectual disciplines—including the discipline of literary studies—"are designed to pick out features of the world of indefinite complexity in ways that transcend our practical understanding" (Mark Platts, cited in Moore 1145).

The Structure of the Argument

I pursue this argument throughout this book. The "Introduction" (Chapter 2)—which grows out of the lectures that occasioned this book altogether—begins by examining the history of the term "literature" in what Hillis Miller calls "our modern sense" of the term in the seventeenth or eighteenth century. Then it sets forth a meditation on experience, including Raymond Williams's suggestion in passing that his well-known conception of "structures of feeling" might have been described as "structures of experience," where "experience" was "the better and wider word" (132). Chapter 3 (based on the first Harbin lecture) catalogues common usages of "discipline" outside its first dictionary definition as "punishment," and in this it examines the humanities—and what I come to call the "human sciences" in the course of this lectures-book—in relation to the nomological and social sciences. Chapter 4 (based on the second lecture) focuses on the relation of language to value, which relation, it contends, is at the heart of speech-act theory and of the value-judgments inherent in language more generally. Chapter 5 (based on the third lecture) focuses on the manner in which material "bases" of experience—the emotional experiences of fear, anger, and awe that promote evolutionary self- and cohort-preservation— are reordered and redescribed in the narrative genres of literary art. This chapter-lecture ends by examining a fine-grained notion of "aesthetics"— an intergenerational notion of "aesthetics"—and its everyday continuity with "experience" in the contexts of the "monumental" categories of genre and death (Sianne Ngai calls such categories "transcendent concepts like democracy and freedom" [187]). And Chapter 6 (based on the concluding fourth lecture) argues that what is usually understood as the "vicarious" experience provoked by literature might be better understood simply as complex "experience" itself, working—as Aristotle argued experience itself does, when properly engaged with, when properly reflected upon—toward *phronesis* or "practical wisdom."

In this book, I follow the palimpsestic format of chapter-lectures for several reasons. Most of all, by doing so I attempt to maintain (or create) the quasi-intimacy of face-to-face presentation, which calls up the "affective rhythm" of drama Richard Kuhns describes (8) and the "invitation" to improvisation Stanley Cavell describes (185) in the very "event" of a lecture. That an argumentative discourse can be grasped as an event—as a "drama" and/or as an "improvisation"—suggests that argument itself can be comprehended as a kind of experience. It suggests that the perlocutionary persuasiveness of argument includes the need to employ a modality of presentation that doesn't depend upon, as a written argument often does, possibilities of pause, re-reading, and meditation. In the course of this book, I contrast "everyday" narratives, whose function evolutionary biology suggests is to promote communal purposes and cooperation, with aesthetic or "art" narratives, whose functions include the expansion of cognitive understanding and affective responses in ways that enrich experience itself. One scholar, contrasting popular music of the dance hall with classical music of the concert hall, calls the latter "museum" music (Hamilton 325; see Jay 131–9 for a thumbnail history of aesthetic-museum experience), and the strict reliance on seemingly timeless written texts, as opposed to the oral-events of lectures, might also be taken to be "museum" discourse. By using the chapter-lecture format, I hope to approximate both goals: communal purposes and cooperation and also a meditative "double-take" on the experienced understanding of literature. This format includes "exhibits": we've already seen eight, whose number here in the Thesis/Contexts discussion, I promise, is significantly larger than their number in the chapter-lectures (since part of the work of Chapter 1 is to *situate* the book's arguments). In any case, the exhibits found throughout these pages at once create possibilities of pausing and meditation—possibilities of a double-take—even as they set forth, as I do in lectures supplemented by powerpoint, moments of shared and focused re-thinking. Moreover, the exhibits create a framework for what I have called "a many-voiced discourse" such as found in Walter Benjamin's conception of the "constellation" of ideas (Wang and Schleifer 34–5; see also Schleifer *Political Economy* 24–31), which—in the many citations found throughout the exhibits—creates a formal structure and discipline for inter-disciplinary and inter-cultural work (see Exhibit 1.9).

Exhibit 1.9: Montaigne's Many-Voiced Style

In *Songs of Experience: Modern American and European Variations on a Universal Theme*, Martin Jay describes the style of Michel de Montaigne's essay "Of Experience." "More like an unruly life than a logical demonstration," he writes, "'Of Experience' meanders digressively, combining anecdotes and *aperçus* with arguments and quotations, reprising themes and coming at them from different angles. Its own temporality, rhythmically uneven and irreducible to a unified narrative, duplicates the unsystematic ruminations on time itself to be found in Montaigne's work as a whole.... [T]he seemingly undisciplined structure of 'Of Experience' ... performatively instantiates what it substantively argues" (25). In her introduction to her translation of "Chinese Poetry and Chinese Painting" by the Chinese novelist and essayist Qian Zhongshu, Zhu Liya similarly notes that "instead of forcing an argument by following its logic, [Qian] invariably comes up with a question or comes to a conclusion in response to the many voices of tradition. Thus, his style is more like that of Montaigne in his familiar essays than Descartes' logic and deductions. Rather than figuring out the logic of phenomena on his own—that quintessentially Cartesian strategy—he is happy to gather around an idea or an argument the traditional debate ... and the many voices of tradition" (230). One of Qian's discursive strategies, as he notes, is "the use of multiple similes to convey a single idea." It is "a technique philosophers use in an attempt to prevent the reader from becoming fixated on a particular analogy and clinging to it rather than the idea .... When analogies and illustrations are presented *en masse*, each vying to be the most apt or alluring, the insights keep shifting and according themselves to different vehicles. In this way, each analogy gives way to the next and none lingers, the writing flows and does not dwell on a single notion, and the thought penetrates to all aspects of the subject and does not guard a single corner" (Qian 137; for an extended analysis of Qian's discursive strategies, see Wang and Schleifer Ch. 4).

In a similar fashion, in the chapters in this book I hope to provoke experience as well as knowledge, or rather, as Jay has it, to provoke, "performatively," instantiations of experience and knowledge and how they hold together. This is one function of palimpsestic "lectures" in a lectures-book and the double-takes they provoke.

What does the lecture format—even the improvised and palimpsestic lecture format I follow in this book—entail? The particular "discipline" of a lecture for people studying the language and literature of English, whose native language is not English, is the constant need to make explicit implicit assumptions about meaning and "common sense." It makes the work of philology particularly important. One strategy to do so, which I follow in these chapters, is the repetition of examples, citation of the same texts several times, sometimes to the same and sometimes to different purposes, versions of the double-take of Benjamin's citations without quotation marks. The global argument of *Literary Studies and Well-Being*—the title of this thesis chapter—is that literature provokes what I call a "second take" or a "double-take" on what we already know. As J. L. Austin notes, in a passage important in these chapters, "A course of E. M. Forster and we see things differently: yet perhaps we know no more and are no cleverer" (*Papers* 194). In discussing panpsychism—which is to say, in discussing the nature of experience—in Marilynne Robinson's novel *Housekeeping*, Kramnick notes that "there are leaves 'as they always are,' and there are leaves as we wondrously attend to them" such that "the physical world on this account includes both the brownness of fallen leaves (a view from one [experiential "first-person"] perspective) *and* the process that empties them of chlorophyll (a view from no perspective)" (154; elsewhere Kramnick calls this second perspective "objective, third-person science" (120)]). As a result, "phenomenal experience seems at once to lace over every object and belong almost to no one" (154; see Exhibit 1.10).

Exhibit 1.10: The Hard Problem of Experience

Kramnick's study focuses on what David Chalmers calls "the hard problem" of experience and consciousness. "For Thomas Nagel and David Chalmers three centuries [after John Locke], consciousness amounts to 'what it is like' to have one experience or another and serves as the prompt for a hard problem: how could the matter of our bodies (our brains especially) have or create experience in the first place?" (Kramnick 4). He goes on to note that Chalmers argues that "there is a disanalogy between the problem of consciousness and problems in other domains." "Life," Kramnick explains, "may be explained entirely in terms of structure and function without any further or open questions, whereas consciousness always brings with it the question of why any relevant function is accompanied by experience" (126). One solution to this problem is the "panpsychism" Kramnick studies in relation to Robinson's novel. Panpsychism is a "radical answer" to the problem, an answer which argues that "experience does not emerge from nonexperiential matter after all but rather is everywhere present in matter itself, each infinitesimal quark also a tiny piece of consciousness" (138). (Alternative explanations are a *dualism* of matter and mind, such as found in Descartes, or a "physicalism," in which experience/consciousness *emerges from* inert matter.)

In fact, the "hard problem" Kramnick brings to bear on the discipline of literary studies is, for the purposes of this book, not a focus of attention. I am not pursuing an ontological (or perhaps a metaphysical) understanding of experience in terms of Kramnick's additional "question of why" in discussing structures of experience. Rather, I examine the "double-take" that experience sometimes—perhaps always—provokes as we wondrously attend to experience. Moreover, I examine the practical work of the disciplined understanding of experience, which examines engagements with experience, rather than inquiring into its essential nature. Kramnick's analyses of fiction and poetry—like Austin's analyses of the "force" of language—pursues a philological working-out of such engagements in the combination of linguistic, historical, and formal investigations he presents. Michael Clune also addresses this problem when he argues that there are "two general approaches to the relation of literature and science" in recent years: one "takes the reading, writing and interpretation of literature to be the objects of scientific study," in which scientific disciplinary models (or vocabularies) are used "to describe literature and literary experience," while the second "argues that literature shows us a gap in scientific knowledge, and an opening for a kind of knowledge peculiar to literary studies." "The gap," he concludes, "is experience": what "neuroscientific descriptions of human thought and behavior leave out ... is what it feels like to think and act" (57). The goals of the health humanities is much less ambitious than the program of addressing the gap in scientific study Clune advocates: it is the "easy" problem of reminding healthcare students and professionals of the "experiences" of feeling, understanding, and value that contributed to their commitment to healthcare in the first place; and for my Chinese friends it is the "easy" problem of setting forth the feeling, understanding, and value that contributed to our shared commitments to the reading and writing of literary studies.

A second strategy of the palimpsestic lecture format in this book—the double-take of its chapter-lectures—which as a whole aims to make the implicit and common-sense assumptions of engagements with literature systematically explicit is to revert to dictionary definitions. Such definitions, as we know, are organized around common usage, with numbered definitions corresponding to the most usual uses of terms. As such, dictionary definitions—and their corresponding philological "usages"—are themselves palimpsestic, and they set forth what we already know about words so that we might, as Austin says, "see things differently." Another version of this strategy is to cite *Wikipedia*, which often also gives us a common-sense handle on understanding. In addition, a third strategy the event-nature of the lecture format calls for is the system of numbered answers to a question, such as the numbered "catalogue" of lecture-features I employ in these paragraphs. Such cataloguing—especially when catalogues are presented as parallel to one another—facilitates the comprehension of what Charles Altieri calls in discussing poetry "relations among facts rather than moments of perception" (5), a strategy which avoids the "self-evidence" of perception.

It is the argument of *Literary Studies and Well-Being* that the discipline of literary studies—and, of course, literature itself and, more importantly, experience itself, when engaged with in a certain way—provokes this kind of "double-take" or "second take," which enriches experience. Syntactically, parenthetical repetition, marked for instance in the dashes of these sentences, reinforces, "orally" as I might say, such double taking. Finally, the palimpsestic format more fully calls for what one art historian describes as the "active absorption" that impressionist painting creates in its "tiny brush strokes that the viewer must visually and actively complete" (Herwitz 184). It calls for, as I do when I lecture, the possibility of questions and clarifications from an audience. The "active absorption" of impressionism demonstrates vividly the manner in which experience is not a passive response to the world, but active participation, which like a speech-act in Shoshana Felman's description, "is a dynamic movement of modification of reality" (51). As the cognitive scientist Alva Noë argues, "consciousness [i.e., conscious experience] is not something that happens inside of us"; it is "something we do or make," "an achievement of the whole animal in its environmental context" (cited in Kramnick 5).

The Stake of the Project: Audience and Purpose

In order to complete this review of my thesis, it is important to articulate what is at stake in this book, which is implicit in the argument I have just set forth, and to discuss why such a study is particularly timely. An important stake in this work, and which, I hope, will allow it to attract an audience beyond those interested simply in literature—my healthcare colleagues are a good example of such an enlarged audience—is its attention to the practical work of literary study, the practical wisdom of *phronesis*, notable in the scene of instruction that arises in the counterpoint between the discipline of literary studies and the practical pedagogy of the health humanities. As I mentioned earlier, this study grows out of my experience in the medical humanities, and I hope this pedigree shows. In other words, an argument for the practical wisdom of the humanities is timely just now when the disciplined study of literature is attracting fewer and fewer practitioners and students. Such practical understanding is implicit in the cross-cultural nature of the chapter-lectures presented here. That is, the social crisis in the humanities in our country is not a crisis in China, as I have argued recently in *Modernist Poetics in China: Consumerist Economics and Chinese Literary Modernism*, a book that is co-authored with Tiao Wang, a Chinese colleague from the Harbin Institute of Technology. In that book, we argue that the experience of social transformations in China for a generation now is analogous to the experience of social transformations in the West at the turn of the twentieth century. In China today, as in London, New York, Paris, in the early twentieth century, literary and narrative arts are important because of the manner in which they reflect and shape lived experience itself, what, as we have seen, Veblen called at the turn of the twentieth century in America "habits of thought." Thus, these chapter-lectures attempt to offer Chinese colleagues and friends a sense of what is at stake in literary studies in America in order to create the opportunity to teach ourselves implicit values in the humanities. Such implicit values warrant a second take on experience that is, I argue, an important goal in the disciplined work of literary studies.

Let me expand upon this. In *Literary Criticism: A Concise Political History*, Joseph North offers a persuasive argument that "the critical revolution of the 1920s was a sharp turn away from what seemed the discipline's obvious trajectory" of "belletristic ... aesthetic appreciation" (22). "The belletristic criticism of the *fin de siècle*," he notes, "had been transformed into something genuinely new" (23), and he spells out this "newness" in terms of the "problem that the critical revolution of the 1920s managed to solve: the problem of creating a true paradigm for criticism—the problem of how to build an institution that would cultivate new, deeper forms of subjectivity and collectivity in a rigorous and repeatable way" (126). It is my contention here—borne of my work teaching and thinking with people committed to the practical wisdom of healthcare and reinforced by my attempt to articulate that work to a sympathetic audience of Chinese teachers of English literature and language—that an emphasis on strategies for spelling out the manner in which the focus on experience in the discipline of literary studies can contribute to caretaking in healthcare (but also in education, legal studies, social work, and even teaching foreign languages and different cultures to fellow citizens). Such strategies themselves offer "something genuinely new" for our work in the humanities and something genuinely timely in the early twenty-first century. In discussing the "critical revolution" in literary studies in the 1920s, North describes the ways in which the "effects of the break" in literary studies "were felt well beyond the bounds of university literature departments" (23), and in order to demonstrate his contention he offers a tangible example of what I describe as "habits of thought." North catalogues these "effects" in cultural studies, particular pedagogical practices throughout the British empire, and even the philosophical and "linguistic" turn of literary studies in the 1970s, and then he notes (without naming it as such) how the "break" helped reshape "habits of thought." "Of course," he says, explicit lists of notable changes in teaching and reading

> fail to do the ["effects" of the break] justice, since the effects that can be traced clearly are naturally less interesting than the subterranean ones—effects less immediately visible, perhaps, but also deeper—the kinds of wide-reaching effects that the disciplined training of multiple generations of minds can have on so many fields and sectors; the effects that a sustained institutional commitment can have, when that commitment is to a transformation of the culture, of the public, or of the common. In this regard, one might say that the most important effects of the critical revolution [of the early twentieth century in Britain] were at the occluded but profound level of the idioms, habits, and sensibilities by which the social body creates, undergoes, and reflects on experiential forms.
>
> (24)

It is my contention here, tutored by work with healthcare students, healthcare teachers, healthcare professionals and by engagements with committed colleagues in China, who are encountering the century-long development of literary studies in the United States anew—it is my contention that an understanding of the discipline of literary studies as fully imbricated in experience and "experiential forms" offers a way of rethinking, in a kind of "double-take," the discipline of the literary studies altogether. Just re-read this paragraph I just cited from North and understand how "the kinds of wide-reaching effects that the disciplined training of multiple generations of minds," and "the effects that a sustained institutional commitment" can have—and throughout the United States has already begun to have—on clinical engagements of patients and healthcare practitioners (see Shakir et al.).

So the audience for this book is complex. It is, of course, my healthcare students and colleagues, who want me to demonstrate as clearly as I can the ways in which literary studies can contribute to the education and practices of healthcare professionals. And it is my Chinese friends and colleagues for whom I organized the lecture series in Harbin in order to present to them my sense of literary studies in the United States. But there is a larger audience as well, defined in three ways: by the "formalism" of literary studies, which, in this book, I articulate in relation to Jonathan Kramnick; by the "politics" of literary studies, which I articulate in relation to Joseph North and, more implicitly, in relation to Sianne Ngai; and by the "materialism" of literary studies, which I articulate in relation to Alvin Goldman. In my work in Irish studies, I came across a wonderful story concerning the collaboration between W. B. Yeats and George Moore, who were writing a play together for the nascent Irish National Theatre. Moore suggested that after the play was complete, he and Yeats should commission its translation into Irish and then its re-translation back into English. Moore said the play would greatly benefit from what he called its "bath" in Irish. My sense—tutored by my collaborative work on Chinese and English literature and my collaborative work on literary narrative and healthcare—is that a sharper sense of our shared discipline of English literary studies benefits from a bath in the work of another pedagogical discipline and of another language and culture altogether. That is, the repeated *materialist aesthetics* that North seeks in reviewing the history of English literary studies since 1920, the repeated *attention to form* Kramnick seeks in engaging in and interrogating interdisciplinary studies in relation to English literary studies, and the repeated widening of the *scope of experience* Goldman seeks in studying simulation and surveying and synthesizing more than a generation of disciplined experiments and arguments focused on simulation in psychology, neurology, and philosophy come into relief and triangulate themselves when we imagine English literary studies for people from another culture or immersed in the assumptions of another (intellectual/pedagogical) discipline (see Exhibit 1.11).

Exhibit 1.11: A Note on Healthcare Practices

As I note in Chapter 2, literature is not only a source of knowledge but also a source of widening sensibility and feeling, what Joseph North, describing mid-twentieth-century criticism, called "an institutional program of aesthetic education—an attempt to enrich the culture directly by cultivating new ranges of sensibility, new modes of subjectivity, new capacities of experience—using works of literature as a means" (6). Were I to replace in this sentence the word "culture" with "healthcare practices," i.e., "an attempt to enrich healthcare practices directly," I would describe the "program"—the goals and purposes—of the chapter-lectures set forth in this book. From pre-med programs to certification exams, healthcare emphasizes the nomological-scientific bases for the treatment of ailments, and in the twentieth century it had done so with astounding success. Still, an important aim of this study (and its palimpsestic lectures) is to re-introduce "experience" into healthcare practices in such a way that "experience" is not simple acquired through long practice but can be systematically acquired by means of programmatic engagements with and cultivation of the facts and experience set forth by literary texts. This contention, I believe, becomes most clear in the final chapter-lecture (Chapter 6) of this book.

The alignment of a materialist aesthetics, the disciplinary attention to form, and interdisciplinary testings and apprehensions of experience uncovers or unpacks for us a working understanding of *phronesis*, practical worldly wisdom, implicit in the inferential and philological work of the discipline of literary studies. Biomedicine organizes itself as a nomological science, which *tests*—literally and repeatedly—members of the healthcare profession. But healthcare often calls upon wider skills and talents beyond (or along with) mastery of nomological logic. The nature of healthcare, then—combining as it does cure, care, and, at times, simple compassion—requires a worldly materialism, attention to form, and an embrace of human experience itself. In fulfilling these requirements, it also allows us to understand in greater detail the worldly work of the discipline of literary studies.

This project, then, suggests that one further stake, implicit in this last observation, is to demonstrate the wider relevance of literary studies beyond a small audience of experts. Perhaps one example of such demonstration is the manner in which *Literary Studies and Well-Being* strives to open up semiotic analysis from its often ivory-tower insulation. Semiotics—the systematic analysis of the generation of the meaningfulness of communicative signs in what the semiotician Louis Hjelmslev describes as the "exact and generalizing" methods (8) of nomological science— often seems to be a project of progressively minute and often precious distinctions, a criticism that can be addressed to other aspects of literary studies as well. But a fine example of productive, "worldly" semiotics is the manner in which this book attempts to articulate what is at stake in close attention to literary forms—their obscure sociality, their provocation of feelings and emotions beyond cliché, their work at moral education. It does so by marshalling the discipline of literary studies to allow readers a stronger sense of how such disciplined understanding participates in the "space of meaning" of lived-lives, in the experience and "habits of thought" literature uncovers and provokes. Many years ago, Lionel Trilling described the way in which literature engages such habits of thought under the category of "manners." Sounding very much like Williams in his descriptions of "structures of feeling" and seeming to unpack Veblen's "habits of thought," Trilling describes manners as

> the great formulated monuments of the present[,] ... all the buzz of implication which always surrounds us in the present, coming to us from what never gets fully stated, coming in the tone of greetings and the tone of quarrels, in slang and humor and popular songs, in the way children play, in the gesture the waiter makes when he puts down the plate, in the nature of the very food we prefer.
>
> ... What I understand as manners, then, is a culture's hum and buzz of implication[,] ... that part of a culture ... hinted at by small actions .... They are things that for good or bad draw the people of a culture together and separate them from the people of another culture. It is the part of a culture which is not art, nor religion, nor morals, nor politics, and yet it relates to all these highly formulated departments of culture. It is modified by them; it modifies them; it is generated by them; it generates them. (200)

Such "manners"—such "structures" of feeling and experience, such "habits of thought"—are not species of idealism, but rather worldly "practices" of life, which embody the value and force that constitute "experience" itself. Charles Taylor's describes this under the French term "idées-forces," by which he means the *practical* "spiritual power" of generally held ideas/thoughts. He describes the power of "idées-forces" within "any cultural phenomenon ... which will show why people found (or find) it convincing/inspiring/moving" (*Sources* 269). Such power-force, I suggest throughout *Literary Studies and Well-Being*, is a defining feature of literature, its "value," which is a significant focus on the discipline of literary studies (see Exhibit 1.12).

Exhibit 1.12: A Note on "Habits of Thought"

In *Sources of the Self* Charles Taylor addresses the problem of idealism in his study in a manner that might clarify the seeming idealism in Peirce's and Veblen's notion of "habits of thought." Veblen addresses this as well, when he argues that "habits of thought" create the bases of human social institutions. Clune offers a simple example of such non-idealistic habits of thought "when Jane Austen tells us Elizabeth Bennet entered a 'handsome modern house'" (117). "To someone familiar with a world," by which Clune means to someone sharing particular habits of thought that make the world "familiar," "the house does not first show up as a gray rectangle subsequently interpreted as a house, but gets immediately recognized as a 'handsome modern house.' These descriptions describe the way things appear as connected to other things in a world, as a knot of cultural associations and connections" (118). Such associations and connections—like associations and connections spelled out in linguistic grammar, in literary genres, even in mathematical physics—constitute *institutions*.

Taylor, however, emphasizes the practical "force" of the ideas he studies in his analysis of the phenomenon of "inward" moral selfhood rather than the force of social and economic institutions, upon which Veblen focuses. "The kinds of ideas I am interested in here," he writes, "—moral ideals, understandings of the human predicament, concepts of the self—for the most part exist in our lives through being embedded in practices. By 'practice', I mean something extremely vague and general: more or less any stable configuration of shared activity, whose shape is defined by a certain pattern of dos and don'ts, can be a practice for my purpose. The way we discipline our children, greet each other in the street, determine group decisions through voting in elections, and exchange things through markets are all practices. And there are practices at all levels of human social life: family, village, national politics, rituals of religious communities, and so on" (270). Taylor goes on to note that such ideas do not necessarily require "some conscious expression [of] the underlying rationale of the patterns [of dos and don'ts] .... A pattern can exist just in the dos and don'ts that people accept and mutually enforce, without there being (yet) an explicit rationale. And as children, we learn some of the most fundamental patterns at first just as such" (271). An instance of such patterned "dos and don'ts" can be discerned in what Wittgenstein calls the "paradigm of our grammar," which Patricia Waugh notes is "used to refer to the fundamental entanglement of the world and language: workable—as opposed to 'idle'—concepts are acquired out of the 'rough ground' of experience …. To learn a grammar is to be assimilated to a world through practical engagement rather than rote or conscious learning of disembodied concepts: [as Wittgenstein notes,] 'to imagine a language means to imagine a form of life" (Waugh 95–6). As such, "dos and don'ts" inhabit the scene of intergenerational learning. Their analysis is the work of worldly semiotics.

The Practical Work of the Thesis

Let me conclude the opening "Thesis" of this book—since such thesis-chapters are rarely encountered in scholarly books, though they might very well do for the first chapter of a lecture series—by noting that it was inspired by Geoffrey Hartman. When I was in graduate school I had the wonderful opportunity of reading Hartman's brilliant phenomenological study—which is to say, his "experiential" philological study—*William Wordsworth's Poetry 1787–1814*. A good part of the wonder of that book was the fact that it opens with "Thesis: The Halted Traveler," which allowed me, I'm just now understanding, to repeatedly take "double-takes" on the rich experience of Wordsworth's poetry. Such "double-takes," I argue here, are called for in the discipline of literary studies—perhaps they constitute the methodology and "feel" of the discipline itself—which I examine in these chapters.

Still, the Thesis here in Chapter 1, supplemented as it is, with Contexts, is considerably longer than Hartman's thesis in *William Wordsworth's Poetry*. In Hartman's phenomenological study, written more than fifty years ago, his purpose was to set forth the "feel" of Wordsworth's poetry by means of superb "close readings" of Wordsworth's poems. My goal has been necessarily larger, to add to the thesis a sense of the wider intellectual contexts—the historicist, interdisciplinary, intercultural, and outright aesthetic-philological work all contributing to literary studies. Thus, there might be a faint homology between "thesis and contexts" and "the real and the construed." That is, since the time of Hartman's study, as many commentators have noted—

commentators who include Jonathan Kramnick, Joseph North, Michael Clune, Sianne Ngai, and the many literary critics they (and I) cite—the discipline of literary studies has answered "close reading" with what North describes as "a scholarly historicist/contextualist approach to literature" (16). North explicitly describes his "concise history" of literary criticism from a leftist political position, even if he does not spell out in any detail the kind of practical, incipient "materialist practice" he repeatedly calls for, something I attempt to suggest in examining the discipline of literary studies from the starting point of healthcare training. Moreover, Jonathan Kramnick and Michael Clune both address another "scholarly historicist/contextualist" approach to literary studies, namely its interdisciplinary engagements with science: Kramnick explicitly distinguishes such interdisciplinary study from formalist aesthetics, while Clune attempts to discover ways that that literary criticism can create "new knowledge ... not in the description of art's embeddedness in contexts recognizable to historians or sociologists, but in the description of the forces by which art attempts to free itself of such contexts and such recognitions" (17). The "aesthetic" project of Ngai is the mirror image of this. Thus, in *Theory of the Gimmick* she claims that the historicist project (she calls it "critical poststructuralism") and "new postcritical" approaches to literary studies (which she claims fly "under the flag of affect theory and aesthetics") are continuous with one another, and that the latter "postcritical" approaches are "fields to which [her own] book also belongs" (35). Still, her analyses do not so much demonstrate a "continuity" between aesthetics and historicism as they present aestheticism and historicism in counterpoint, where close readings of aesthetic objects—novels, stories, poems, photographs, etc.—and abstract Marxist social analyses alternate throughout her discussion. Thus, rather than to free literary criticism, as Clune says, from sociology, Ngai seeks their "continuity" where a Marxist "base" is purported to ground an aesthetic "superstructure" in a counterpoint, as her subtitle has it, between *Aesthetic Judgment and Capitalist Form*. This deployment of aesthetic analysis in the service of a Marxist critique of consumerist capitalism is perhaps most pronounced in the final chapter of her book, which offers philological/aesthetic "close readings" of late novels of Henry James, readings which focus on the "secret structure" of James's work, its style, the aesthetic term *ficelle*, which James developed to explain his narrative strategy and which Ngai argues is "'cheaply' employed for expository or plot-advancing reasons" (293). At the end of her engagement with James—and, in fact, at the end of almost every chapter examining aesthetic phenomena—her philological/aesthetic "close readings" reveal, after all, "the representation of capitalist totality" (298) in James and in the various aesthetic texts she analyzes.

I detail Ngai's study at some length, because it and the other studies I engage with throughout *Literary Studies and Well-Being*—in aesthetics, historicism, literary history, interdisciplinary literary studies, all of which taken together can stand, synecdochally, for the function of literary studies at the present time—all these projects can benefit, as I have suggested, by taking the worldly, practical work of the health humanities as a starting point of understanding. Particularly, I believe that my engagements with Alvin Goldman's synthesizing work in psychology, neuroscience, and philosophy, which is focused upon simulated "experience," can and should be "recognizable" for people in biomedicine—and implicitly, in law, social sciences, engineering, and in practical applied sciences more generally— pursuing worldly, practical wisdom. That is, unlike Hartman's 1965 study, *Literary Studies and Well-Being* addresses the twenty-first-century divide in literary studies between historicist scholarship and aesthetic analysis. In doing so, it addresses the ways in which the aesthetics of literary form conditions the "experience" of reading—and especially "close reading"— even while historicist/contextualist approaches focus on the ways that literature in its aesthetic forms reflects the culture in which and the psychology from which it arises—what Trilling describes as the "hum and buzz" of a culture and what I might call the "hum and buzz" of thinking and experience. But the worldly work of literature, like that of healthcare, aims to go beyond "reflection" in order, as Shoshana Felman argues about speech acts, to *enact*—particularly in small everyday gestures—a "modification of reality" itself (51; see Exhibit 1.13).

Exhibit 1.13: Everyday Ethics in Healthcare

In *Stories of Sickness*, Howard Brody notes that V. I. Warren, in "Feminist Directions in Medical Ethics," likens the everyday ethics of healthcare to the everyday activity of housekeeping, a notable example of the "everyday gestures" I mention. "Housekeeping," he writes, "signifies that portion of ethical behavior that is like mopping the floor: no one will praise you for mopping the floor; everyone will blame you for failing to mop the floor; and no matter how good a job you did yesterday of mopping the floor, it still has to be done all over again, indefinitely. The physician does many things on a day-to-day basis purely out of habit and without any explicit analysis .... The physician, for instance, does not choose each time she encounters a patient whether to smile and offer a friendly, warm greeting, but her doing so means both that things will happen afterward in certain ways and not in other ways and that a certain set of ethical dilemmas will arise very seldom in her practice" (208; see also Warren; and Schleifer and Vannatta *Chief Concern* Ch. 9).

Thus, one final purpose of this lectures-book, with this lengthy Thesis, the Introduction (Chapter 2) presenting a sketch of literature and literary studies, and the chapter-lectures that follow, is to obviate the divide between "contextualist" and "aesthetic" understandings of literature, found in North, Clune, and in the very expository counterpoint of Ngai and the many other contemporary literary critics they cite. In *Literary Studies and Well-Being* I pursue the connection between the knowledge of historicism and the power of aesthetics in the practical, philological work—the *worldly* work—of literature in its engagements with wider education, including healthcare, but also including the cross-cultural engagement with Chinese colleagues, which occasioned the lecture series in Harbin. Implicit in these chapter-lectures, then, is my contention that the opposition between aesthetic experience and historicist recovery, which seems to shape understandings of literary studies at the present time, can be more clearly grasped, in the context of the health humanities, not as a breach and divide but as a "double-take" of knowledge and power, which Yeats describes in "Leda and the Swan," so that the close reading of that poem and the larger arguments of the book as a whole, can help us apprehend the worldly work literature.

CHAPTER 2
INTRODUCTION: ON THE DISCIPLINE
OF LITERARY STUDIES

Literature and Discipline

J. Hillis Miller begins his book *On Literature* by discussing the ways in which our modern sense of literature developed in relation to the formal study of imaginative writing in institutions of higher education and institutions of "lower-school training in preparation for the university" (2) in the eighteenth and nineteenth centuries. "Literature in our modern sense," he writes, "appeared in the European West and began in the late seventeenth century, at the earliest" in "the relatively brief historical period of a predominantly paper culture" (1, 81–2). In his discussion he catalogues phenomena that "made literature possible": they include technologies of printing, "vernacular" literacy that grew to be "almost universal," transformations of political systems into "Western-style democracies" (i.e., "regimes with expanded suffrage, government by legislatures, regulated judicial systems, fundamental human rights"), and "the appearance of the modern nation-state" (2–3). Most importantly for the chapter-lectures set forth here, he argues that

> the modern Western concept of literature became firmly established at the same time as the appearance of the modern research university. The latter is commonly identified with the founding of the University of Berlin around 1810, under the guidance of a plan devised by Wilhelm von Humboldt. The modern research university has a double charge. One is *Wissenschaft*, finding out the truth about everything. The other is *Bildung*, training citizens (originally almost exclusively male ones) of a given nation-state in the ethos appropriate for that state.
>
> (4)

In describing the "double charge" of higher education—*Wissenschaft* and *Bildung*—Miller repeats the double-take of literature I set forth in Chapter 1.

Still, in his study Miller doesn't mention the relation of the phenomenon of literature as an institution to the development of what Adam Smith called "commercial society" in 1776 and what came to be called "capitalism" in Britain around 1833 (OED).

In my recent work I have focused on the relationship between cultural institutions, including institutions of literature and the arts, and economic institutions. I touch upon this relationship throughout the chapter-lectures that comprise *Literary Studies and Well-Being*. What is only implied in my earlier studies, however, is the ways in which the notion of *institution*, which is central to this constellation of phenomena—print culture, literature, literacy, nation-state, democracy, capitalism, etc.—can be understood in relation to various forms of discipline, including intellectual discipline. "Institutions," Douglas North has argued in studying perspectives in economics,

> are the humanly devised constraints that structure political, economic and social interaction. They consist of both informal constraints (sanctions, taboos, customs, traditions, and codes of conduct), and formal rules (constitutions, laws, property rights). Throughout history, institutions have been devised by human beings to create order and reduce uncertainty in exchange.
>
> (97)

Discipline comprises informal constraints, such as how we might begin a scholarly essay, and formal rules, such as the prefatory abstract required by most scholarly journals these days. But North's strict distinction between informal customs and taboos and formally itemized laws and rights breaks down in the lived-life of experience (see Exhibit 1.12: A Note on "Habits of Thought"). We can discern this breakdown in the rules implicit in what Thorstein Veblen describes as "settled habits of thought" that define social institutions (*Modern Civilization* 239) in his study of economics—what came to be called "Institutional Economics"—at the turn of the twentieth century. In the chapter-lectures that follow, in large part I focus on this combination of formal understanding and informal habitual behavior because, as I note in the Chapter 3, I hope to develop an understanding of the connection between the seeming spontaneity of experience and shared but unspontaneous "rules"—rules that do not always need "an explicit rationale" (Taylor *Sources* 271)—which condition the qualities of experience themselves.

In his definition, North focuses on economic institutions and "wealth maximizing behavior" (98) in economics, which is related to, but different from, the experience of the power of wealth in Veblen's economics. Still, North's definition also fits intellectual institutions—i.e., intellectual *disciplines*—or what I might call "knowledge-maximizing behavior." In the discipline of literary studies, this includes "affect-maximizing behavior" as well. That is, literature is not only a source of knowledge but also a source of widening sensibility, widening feeling, widening experience, what Joseph North, describing mid-twentieth-century criticism, called "an institutional program of aesthetic education—an attempt to enrich the culture directly by cultivating new ranges of sensibility, new modes of subjectivity, new capacities of experience—using works of literature as a means" (6). (This is a version of the *Bildung* that Hillis Miller argues was one of the roles of higher education—and particularly literary education—in the nineteenth century.) Were I to replace the word *culture* in Joseph North's sentence with *healthcare practices*—i.e., "an attempt to enrich healthcare practices directly"—I would describe the "program" of the chapter-lectures set forth in this book insofar as my examination of the discipline of literary studies takes its motive from my work with healthcare students and professionals. Thus, it is perfectly apt, for both Joseph North and myself, that Jane Austen entitled one of her novels *Sense and Sensibility*. In "A Plea for Excuses"—an essay that looms large in the chapters that follow—J. L. Austin argues that we seldom ponder on "whether flames are things or events" (179), and answering his question about the nature or quality of flames—his question about the "self-evident" nature of flames—might allow us to more fully plumb the role of judgment and value in seeming self-evident experience. That is, Austin's question about flames—to which I return in the final chapter of this book—offers a question *about* experience, rather than taking experience to be self-evidently given.

The Event of Experience

Austin's question about the "fact" and "event" of flames is a good place to begin a discussion of experience and literary studies. In my examination of experience and literary studies, I am suggesting that the fact and event of experience raises rather than answers questions about the world, that "experience" is not an explanation but something that calls for explanation. Thus, it is my starting assumption in these chapters that literary studies, more or less explicitly, focus on *experience* understood as facts and events, knowledge and affect. Hans-George Gadamer suggests as much when he argues in *Truth and Method* that experience brings nothing to a close. "Being experienced," he writes,

> does not mean that one now knows something once and for all and becomes rigid in this knowledge; rather, one becomes more open to new experiences. A person who is experienced is undogmatic. Experience has the effect of freeing one to be open to new experience .... In our experience we bring nothing to a close; we are constantly learning new things from our experience ... this I call the interminability of all experience.
>
> (cited in Jay 402)

Take, for instance, as Stanley Cavell does in analyzing Wittgenstein, the experience of expectation as an event. (This experience is closely related to what the neurologist David Huron calls "a *sense of future*" [355], which I examine in several chapters. Huron argues, as I do, that aesthetic experience—his focus is on the experience of music—builds upon evolutionarily adaptive strategies of anticipating dangers.) Cavell examines the everyday occurrence of "expecting someone to tea," and he wonders "whether expecting [is or] isn't really a particular feeling (say the one developed in waiting in the dark with others for the birthday person to open the door ...)" (205). Is such a "feeling" an event? And, if so, is the "event" of experience *always* somehow anticipatory, as if "experience" is not as self-contained as it sometimes feels? Cavell goes on to wonder whether "the concept expressed in the ordinary world 'expecting' is basically vague or grossly conventional ... or else there really is no such thing as expecting, but at best a collection on unnamed and perhaps unnamable inclinations." He concludes: "if I say to myself 'Still, *I* know what expecting is,' I am at the verge of an intellectual crisis. It is not *I* who know this. This is what expecting *is*. Everyone knows it. Except, evidently, for some people" (205). What Cavell is doing—what Wittgenstein does—is complicating the *event* of experience and in so doing complicating "experience" itself.

But let me return to literary studies. In Chapter 1 I have already touched upon Jonathan Kramnick's synthesizing account of the relationship between the ways we might understand what he calls "experiential consciousness" (3) provoked and set forth by literary texts in relation to psychological and neurological research focused on consciousness, the "way," as he notes, that "mere marks on the page strive to create perceptual objects" (166). My task is somewhat different: I hope to demonstrate how disciplined literary study works to make "experience" part of healthcare rather than to bracket "immediate sensations of experience," as Frye and the nomological sciences do. Kramnick offers a fine definition of "experience" in relation to the discipline of literary studies: "experience," he writes, "is originary and the stuff of life but it is also achieved through skilled attunement to a world in which one is embedded" (76). The *Oxford English Dictionary* defines the noun "experience" more generally as "**3**. The actual observation of facts or events, considered as a source of knowledge." (This third definition presents the earliest instance of the word in English, 1377.) And it adds "**4a**. The fact of being consciously the subject of a state or condition, or of being consciously affected by an event." As a verb, it notes "**2a**. To have experience of; to meet with; to feel, suffer, undergo" and "**2b**. To learn (a fact) by experience." Generally speaking, as both noun and verb—as both a fact and an event—experience designates active awareness.

More technically, David Chalmers begins his monumental philosophical study, *The Conscious Mind*, with "a catalog of conscious experiences." Although I do not share Chalmers early conclusions concerning the metaphysical "dualism" he espouses (see Exhibit 2.1), his catalogue offers a comprehensive sense of experience. It includes visual experiences, auditory experiences (particularly music), tactile experiences, olfactory experiences, taste experiences, experiences of hot and cold, pain, and other bodily sensations. In addition to these "sensational" or "perceptual" notions of experience, he also catalogues mental imagery, conscious thought, emotions, and the sense of self (6–11).

Exhibit 2.1: Chalmers' Dualism

For Chalmers, at least in his early ground-breaking study *The Conscious Mind*, consciousness—including, by implication, the *experience* of meaning I touched upon at the beginning of Chapter 1—is immediate and unanalyzable: it is not subject to scientific (e.g., *semiotic*) analysis or to physicalist reductionism, the latter of which I describe in these chapters as scientific positivism. For Chalmers, consciousness is simply a given, a "further fact" as he calls it (*Conscious Mind* 107) beyond any accompanying physical processes. Hence his early "dualism."

In his analysis, he sets forth the intuition—he claims throughout *The Conscious Mind* that conscious experience itself is necessarily "intuitive"—that the felt qualities of experience such as the color red, harmonies of sound, or pain (146) are not reducible to the mechanical explanations of materialism. Thus, he notes that "all it means to be a conscious experience, in any possible world, is to have a certain feel" (133). In work subsequent to *The Conscious Mind*, Chalmers more fully contemplates the possibility of panpsychism as noted in Exhibit 1.10 and also in Chapter 6. In *Intangible Materialism*, as in this book, I argue that experience is susceptible to systematic analysis beyond the bald assertion of "intuition" even if I believe, as does Chalmers, that it cannot be adequately analyzed by the systematic positivism of purely "physicalist" reductionism. In an essay in *Scientific American* that Chalmers published just before *The Conscious Mind* appeared, he "speculates" on a "grand theory" beyond intuition to account for conscious experience ("Puzzle" 86). I examine this essay more fully at the end of Chapter 6.

I first began to focus systematically on the nature of experience when I was working on my book *Pain and Suffering* in the Routledge Series Integrating Science and Culture. I found that people who study pain—psychologists, philosophers, medical researchers, even semioticians, and literary critics—observe that *pain is by definition a conscious experience*. Moreover, I discovered that the phenomenon of pain raises questions concerning the integration of the sciences and the humanities that is the focus of the Routledge Series. As fact and event, pain is subject to scientific analysis; yet because it is necessarily conscious, necessarily experienced, it is intimately tied up with any experience we might have of self or personhood, with the meanings and values—the *meaningful value*—with which the humanities and cultural studies engage. In studying pain, I came across a bizarre case of a man who, in an emergency open-heart surgery performed *without anesthetic*, which seemed to occasion excruciating pain, was given a drug inducing amnesia. What was bizarre was that fact that afterwards he felt that he had not experienced any pain at all. I also encountered the equally bizarre use of lobotomy as pain relief. The terrible surgery of lobotomy results in what is described as a complete indifference to pain. One woman, who underwent a lobotomy to relieve intractable pain, answered, when her doctor asked her about her pain, that "yes, it's still there. I just don't worry about it anymore." Then, she smiled sweetly and chuckled to herself: "In fact, it's still agonizing. But I don't mind" (see *Pain and Suffering* 10, 6–7, 59, 60).

Both of these cases—the loss of the sensation-experience by means of an amnesiac drug and loss of the affect-experience related to pain by means of a lobotomy—seem to erase both of Chalmers' categories of experience: "perceptual experience," experience that seems to come through the senses, and "affective experience," experience that presents itself as meaningful. In Chapter 3, I cite (more fully than in Chapter 1) Northrop Frye's examination of "naïve science," which focused on "the immediate sensations of experience" (44), and his distinction between "immediate sensations" and a more complex—a "mediated" and often "affective"—sense of "experience," which is important in understanding both discipline and literature. In this book, I strive to replace the notion of "sensation-perception" with that of "experience" because sensation-perceptions present themselves as simply self-evidently true, even when they are not "experienced," as in the two bizarre examples I set forth. I argue that while pain clearly presents itself as immediate sensation, there is good evidence that such immediacy is mediated through neurological and cultural schemas that condition different experiences of pain from one community to another and one time to another. "Experience" is more complex than apparently immediate self-evident sensation in other ways as well. Along with *perceptual experience*, in these chapter-lectures I also touch upon *intellectual experience* (citing Ludwig Wittgenstein's meditation on the "*experience* [of] the meaning of a word" [§261] in Chapter 3), *social experience* (applying Veblen's "habits of thought" in Chapter 4), *affective experience* (reviewing neurological studies of affect and aesthetics in Chapter 5), and *vicarious experience* (to which I devote the final Chapter 6).

In *Marxism and Literature* Raymond Williams sets forth his fecund and widely cited notion of "structures of feeling" in a passage that led me to the "allusive" subtitle for this book. "Structures of feeling," he writes, are

> concerned with meanings and values as they are actively lived and felt .... An alternative definition would be structures of experience: in one sense the better and wider word, but with the difficulty that one of its senses has that past tense which is the most important obstacle to recognition of the area of social experience which is being defined. We are talking about characteristic elements of impulse, restraint, and tone; specifically affective elements of consciousness

and relationships: not feeling against thought, but thought as felt and feeling as thought: practical consciousness of a present kind, in a living and inter-relating continuity.... [In this], we are also defining a social experience which is still in process, often indeed not yet recognized as social but taken to be private, idiosyncratic, and isolating, but which in analysis (though rarely otherwise) has its emergent, connecting, and dominant characteristics.

(132)

Williams rejects "the better and wider" terminology of "structures of experience" because, I suspect, it is so easy to confuse "experience" with "immediate sensation." That is, the "past tense" of experience he describes is the fact that experience seems both individual and always already completed and remembered—which is why that stories of unremembered and non-affective pain I mention are so bizarre.

Yet, as Williams's longer meditation on "structure of feeling" suggests—along with enormous advances in understandings of neurological subroutines and subsystems (see Hardcastle, Huron, Goldman, Damasio) and along with more fine-grained understandings of cultural "habits of thought" or the cultural "space of meaning" (see Veblen, Harris, Flanagan)—the concern Williams felt about the term "experience" in 1977 is less apposite now almost a half a century later. Thus, Lauren Berlant notes the ways in which we might understand Williams in relation to "affect" studies that have arisen in the wake of "critical poststructuralism" (Ngai 35), which was, as Joseph North points out, initiated in large part in the work of Williams. "Williams' model" of "structures of feeling" as opposed to the "intensities" of affect, upon which affect theory focuses, Berlant notes, "places the historical present in the affective presence of an atmosphere that is sensed rather than known and enacted, a space of affective residue that constitutes what is shared among strangers" ("Unfeeling" 194). Such a space, she contends—which I am arguing is the "space" of "experience" writ large—develops "an affective common [by means of] a process of jointly gathered implicitation" (194), which is to say joint engagements with the implicit—and the *inferential*—within experience. It is precisely to develop or strengthen this common and communal ("jointly gathered") sense of possibly shared experience, I am arguing, that is the explicit work of the health humanities just as, in my argument, it is the implicit work of literature. Thus, in many ways, Williams—along with the philosophy of science, neurology, economics, moral philosophy, and the practical reasoning pursued in the health humanities—has taught us to look twice at "experience," to think of both the intensities and the future of "experience" itself in the double-take I describe in Chapter 1. Finally, I should also note that Williams's emphasis on the recognition of features of experience in "analysis (though rarely otherwise)" is an emphasis on *disciplined* understanding (see Exhibit 2.2).

Exhibit 2.2: Cultural Studies and Aesthetic Studies

A major theme of Joseph North's argument in *Literary Criticism: A Concise Political History* is that the cultural studies of Williams offers an extreme antithesis to the aesthetics and practical criticism of I. A. Richards and the far more conservative Kantian idealism of the American New Criticism. He argues that Williams is the "emblem" of "the current consensus around a scholarly historicist/contextualist approach to literature," which was "a rejection of the category of the aesthetic" (16). "For Williams," North notes, "... the critique of idealist aesthetics ended with the wholesale rejection of aesthetics, and its replacement with a thorough-going historicism" (68). This opposition in recent literary studies had led some scholars, as Jonathan Kramnick notes, to focus on "the fundamentality of form" rather than historicism in studying literature (43). (He examines Sandra Macpherson and Caroline Levine to this effect in some detail.) While historicism—in Williams, Fredric Jameson, and many others—seeks explanations that sometimes seem more sociological than "literary," formalism commits itself (in many instances) to "surface" reading. In another way to describe this opposition, historicism has a tendency to emphasize the cognitive, what we can learn from literature, while aestheticism tends to emphasize the experiential, how literature provokes the simulated (vicarious) "feel" of things. For my purposes, however, the distinction is somewhat besides the point. For in educating healthcare students and professionals—and, as Dr. Robert Coles says, for educating "every medical student, law student, or business school student, every man or woman studying at a graduate school of education or learning to be an architect" (160) as well—one can see that vicarious experience contributes to empathetic engagements while cognitive comprehension contributes to what I describe in Chapter 6 as "moral education." As such, it is not necessary to situate Williams as an "emblem" of a seemingly "fundamental" opposition in literary studies, but rather to see him, as I implicitly do, as taking up literary texts to the end of contributing to moral—what he would call "political"— education. Moral education, after all—and, for that matter, political education—traffic in the "experience" of value.

At least one purpose of these chapter-lectures on the discipline of literary studies is to participate in the disciplined "double-take" of what we think we already know. Such a "double-take," as Rita Felski notes in *Uses of Literature*, defines literature itself as offering the combination of facts and events, the experiential rediscovery of "things as we know them to be, yet reordered and redescribed, shimmering in a transformed light" (102). When the neuroscientist Antonio Damasio describes the self as "witness" (*Self* 12), he is also suggesting the necessary conscious and reflective nature of experience. He extends this notion when he distinguishes between "emotion" ("the world of emotion," he says, "is largely one of action carried out in our bodies") and "feelings" ("composite *perceptions* of what happens in our body and mind when we are emoting)" (109). "A discussion on the topic of emotion," he says, "returns us to the matter of life and value" (108). In Chapter 6, I examine one "feature" of literary narrative under the category of "the witness who learns," something that Felski describes in her study of literature. In Chapter 5, I attempt to bring together the way that literary genre captures the *perceptions* of feeling. A significant theme in all these chapter-lectures is the contention that semiotics is the systematic study of perception, the systematic study of the necessary *meaningful* nature of experience, which is erased by amnesia and lobotomy.

The Representation of Experience

In order to develop a more detailed sense of "literature," I should set forth a short analysis of the representation of experience—the extreme "experience" of pain—in the discursive arts of poetry and fiction. A strictly semiotic account of the experience of poetry—what one might call a strict "surface" reading of language—clarifies, I think, the double-take of aesthetic experience I have been describing. "What is common to all [poetic] phenomena," A. J. Greimas argues in an attempt to articulate a precise semiotic description poetry,

> is the shortening of the distance between the signifier and the signified: one could say that poetic language, while remaining part of language, seeks to reachieve the "primal cry," and thus is situated midway between simple articulation and a linguistic double articulation. It results in a meaning-effect ... which is that of "rediscovered truth" which is original and originary .... It is an illusory signification of a "deep meaning," hidden and inherent in the [phonological—which is to say the "surface"] plane of expression.
>
> ("*La linguistique*" 279; my translation)

The double articulation of language is the opposition between the material signifier (the phoneme, which, as I mention in Chapter 4, is a mechanism of *attention*) and the immaterial signified (meaning, which, under the category of *purport* described in Chapter 3, is a mechanism of *expectation*). Poetry, in this definition, attempts to create the "illusion" of the immediate experienced value of a "meaning-effect" simply on the surface. Such a meaning-effect suggests that the signifier of the symbolic and communicative system of language can be taken to be what cognitive neuroscience calls the simple "vocal signals" of primates (Emery and Amaral 174), a seemingly momentary—seemingly immediate and unmediated—"fact." These two "planes" of language—that of phonological "sound-distinction" and that of semantic "meaning"—describe "linguistic double articulation." In this, the "phonological sound-distinction" is best understood as a phonological *force*, a phenomenon that, I note in Chapter 5, is neither physical nor psychological but rather a complex mediated "fact" that is felt to be immediate. Moreover, what is felt in semiosis and in Greimas's semiotic analysis of poetry is the promise—the expectation—of meaning, the "particular feeling" of expectation (205), which Cavell discusses.

As Greimas suggest, one such human primal "vocal signal," outside systematic meaningfulness, is the very scream of pain. Thus, David Morris remarks that tragedy enacts suffering and, at its heights, as in *Oedipus*, it sets forth a "cry of agony: speech rolled back into mere sound and torment"; and he adds that Lear, holding the corpse of his dead daughter, "utters three words, but they are not so much words as sounds, less spoken than bellowed like an animal cry: 'Howl, howl, howl.' As with Oedipus," he concludes, "we witness simply the ruined human body and the sound of suffering. Nothing more"

(248). Whether or not Lear's "Howl" is a primal cry—in this scene he may be enjoining his audience to howl in an imperative perlocutionary speech act rather than a cry—the "vocal signals" of primates that neuroscience describes are *literally* "primal cries," in which the distance between signifier and signified, between sound and import, does not exist, in which, that is, the momentary scream contains no promise of meaning. Thus, Greimas's semiotic description of poetry, like Viktor Zuckerkandl's descriptions of music I examine in Chapter 4, attempts to delineate the power and force of a primal cry as part of an (aesthetic) experience rather than taking it to be "nothing more" than "the sound of suffering."

In his masterful study *Pain: A Cultural History*, Javier Moscoso has argued that there is strong historical evidence for aesthetic transformations of the "objectified content" of pain, what he calls its "imitation" (or what I might call its "analogical grasping") and the "narrative recounting" of pain itself. In fact, he takes up complex combinations of attention and expectation that are caught up in "experience," which I have already touched upon, in the phenomenon of pain. Moscoso's study, ranging through a long history of artistic forms, attempts to categorize forms of representation of pain. His extended discursive example is *Don Quixote*, where he focuses on the inability of recent literary criticism to attend to the mimetic representation of Quixote's pain (34–43). He notices the ways that modern readers "lose sight of the extent to which Cervantes represented his protagonist in confrontation with the *tyranny of matter*" (38; italics added), what I have called the force and dynamism of the *facticity* of pain ("Aesthetics of Pain" 472). That is, he notices the ways that modern readers are less likely to attend to the *fact* of pain in a quest to anticipate its meaning.

More contemporaneous narrative accounts of pain than Cervantes's confrontation with the materiality of pain emphasize its discursive/semiotic representation rather than its mimetic representation Moscoso nicely pursues. In a powerful and harrowing novel, *The Woman Who Walked into Doors*, Roddy Doyle recounts the life of a working-class woman in Dublin who suffers through decades of physical and sexual abuse from her husband. It is a novel I regularly read with pre-med and medical students. In the novel, Paula Spencer narrates her life from adolescence—when her father called her a "slut" for putting on makeup—through her marriage, separation from her husband, and finally his death. The novel builds toward the pain and violence that was always, silently and implicitly, a part of her life. Toward the end of the novel, Paula remembers a particularly terrible beating she suffers at the hands of her husband, Charlo. This passage is striking because

Paula juxtaposes two accounts of her painful experience: first a narrative presentation of a terrible beating, which sets forth the overwhelming of any sense of expectation—any sense of "the promise of happiness," by which, as we have seen, Stendhal defines beauty (66)—in its insistent attention to (Moscoso's "imitation" of) pain itself; and second, Paula's reflection on the story she is telling, in which she "cannot recollect" the difference between one beating and another in her long experience of spousal abuse. In other words, the novel—and particularly this long passage—in its "double articulation" of Paula's pain experience offers an aesthetic "double-take" on experience itself.

> He's seen me looking at a man. In the pub; we're just back from the pub, just in the door.
> —I didn't look at anyone, Charlo.
> He opened his hand. The sting and the shock, the noise, the smack. He's too fast.
> —Say that again.
> You never get used to it. Predicting it doesn't matter. Nothing I can do; he has complete control. It's always fresh, always dreadful.
> Again.
> Always a brand new pain.
> The skin doesn't get any harder ....
> Pushes me, drops me into the corner. Hair rips. A sharper pain. His shoe into my arm, like a cut with a knife. His grunt. He leans on the wall, one hand. His kick hits the fingers holding my arm. I lose them; the agony takes them away. Leans over me. Another grunt, a slash across my chin. My head thrown back. I'm everywhere. Another. Another. I curl away. I close my eyes. My back. Another. My back. My back. My back. My back. Back shatters.
> The grunting stops. Breaths. Deep breaths. Wheezing. A moan. I wait. I curl up. My back screams. I don't think, I don't look. I gather the pain. I smooth it.
> Noises from far away. Creaks. Lights turned on, off. Water. I'm everywhere. I'm nothing. Someone is crying. It isn't me yet. I'm under everything. I won't move; I don't know how to. Someone's in pain. Someone is crying. It isn't me yet. I'm under everything. I'm in black air. Someone is crying. Someone is vomiting. It will be me but not yet. (183–4)

The pain described in this passage is so overwhelming to Paula that both she and the "future-oriented construals" of meaning and discipline I discuss throughout this book disappear in the face of it—"it will be me but not yet," she says—as the experience of pain itself, like a primal cry, becomes *everything*. This passage offers a crescendo of pain, as expectation is repeatedly violated: Doyle captures the first-person voice of his protagonist even as the "person" speaking seems to disappear in the face of pain. That is, in this passage the first-person—the experiential first-person "perspective" Kramnick describes (120) discussed earlier—is lost and overwhelmed in sentence fragments, "gestures" of meaning, "prelingual" free-floating sounds that Dr. Rita Charon and Maura Spiegel describe (v), in which paradoxically habituation, as Clune argues, overwhelms experience.

But the next passage in Doyle's novel is even more striking. Here, Paula reflects on her pain in a manner that substantiates Clune's contention that the goal of aesthetics—or at least Romantic and Post-Romantic aesthetics—is to "write against" the ways that the "familiar object," though time, becomes "a cognitive whole practically sealed off from direct perceptual contact" (3). In his argument, he favorably quotes Proust, who observes that "the only true voyage, the only bath in the Fountain of Youth, would be not to visit strange lands but to possess other eyes, to see the universe through the eyes of another" (cited by Clune 28; remember also the "bath in Irish" defining interdisciplinary studies I mentioned in Chapter 1). In this passage, Doyle seems to simultaneously depict Paula as "sealed off" from particular experience and, at the same time, to present his readers with "new eyes" that "open up" the *verbal* experience of her discourse. "Do I actually remember that?" Paula asks herself.

Is that exactly how it happened? Did my hair *rip*? Did my back *scream*? Did he call me a cunt? Yes, often; all the time. Right then? I don't know. Which time was that anyway? I don't know? How can I separate one time from the lot and describe it? I want to be honest. How can I be sure? It went on for seventeen years. Seventeen years of being hit and kicked. How can I tell? How many times did he kick me in the back? How many times did I curl up on the floor? How can I remember one time? When did it happen? What date? What day? I don't know. What age was I? I don't know. *It will be me but not yet*. What is that supposed to mean? That I was nearly unconscious; that the pain was unbearable? I'm messing around here. Making things up; a story. I'm beginning to enjoy it. Hair *rips*. Why don't I just say He pulled my hair? *Someone is crying. Someone is vomiting*. I cried, *I* fuckin' well vomited. I choose one word and end up telling a different story. I end up making it up instead of just telling it. *The sting and the shock, the noise, the smack.* I don't want to make it up. I don't want to add to it. I don't want to lie. I don't have to; there's no need. I want to tell the truth. Like it happened. Plain and simple. *My husband is beating me up. A horrible fact. A stranger.* Did any of this actually happen? Yes. Am I sure? Yes. *Absolutely sure, Paula?*

(184–5)

"I want to tell the truth" has the force of the future, the force of a promise. That is, these passages taken together attempt to enact Greimas's illusion of a primal cry and to reflect upon that illusion in order to transform, somehow, the terrible facticity of pain into what I have called "affective comprehension" (see "Aesthetics of Pain" but also Chapter 5). Such comprehension, and the future-oriented transformations upon which it builds, allows us to grasp and represent the dynamism and force of pain, the "third thing" I describe in Chapter 4, which is not simply reducible to natural fact or social construction.

In the two versions of Paula's pain Doyle presents, he enacts both an illusory "simple articulation" of her pain and its second, "double articulation" that Greimas describes in his semiotic description of poetry. That is, in the first passage Paula narrates material embodiments, vocal signals of pain: grunting, wheezing, crying. Yet she does so in the manner in which semiotic systems create material (phonemic) signs—realized *through* the materiality of physical of sounds, inscriptions, gestures—and organize them into systems of signification, paradigms of grammar. Paula's direct description functions like the articulation of seeming "material embodiments" of apparent sound, which constitute phonemes in the linguistics of Ferdinand de Saussure. In this, linguistic phonemes are not *simply* physical air vibration or psychic apprehension but "a third thing, which [as we shall see] belongs to neither the physical nor the psychic context" (Zuckerkandl 60). With the second passage—which directly follows the first—Doyle creates a discursive double articulation of Paula's pain. Here, I want to argue that pain—the complex *experience* of pain—is necessarily inhabited by signification, meaning, purport. In this, we can see, everyday "experience" is continuous with aesthetic "experience": Paula is seemingly "sealed off" from the particularities of her experience while Doyle's reader is offered "other eyes" to engage that very experience *in the future reading of his text.* (Such "future reading," as we shall see, warrants the linguist Louis Hjelmslev to replace the word *meaning* with *purport* in his systematic account of Saussurean semiotics. In a larger register, it can be discerned in the intergenerational caring—the "keyings" of the real—described throughout this book.) In the second passage, Paula

55

transforms into meaningful *expectations* for her readers or interlocutor the seeming momentary overwhelming attention that pain demands. (One of the essential aspects of meaningful discourse, both everyday discourse and aesthetic discourse, as I have already suggested, is the interlocutor, what I call "the witness who learns.") Moreover, in its explicit struggle for a "double articulation"—in its "double-take" on experience—the discourse of Doyle's novel describes the *situation* of experience, which is neither psychological nor physical, neither "subjective" nor "objective." That is, experience is *dynamic*—as Gadamer says, it brings "nothing to close" (cited in Jay 402)— but rather is a site of interaction and feedback.

The Chapter-Lectures

In *Literary Studies and Well-Being*, then—and especially in the chapters based upon the Harbin lectures, which follow this chapter—I focus on aspects of the discipline of literary studies. The term "aspects" itself, which I borrow from Wittgenstein, is a way of engaging and understanding experience that helps shape the discipline of literary studies altogether. In Chapter 3 I examine the humanities in relation both to the nomological sciences and to "retrospective" sciences such as the social sciences or evolutionary biology. I argue while the nomological sciences focus on unchanging "facts"—and "events" understood primarily as "facts"—and while the social sciences focus on "events" also understood primarily as "facts," which develop through time, and which social sciences analyze in terms of statistics or function, the humanities in general, and the discipline of literary studies more particularly, focus on the relationship between facts and events—knowledge and affect— which is to be understood as *experience*. Such experience, as Charles Altieri has argued in discussing the meaning and force of the poetry of Ezra Pound, can be grasped as "relations among facts rather than moments of perception" (5); his refusal to take self-evident "moments of perception" as an adequate description of experience reinforces the substitution of the term *experience* for the narrower term *sensation* throughout this book. It is my contention that relations among facts can be understood as "structures of experience." The discipline of literary studies, then, is the systematic study of the nature—which is to say, the "structure"—of experience and the rules and institutions which condition experience.

Chapter 4 focuses on value and language, with value understood as the *qualities* that inform experience. In doing so, it considers speech-act theory and its analyses of values and qualities as ways of understanding facts and events. It discovers in speech-act theory—and in the discipline of literary studies more generally—an alternative to the philosophical and scientific positivism inherited from Enlightenment Modernity. In the early twentieth century, in developing what came to be called "Institutional Economics," Veblen argued that we should understand that most (if not all) phenomena we experience are "institutional" facts rather than what John Searle calls positive "brute" facts (50–3). Such institutional facts come to be through performance—actions in the world—rather than the "myth" of self-evident truths, "the myth of that which is the case," which Max Horkheimer and Theodor Adorno critique in *Dialectics of Enlightenment* (ix). Hilary Putnam describes the self-evident truths of positivism as "empiricism's sensationalistic epistemology" (loc 83), a description which reiterates the importance, throughout this book, of replacing the notion of seeming immediate *sensation* with a sense of the rich complexity of *experience*.

Chapter 5 focuses on narrative genres in relation to literary studies. Genre, it contends, is the bedrock of the discipline of literary studies—along with a parallel bedrock found in semantics—in the same way that formulaic mathematics is the foundation of the nomological sciences and retrospective statistical analysis is the foundation of the social sciences. As I have already suggested and elaborate more fully in Chapter 3, Frye argues that disciplines do not organize themselves in relation to "the immediate sensations of experience" but rather seek to analyze in an organized "institutional" fashion what gives rise to facts of experience. In Frye's examples, physics becomes a thorough-going intellectual disciplinary when it questions the nature of self-evident sensations, "hot, cold, moist, and dry" and discovers "that its real function was to explain what heat and moisture were." Similarly, he argues

> as long as biology thought of animal and vegetable forms of life as constituting its subject, the different branches of biology were largely efforts of cataloguing. As soon as it was the existence of forms of life themselves that had to be explained, the theory of evolution and the conceptions of protoplasm and the cell poured into biology and completely revitalized it.

> (45)

In same way, genres focus on the "forms" of literature. Thus, in engaging with and understanding phenomena beyond the self-evidence of "immediate sensations of experience" (44) in Frye's examples of physics and biology, literature can be studied in a disciplined institutional fashion that systematically analyzes the seeming "immediate sensations of experience" that literature provokes, including aesthetic experiences of frisson, awe, and laughter organized in relation to literary genres. The systematic analysis of language takes place on many levels—see the catalogue of features of semantic analysis beginning with the "distinctive features" of phonemes in Chapter 4—but the most encompassing, I contend, is genre, especially when genre is understood as related to the "habits of thought" and the "space of meaning" of ideology (see Frow *Genre*). I think it is no accident that the systematic analysis of the modes, symbols, archetypal myths, and genres of literature that Frye undertakes in *Anatomy of Criticism* concludes with the "Fourth Essay: Rhetorical Criticism: Theory of Genre." (The link between rhetoric and genre also underlines the connection between genre and ideology John Frow examines and the connection between genre and semantics I mention here.)

Thus, the first three chapters based upon the Harbin lectures (Chapters 3, 4, 5) focus on the experience of "action" and "acts": the work of discipline, speech-acts generating value and meaning in language and discourse, and narrative genres generating value and meaning in discursive art-forms and social situations. The final chapter examines the value of action in terms of defining "events"—including "events" of vicarious experience—conceived as contributing to a moral education, an education for the future. It pursues a sense of morality and ethics that is "worldly" in Edward Said's sense of the term, which I take up in the Chapter 3 (and which we already encountered in Said's definition of philology). In doing so, I concur with Sam Harris's argument that worldly morality is intimately related to the real or potential lived experience of well-being—Hilary Putnam describes this as "the great Aristotelian definition of human flourishing (*eudaimonia*)" (loc 244). Such flourishing, like morality itself, is always future-oriented (Flanagan 58; Flanagan also notes that for John Dewey "the moral problem concerns the future" [35]). Chapter 6 pursues this argument about moral education in order to suggest the ways that literature creates occasions for developing what Aristotle calls *phronesis* or "practical wisdom," which itself is at the base of the well-being (or "happiness") of *eudaimonia*. Most, including Aristotle, believe that *phronesis* is the product of long experience, but insofar as literature traffics in experience, I argue—based upon years of experience engaging people pursuing careers in healthcare with literary and non-literary narratives (see Shakir et al.)—that the vicarious experience provoked by literature can inform the practical future just as the wisdom of *phronesis* does.

The Discipline of Literary Studies

If the formulas of the nomological sciences are basically "timeless," and the analyses of the social sciences are basically "retrospective," then the discipline of literary studies confronts (vicarious) experience of the present with an eye toward the future. Its aim, then, as I suggest in Chapter 6, is practical reasoning or practical wisdom, which is after all, the worldly wisdom of *phronesis*. As such, the discipline of literary studies combines pure reasoning, aesthetics, and practical reasoning, which Immanuel Kant and Enlightenment Modernity took such pains to separate from one another (see Latour for a fine historical analysis of this pursuit of the systematic separation of fact, event, and value). Thus, the discipline of literary studies brings together the structure of language and narrative (pure abstractions), the order of genres (aesthetics), and the worldly work of *phronesis* (practical reasoning) in order to investigate the imbrication of the knowledge of facts and events, the pleasures (and displeasures) of aesthetic experience, and the practical reasoning of moral education all at once. (See Exhibit 2.3.)

Exhibit 2.3: Moral Reality

In his meticulous study arguing that moral values are no less "real" than the seeming self-evident facts of positive science, Michael Moore contends that positive facts are no less imbued with the experience of belief than are seeming subjective value judgments. He notes that "unlike the timeless *propositions* that we believe, our *beliefs* are states that occur in history. Like all states, they both cause other states or events and are caused by them" (1098). Moore's study is undertaken with the practical goal of analyzing the nature of "legal reasoning" just as the practical goal of much of my career has been the "clinical reasoning" of health care (see *Literature and Medicine* and "The Role of Narrative Structures in Healthcare Education"). As I have noted, Aristotle describes the goal of "practical reasoning"—knowledge that acts in the world—as *phronesis*.

In *On Literature*, Miller suggests that interest in a book like his focusing on the "concept" of literature is a sign of the waning of the function of literature "as a primary force in Western culture": he remarks that the invitation he received to write a book "on literature" was a symptom of what he calls "the death of literature" (35). That "death," he observes, is a function of new technologies, mostly digital, that are replacing the "predominantly paper culture" of books (82) and that are also replacing the collection, preservation, and study of such documents in institutions of higher learning. But what is to be made of a series of lectures on the "discipline" of literary studies offered in China during the great boom of wealth and leisure in that country, comparable, Professor Wang and I argue in *Modernist Poetics in China*, to the boom in wealth and leisure of Western cultural modernism at the beginning of the twentieth century? In other words, my concentration on the basic organization and focus of the discipline of literary studies as it developed in the twentieth and early twenty-first centuries in lectures presented to an audience of Chinese colleagues and friends is less, I think, a signal that "the end of literature is at hand" or "literature's time is almost up. It is about time" (Miller 1) than it is a way of re-thinking the "immediate sensations" of experience themselves in terms of the disciplined institutions of their study.

In his argument, Miller contends that "literary theory contributes to [the] death of literature [announced in] the first sentence of [my] book." Literary theory arose, he argues, "in its contemporary form just at the time literature's social role was weakening. If literature's power and role could be taken for granted as still in full force, it would not be necessary to theorize about it" (35). The chapter-lectures here, however, are not much concerned with "theorizing" about literature, and less concerned with "the end of the print age," "literature's strangeness," "the secret of literature," "why read literature," "how to read literature," and "how to read comparatively"—to list chapter titles and subtitles in Miller's book. Rather, they are concerned with the formal, institutional assumptions and organization of the study of literature in a time and place—in twenty-first century China, which is encountering, pursuing, and, indeed, transforming the formal study of literature as it developed in the West during the second Industrial Revolution of the early twentieth century and in expanded healthcare training programs throughout the United States, Europe, and Asia. Analyzing the discipline of literary studies in dialogue with Chinese colleagues and friends and healthcare colleagues and friends at this particular time allows us, together, to situate the study of literature and educated understanding more generally within the broader pursuits of higher education altogether. As I have already noted, it is striking to me how easily—and how cavalierly—Joseph North dismisses the health humanities as among "the various new discourses of 'literature as therapy' that have sprung up recently on the margins of literary study, often in the gap between our discipline and more directly therapeutic ones: the field of 'narrative medicine,' for instance" (188). It is my argument throughout this book that engagement with the practical understanding of healthcare sharpens ways of understanding the discipline of literary studies rather than creating a "marginal" application of literature in the service of other disciplines.

This larger project touches upon the nature of intercultural and interdisciplinary work. *Literary Studies and Well-Being* is fully inter-disciplinary, and, as readers will see, it takes up neuroscience, evolutionary biology, linguistics, philosophy, even economics, in its attempt to examine the formal institutional study of imaginative texts. But such "taking up" is not as simple as the notion of interdisciplinarity sometimes suggests. Kramnick is particularly anxious, as I note in Chapter 1, to maintain the disciplinary independence of literary studies from other—mostly scientific—disciplines with which it has recently engaged. And Michael Clune is also particularly anxious to distinguish the ways that the discipline of literary studies has either based its work on scientific understandings, to which it appears to be subservient, or—in his preferred understanding—remains independent insofar as literary studies "seek to open a special place for literature and art in scientific discourse by pointing to a particular caesura in the scientific study of human life. This gap," he concludes, "is experience. What cognitive, biological, and neuroscientific descriptions of human thought and behavior leave out ... is what it feels like to think and act" (57). Some years ago, in *Essays on Actions and Events*, Donald Davidson thoroughly examined such disciplinary independence. He takes it for granted, as he says,

> that detailed knowledge of the neurophysiology of the brain will make a difference ... to the study of such subjects as perception, memory, dreaming and perhaps of inference. But it is one thing for developments in one field to affect changes in a related field, and another thing for knowledge gained in one area to constitute knowledge of another.
>
> (247)

Davidson's inclusion of "inference" in his list of subjects connected to neurophysiology is illuminating in the context of this book. Charles Sanders

Peirce—Veblen's one-time teacher at Johns Hopkins and a person, along with Ferdinand de Saussure, who coined the term "semiotics" in the early twentieth century—spent some time examining the logic of "abduction," which later came to be known as "inference to the best explanation."

Michael Moore argues that "the inferential nature of perception" offers a powerful alternative to the positivist self-evidence of perception. His study of "Moral Reality" suggests that the self-evidence of "immediate experience" can be replaced by an understanding of the mediated-social nature of perception and experience, which entails the habits of (shared) thoughts governing more or less unconscious—or unreflected upon—inference. "Much of the work of the psychology of perception in the last forty years," he wrote in 1982,

> has shown the inferential nature of perception. We correct perception constantly, in light of our antecedently held background beliefs about how the world is. Much of the correction is not conscious .... Such work in psychology only dramatizes what we knew anyway; namely, that no factual beliefs are just inferenceless readoffs of reality .... While our retinal images may be unmediated reflections of reality, our beliefs about what we see are formed not only from retinal images but also from our more general beliefs.
>
> (1110)

The replacement of "inferenceless" self-evidence by experience conditioned by inference allows us to see the color brown in a different way—this is Moore's example—even though we also "*see* that it has not changed" (Wittgenstein §113). Moreover, the study of inference—of the devices of *construal*—is of great importance in understanding the work of literary studies in relation to healthcare. Jerry Vannatta and I devote a chapter of *The Chief Concern of Medicine* to Peirce's notion of "abduction," since it is a formal, disciplined, and, for the larger purposes of the healthcare humanities, a *narrative* way of understanding the so-called art of diagnosis, which in medical training is usually based upon the "unfiltered" apprenticeship of fostering seeming immediate experience. As Moore suggests, inference is built into experience, and the systematic analysis of its features and functioning suggests an important aspect of disciplined study and understanding.

What Davidson says about different "fields"—which is to say, different "disciplines"—could even more forcefully be said about different cultures, and in these chapters I hope, if not to affect changes, at least to provoke renewed examination of the formal, institutional assumptions and organization of the study of literature in China—and, in addition, the organization of the study of literature in relation to healthcare—by studying the organized assumptions about the study of literature in the United States at the present time. Unpacking, philologically, what Davidson says about the "constitution" of knowledge within disciplines is a goal of this book; it is part and parcel of my contention that "knowledge," for the humanities, includes the experience of affect as well as the knowledge of facts, the very engagement with what Wittgenstein calls the "*experience* [of] the meaning of a word" (§261). If this is so, then the analysis of the discipline of literary studies might allow us to see the work of other disciplines in a new light, what Wittgenstein also describes as the experience of "lighting up" of phenomena (§118) when we "see [them] differently" even though we also "*see* that [they have] not changed" (§113). In any case, this was and remains my hope for this book, initiated in my work in the health humanities and shared with colleagues and friends at the Harbin Institute of Technology on cold and bright wintery days.

* * *

The chapter-lectures that follow are based upon lectures that I offered at the Harbin Institute of Technology in January 2020. My hosts—particularly Lui Kedong, Wang Tiao, Huang Furong, Meng Meng, Han Xiaohui, among others—graciously asked if I might offer a series of lectures that would tie together some of the strands of my teaching and writing in several different fields over the years: the "culture of modernism" in the early twentieth century, semiotics, the medical humanities. The invitation was a wonderful opportunity for me to think about connections in various areas of study that seemed, when I undertook them, to be almost accidental: the sad death of Earl Wasserman, while I was in graduate school, that turned my doctoral work from Shelley to Yeats and Irish literature; the chance opportunity to work on a team, initiated by Alan Velie, that translated A. J. Greimas's *Structural Semantics* into English; the fortuitous meeting of my wife, Nancy Mergler, then Provost of the University of Oklahoma, with the Dean of our College of Medicine, Dr. Jerry Vannatta, which turned into decades of team-teaching, team-writing, and the widening of understanding of both of us. More specifically, in the Harbin lectures—and now in this book—I thought I would undertake the systematic pursuit of elaborating the appendix of *The Chief Concern of Medicine*, which I wrote with Jerry, entitled "Humanities as a Discipline," and an additional appendix of my book *Pain and Suffering*, entitled "Pain, Science, and the Humanities."

With the opportunity of looking back and across the discipline of literary studies, I find that transforming lectures into a book has afforded me the possibility of apprehending what Paul Klee described as the work of the modernist arts, namely "a striving to emphasize the essential character of the accidental" (cited in Bradbury and McFarlane 48; for a clear analysis, which offers a detailed exposition of the relation of accident to essence, see Ngai's discussion of Torbjørn Rødland's photograph *Baby* 211–12). But, of course, the essential character of the accidental is the character of experience itself. This is clear in engagements with impressionistic painting I touch upon in these chapters, which calls upon the pursuit and experience of "active absorption"; but it is also clear in the "active absorption" James Joyce demands of us: "it has been an unusually fatiguing day," Bloom reflects in *Ulysses*, "a chapter of accidents" (514). In addition, the essential nature of the accidental is also discernible in the active, contextual work of improvisation, of which this transformation of an "occasional" series of lectures into a book stands as an example. After all, the apprehension of the accidental as "essential" engages and organizes the lives and meanings we live and anticipate. In any case, it was with a real sense of gratitude that I undertook these lectures for my friends and colleagues in China, whose questions and discussions have deeply enriched my engagements with these matters in these chapters and exhibits.

CHAPTER 3
DISCIPLINED KNOWLEDGE AND THE EXPERIENCE OF MEANING

The Harbin Lectures

With this chapter, I begin four chapter-lectures based upon on a series of lectures entitled "The Discipline of Literary Studies" presented at the Harbin Institute of Technology. In the Harbin lectures I had returned to the theme of what Robert Con Davis-Undiano and I called "Literature as an Institution" in our text-anthology of more than twenty years ago, *Contemporary Literary Criticism*. In that book, we were thinking of a series of important statements about the study of literature, beginning perhaps with Matthew Arnold's attempt to define the discipline of literary studies in his essay "The Function of Criticism at the Present Time," written in 1865 from his position as the first scholar of modern (as opposed to classical) literature in Britain. In touching on Arnold, RC and I traced various ways that scholars in the late twentieth century focused on disciplined engagements with literature, what Joseph North has recently described as the "scholarly historicist/ contextualist approach to literature" (16). These included literary historians like Gerald Graff, who trace the institutional approaches to literature in American higher education; philosophers, like Cornel West, who situate literary studies in relation to race relations in my country; literary critics like Nancy Armstrong, who analyze the implicit ideologies of literary texts in relation to gender and class in Western culture; postcolonial scholars, like Gauri Viswanathan, who study the wider place of literature in creating colonial subjects; and literary critics like Northrop Frye, whose "Polemical Introduction" to *Anatomy of Criticism*, published in 1957, was adapted from his own 1949 essay rethinking Arnold's Victorian argument, also entitled "The Function of Criticism at the Present Time."

The Harbin lectures built upon this theme of the institutional nature of literary studies, including, as I already noted in the first two chapters of this book, the return to aesthetics and "close reading" and the turn to more thoroughgoing interdisciplinary studies in the early twenty-first century. Many scholars have remarked that these "turns" in literary studies mark a crisis in our discipline—as I note in Chapter 2, Hillis Miller explicitly proclaims that "literature's time is almost up" (1)—but it was my hope in the Harbin lectures, as it is in *Literary Studies and Well-Being* as a whole, to emphasize the practical wisdom of literary studies, particularly as I have already suggested, in its reality as a form of transgenerational caring, a feature it shares with the health humanities.

In this book, then, I am particularly interested in the institutional nature of value in literary studies. Since I describe in some detail this short series of chapter-lectures in Chapter 2, I only need to mention the trajectory of the Harbin series, beginning with a first lecture on the institution of literary studies in relation to other disciplines; a second lecture on the relationship between value and language; a third lecture that studies the discipline of literary genres in relation to neuroscience, the health humanities, and a materialist aesthetics; and a final lecture on the extension of value to ethics and morality, which focuses on the special "worldliness" of the discipline of literary studies, including the worldliness of ethics and literature. In the conclusion to the final chapter of this book—based upon the final Harbin lecture—I also return to Aristotle's notion of *phronesis*, which is sometimes translated as "practical wisdom" and to Aristotle's notion of *eudaimonia*, which, as I noted in the first pages of this book, is sometimes translated as "well-being," "flourishing," or "happiness." At Harbin—and also in the first pages of this book—I also mentioned the related Chinese term *le* (乐), which, as my Chinese audience understood, describes "feelings of joy, happiness, optimism and well-being" in relation to "the well-being gained when recovering from illness and when finally healing" (Yang and Zhou 182). "Flourishing," "well-being," and "healing"—particularly the last as the simpler "absence of disease"—are also three distinct definitions of "health" (see Schleifer and Vannatta *Chief Concern* 3–7). Thus, as this summary of the Harbin lectures might come to suggest—it outlines the "future" of the book based upon these lectures and based, as well, upon the rich colloquy accompanying these lectures—I have taken the opportunity afforded me by the invitation to lecture in Harbin to reconsider, in *Literary Studies and Well-Being* as a whole, my thinking about literary studies since *Contemporary Literary Criticism*, rethinking which is inflected by my now long-term collaborations with Dr. Jerry Vannatta in our work on literature and narrative in relation to clinical medicine, which began the very year the last edition of *Contemporary Literary Criticism* appeared, 1998.

The Nature of Discipline

Before I begin my examination of the discipline of literary studies in these chapter-lectures, let me take a few moments to examine discipline in general, and particularly the future-oriented nature of discipline, about which I hinted in the first two chapters. *The Oxford English Dictionary* offers twelve definitions of "discipline" as a noun, divided into three categories. They include "**II.6.** A system or method for the maintenance of order; a body of rules for conduct or action; a way of doing things"; and it describes "discipline" as related to "**III.12** .... some kind of control or command," including "**III.11** ... self-control, self-discipline." Its first set of definitions, "**I.** Senses relating to punishment," offers a region of meanings I do not touch upon in these chapters. To justify this exclusion of senses of "discipline" related to punishment in my argument, I implore you to remember the wonderful observation of Stanley Cavell, which I mentioned in Chapter 1, who notes that in "emphasizing society's resemblance to a prison rather than to a schoolroom, [philosophical thinking] may push too hard to fix the power between generations" (207). Walter Benjamin also asks in a similar fashion: "who would trust a cane wielder who proclaimed the mastery of children by adults to be the purpose of education? Is not education, above all, the indispensable ordering of the relationship between generations and therefore mastery (if we are to use this term) of that relationship and not of children?" (*Street* 487). The OED offers two other sets of definitions of "discipline": "**II.** Senses relating to training, instruction, or method" and "**III.** Senses relation to order arising from training or instruction," which more fully touch upon intellectual disciplines. These abstract definitions suggest five categories of "discipline": discipline—or what I might call "the challenges of discipline"—can be thought of in the following five ways.

1. Work and Toolmaking: Building Bridges from Goal to Accomplishment. The first aspect of discipline is perhaps the most concrete, even if I present it under the metaphor of "bridge-building," namely the discipline of trying to create something, to build something. In thinking about this, we should remember that the ancient Greek term ποιεῖν (poieó), from which we derive our English word *poetry*, means "to make" or more specifically "the activity in which a person brings something into being that did not exist before" (Polkinghorne 115). Some years ago—long before my first visit to China—I was invited to write a short article on "Literature" for the *Encyclopedia Americana*, which I began by comparing the Western notion of *poesis* to the Chinese term *wen* (文), which is variously translated as "text" and "pattern," and exists within what Ludwig Wittgenstein calls "a family of meanings" (§77) that includes "culture," "language," "writing." "Ancient Chinese culture," my encyclopedic entry notes,

> developed the term *wen*, which referred to "patterned" or rhymed language, what we might call "literary language," or "poetry." (*Wen* also referred to patterns or markings on natural objects, to inherited cultural traditions, and to the order of the cosmos.)
>
> (22.559)

Such patterning calls upon the "bridge-building" discipline I am describing, pursuing a goal and transforming the world. Even the patterns or markings of natural objects—especially on biological "objects"—are often "the fine-tuned product of hundreds of millions of years of [biological] evolution, presenting an orderly world of objects, agents, and events" (Steen 95), which follows the ruthless discipline of natural selection. (For a fine philological unpacking of *wen*, see Saussy.)

An important aspect of human "making" is the discipline of human toolmaking, which includes the truly amazing fact that tools—flint knives, stone blades, even musical instruments—were made *in anticipation of their use* (Donald 179; see also Schleifer *Intangible* 118). Moreover, such toolmaking is communal as much as individual, inherited from long social use, the "cultural traditions" of *wen* and "cultural inheritance," which contributes to the wealth of a community. In this, human toolmaking—beyond the ingenious "tools" of other primates, such as using sticks to get ants out of an ant colony—entails the creation of tools outside the immediate material situation of their necessity, so that the discipline of toolmaking is not "dependent on immediate environmental reinforcers or contingencies" (Donald 179). That is, human toolmaking is organized in relation to an imagined future—what the neurologist David Huron calls "a *sense of future*" (355)—a matter to which I return toward the end of this chapter. In fact, I might say that the concept of *discipline* altogether—its "method," its "control," and "self-control"—is precisely the manner in which disciplined work often begins in a detachment from *immediate* experience and need in the disciplined work of imagining a future. The future orientation of toolmaking is closely related to a central issue in Chapter 4, namely the future-oriented nature of language and meaning. There I note Charles Sanders Peirce's contention that the semiotic *symbol* in language is defined as "the law that will govern the future" (I, 23). It is also closely related to other chapter-lectures insofar as the aesthetics of literary genre—the focus of Chapter 5—participates in Stendhal's definition of beauty as simply "nothing other than the promise of happiness" (66) and moral education—the focus on Chapter 6—organizes itself in relation to future behavior.

2. Restraint: The Discipline of Resisting Instinct. A second aspect of discipline, closely related to toolmaking as I am describing it, is the discipline of resisting instinct. Here, we can see detachment from immediate need is closely related to detachment from immediate impulse with an orientation toward future activity. There is often great discipline involved in resisting impulse. This can be seen in the creation of tools outside of the pressing need dictated by environmental reinforcers or contingencies, but more notably in the general discipline of deferred gratification. Later in Chapter 5 I discuss the work of David Huron in his neurological analysis of the experience of music in which he describes the transformation of "instinctual" reactions to the world into "aesthetic" reactions to natural and made objects. He focuses on the transformation of *flight, fight,* and *freeze* reactions to danger, conditioned by neurological reactions to the environment, into vehicles for enlarging experience. The function of these so-called neurological instincts is to protect the individual and, in human communities, the cohort, from life-threatening dangers, while the function of the arts—the music Huron studies, the plastic arts of museums and architecture, and the discursive literary arts—is to expand possibilities of experience and affect, to create what Michael Clune calls "real human experience [which] is not natural but—in Coleridge's word—'supernatural'" (59). (He adds, such "perception is supernatural not in the sense of revealing another world, but in the sense of genuinely experiencing this world" [59].) The "supernatural"—or at least unnatural—resistance to so-called instincts embodied in the arts (although Huron doesn't explore this aspect of the aesthetics of music) entails great discipline, like that of toolmaking, of putting off immediate engagements with the environment in light of future purposes. (See Exhibit 3.1.)

Exhibit 3.1: On Instincts

I say "so-called" instincts, because the language of "instincts" seems to posit a positive fact rather than phenomena—the combination of fact and event—that call for further analysis. Thus, Francis Steen suggests that the conventional language of neurological "modules" should be replaced by conceiving these sources of behavior as neurological "sub-routines": "a key argument in evolutionary psychology," he writes, "is that natural selection will tend to produce highly specialized cognitive subsystems, each of which is optimized for solving recurring problems within a narrow domain" (94). To describe neural "modules" as subroutines and subsystems emphasizes inherited functions and human predispositions without positing a sense of the inheritance of strict "faculties" of mind, as if they were "facts" rather than processes (or "events"). Clune argues that such subroutines replace the "the high 'metabolic costs' of intense sensory engagement" (3) with experience-dulling habitual responses to the world. That is, his argument in *Writing Against Time*, as we have seen, is that artworks—objects of aesthetic attention—are designed to provoke the experience of perceiving "something for the first time" (4). His study is an extended discussion of the conception of "defamiliarization," developed by the Russian Formalists in the early twentieth century.

3. Ideas: Intellectual Discipline. In *Paper Minds*, Jonathan Kramnick offers a concise definition of intellectual discipline. "A discipline," he writes,

is an academic unit. It is neither a natural kind nor an arbitrary relic of the history of higher learning. Rather, any given discipline is a body of skills, methods, and norms able to sustain internal discussions and do explanatory work in a manner subject to its own consensus acts of judgment.

(18)

Kramnick offers a precise definition of an intellectual discipline, but it is striking—particularly because the subtitle of his book is *Literature and the Ecology of Consciousness*—that in this definition he does not coordinate his definition of intellectual discipline with any notion of experience. As I have already mentioned, two generations ago, in "The Function of Criticism at the Present Time"—later the "Polemical Introduction" to his enormously influential book, *Anatomy of Criticism* (1957)—Northrop Frye did precisely this. He argued that intellectual disciplines must create a systematic framework of symbols and procedures, which are fundamentally different from the worldly phenomena they seek to explain and understand. Thus, the *discipline* of an intellectual understanding, like toolmaking removed from immediate environmental needs and action removed from immediate impulse, is the rigorous separation from immediacy in a quest to develop and understand an intervening medium or agency. (The OED defines "immediate" as "**2a** .... acting or existing without any intervening medium or agency.") "Sciences," Frye writes,

> normally begin in a state of naïve induction: they come immediately in contact with phenomena and take the things to be explained as their immediate data. Thus physics began by taking the immediate sensations of experience, classified as hot, cold, moist, and dry, as fundamental principles. Eventually physics turned inside out, and discovered that its real function was to explain what heat and moisture were. History began as chronicle; but the difference between the old chronicler and the modern historian is that to the chronicler the events he recorded were also the structure of history, whereas the historian sees these events as historical phenomena, to be explained in terms of a conceptual framework different in shape from them.
>
> (44)

It is just such a disciplined framework that Frye develops for the study of literature in *Anatomy of Criticism*. This book, as James Comas argues, gained its importance because it offered a "science" of the humanities in 1957—what I am calling in this book "the human sciences"—just when the US Congress was passing the National Defense Education Act in response to the Russian sputnik (Comas 69–71). The final NDEA, which Congress passed in 1958, Comas argues, included the humanities in large part because of the disciplined systematic nature of Frye's analysis of literature. (I should also add in passing that it is striking to me that Joseph North fails to mention Frye at all in his concise history of literary criticism in the twentieth century. Perhaps North's strict opposition of historicist/contextualist approaches to literature and aesthetic approaches to literature is somehow confounded by Frye's systematic aesthetics and implicit literary history. See Exhibit 4.4: Northrop Frye.)

The difficulty of Frye's analysis of disciplines, however, is his metaphorical notion of turning understanding—in this instance, the understandings of physics—"inside out." What might this mean? Later in this chapter, I quote Charles Taylor describing the "renewals" of language. "Languages," he argues, "live only through successive renewals, each of which is a risk, for it runs the risk of not coming through this renewal unharmed" ("Discussion"

176), and certainly one sense of turning understanding "inside out" is to create a "renewal" of understanding. But perhaps more illuminating of Frye's metaphor is what philosophers call "semantic depth," an idea closely related to Taylor's sense of renewal (and closely related to the sense of the work and discipline of philology examined throughout Chapter 1). In arguing for "moral realism"—the reality of the status of judgments of value equal to the reality of the status of facts—Michael Moore cites Mark Platts's analysis of the nature of meaning. "Moral concepts," Platts writes,

> have a kind of semantic depth. Starting from our austere grasp upon these concepts, together perhaps with some practical grasp upon the conditions of their application, we can proceed to investigate, to experience, the features of the real world answering to these concepts. Precisely because of the realistic account given of these concepts and of our grasp upon them—precisely because they are designed to pick out features of the world of indefinite complexity in ways that transcend our practical understanding—this process of investigation through experience can, and should proceed without end.
>
> (Cited by Moore 1145)

In this account, Platts—and Michael Moore—offers a strong definition of what is meant by understanding altogether and specifically what he calls "investigation through experience": namely, strategies "designed to pick out features of the world of indefinite complexity in ways that transcend our practical understanding." Later Moore describes this as the repeated possibility "of more complex elaboration" of features or distinctions that shape understanding (1151); from the beginning of this book, I have described this "complex elaboration" as "philological unpacking." In this manner, the moisture and heat of naïve physics, the "immediate sensations of experience" which constitute "practical understanding," are transcended by accounts that allow us to *see* or *grasp* more, to see or grasp what had not been noticed before (see Exhibit 3.2).

Exhibit 3.2: The Discipline of "Features" and the Concept of *Geistigkeit*

In his history of the "universal theme" of experience in America and Europe, Martin Jay describes the organization of understanding in relation to features and distinctions as "the modalization of experience, its fracturing into the discrete sub-categories we have designated as epistemological, religious, aesthetic, political, and historical, ... [which allows] the inherent logic of each variant to be isolated and developed in its own immanent terms" (261). "More than merely discursive distinctions," he concludes, "these differentiated notions of experience also operated as normative guides for practices sanctioned by the distinct social and cultural institutions that emerged to propagate and regulate them. What came to count as a legitimate scientific experiment [for instance] was not the same as the mystic's attempt to merge with divinity by deliberately disorienting his sensorium, even if both could justifiably be called experiences" (262).

In some ways, such modalization allows the "ideas" of intellectual discipline to govern the experience that gives rise to those ideas. In *Freud: An Intellectual Biography*, Joel Whitebook analyzes a presentation Freud made toward the end of his life, which described what Freud called "an advance in *Geistigkeit*." *Geistigkeit*, Freud wrote, "meant that a sensory perception was given second place to what may be called an abstract idea—a triumph of *Geistigkeit* over sensuality, or strictly speaking, an instinctual renunciation, with all its necessary psychological consequences" (cited in Whitebook 489). Whitebook goes on to note that *Geistigkeit* is "richly polysemic," having been translated as both "spirituality" and "intellectuality" (440), but most importantly for my purposes, it entails both the making of things outside of the context of need and the resistance to instinct I have described in this catalogue of "discipline." In addition, Whitebook argues, it participates in a "second-order being and thinking" that characterizes the transformation of human engagements with the world, which first found world-wide instances in the Axial Age of the ancient world, and which manifests itself in the Enlightenment science Frye describes. (The "Axial Age"—a term coined by Karl Jaspers—designates the period of ancient history from about the eighth to the third century BCE that characterizes a period in which new ways of thinking in religion and philosophy appeared in Persia, India, China, ancient Israel, and the Greco-Roman world.) Second-order thinking, Whitebook goes on, "made it possible to both understand and criticize first-order thinking and the world as it is given. To use Hegel's language, this breakthrough to transcendence raised the human species out of its immediate natural existence and elevated it to the level of self-reflective *Geist* [spirit, ghost, mind]. The point to be stressed is that positing the existence of a transcendent sphere creates a standpoint from which 'actually existing thinking and reality can be criticized" (400). This second-order thinking characterizes Frye's notion of "inside out."

It is my contention that such "transcendence," at least in the human sciences, does not *abandon* experience but "picks out features" of the indefinite complexity of experience. Thus, it is my argument throughout this book that the discipline of literary studies pursues such a "realistic account" of experience itself—"the process of investigation through experience"— in a manner homologous to the "realistic accounts" of the physical world pursued by physics and of the social world pursued by the social sciences. Although Frye's "inside out" seems to advocate a systematic framework of symbols and procedures, which seem fundamentally different from the worldly phenomena they seek to explain and understand, Michael Moore (citing Mark Platts) suggests that this framework is not fundamentally different from worldly experience—in the way that the formulas of mathematical physics are fundamentally different from the experience of moisture or heat—but simply a more precise and systematic constellation and analysis of the complexity of phenomenal experience. (Moore, as I mentioned earlier, is a legal scholar marshalling philosophic arguments about understanding and reality to the practical ends of moral judgments in the context of legal practices, a fine example of *phronesis*. The anti-Kantian/ anti-Enlightenment contention of the continuity of worldly phenomena and aesthetic phenomena—including the framework of symbols and procedures developed by intellectual disciplines I am describing here—is a major theme of the rethinking of literary studies in the twenty-first century: see Kramnick, Clune, Joseph North, and especially Martin Jay and the many scholars they cite.)

As I have noted, intellectual discipline is homologous to the disciplines I have described so far, that of toolmaking and that of resisting impulse. The discipline of work, anticipated by tools, creates things that did not exist before, and that of resisting impulse creates possibilities of wider engagements with the world, wider sensibilities. Both disciplines are essentially *worldly*. Intellectual disciplines, as Frye suggests, often seem to strive for a separation from the immediate world in a "theoretical ideal," to use a phrase of Edward Said, an ideal that seeks a simple framework of understanding, a "simple additive or mechanical notion of what is or is not factual," as Said says ("Politics" 159). Such an ideal, as I note later in this chapter tutored by the analysis of Charles Taylor, "subsumes" worldly phenomena by means of explicit and sometimes implicit rules that are part of the disciplinary frameworks Frye describes. However, in his meditation on what he calls "the politics of knowledge," Said claims that the "intellectual work" in the humanities—unlike, perhaps, work in the "pure" nomological sciences—is always *worldly*. The theoretical "purity" of the nomological sciences is particularly notable in the creation of the discipline of economics in Europe. The late nineteenth century saw the transformation of "political economy" to "economic science"—the transformation of the study of wealth and value in human affairs to the creation of a mathematical economics purportedly indifferent to value judgments, which was, I have argued, "an attempt to squeeze experience out of understanding" (*Political Economy* 59).

Said makes his claim about worldliness in order to maintain a sense of experience within the purview of the intellectual discipline of the humanities. To do so, he advocates the development of a way of understanding knowledge and value in a manner that is commensurate with "the central factor of human work, the actual participation of peoples in the making of human life" beyond any theoretical "notion of what is or is not factual." In calling upon "human work" and "human life," Said touches upon the first two conceptions of "discipline" I am setting forth, and he emphasizes that their intellectual understanding must take up worldly behavior and worldly experience rather than explaining them away in theoretical (or mathematical or even aesthetic) idealizations. For Said, then, intellectual work focuses on human life—like these other disciplines, the human work of toolmaking and the human work beyond impulse—and it should not lose sight of the immanence of human activities. Such a goal in intellectual work, he says, "is worldly, that it is situated in the world, and about that world" ("Politics" 159-60; see also *Humanism*).

Sam Harris offers an extended example of worldliness—particularly in the way it emphasizes the connection between worldliness and human experience—in a catalogue of criteria often assumed in moral philosophy.

In discussing how "a practice like the forced veiling of women" might be "objectively wrong," he asks:

> Would the practice have to cause [the experience of] unnecessary suffering in *all possible worlds*? No. It only need cause unnecessary suffering in this world. Must it be *analytically* true that compulsory veiling is immoral—that is, must the wrongness of this act be built into the meaning of the word 'veil'? No. Must it be true *a priori*—that is, must this practice be wrong independent of human experience? No. The wrongness of the act very much depends on human experience. It is wrong to force women and girls to wear burqas because it is unpleasant and impractical to live fully veiled, because this practice perpetuates a view of women as being the property of men, and because it keeps the men who enforce it brutally obtuse to the possibility of real equality and communication between the sexes .... Does this slide from brute, analytic, *a priori*, and necessary truth to synthetic, *a posteriori*, contingent, exception-ridden truth pose a problem for moral realism? Recall the analogy I drew between morality and chess. Is it *always* wrong to surrender your Queen in a game of chess? No. But generally speaking, it is a terrible idea.
>
> (266–7)

Harris, then, like Said, pursues a kind of *worldliness*—here in ethics rather than in the more generally worldliness of discipline—in the disciplined investigations of human experience.

There is something more to this as well. The vicarious experience occasioned by literature, which I discuss at some length in the final chapter, is essentially worldly. This is the general purport of the enormous amount of work in psychology, neuroscience, and philosophy that Alvin Goldman surveys and synthesizes in *Simulating Minds*, which I touch upon in the early chapters of this book and repeatedly return to. Moreover, the simulated "vicarious" experience this work demonstrates in ordinary life as well as in literary "experience" emphasizes the *continuity* between worldly experience and aesthetic experience I mentioned earlier. And when I note in the final chapter how literary scholars often explain away (often in footnotes) as quickly as possible the experience of visceral violence, which literature, such as Yeats's "Leda and the Swan," provokes, I offer an example of the rejection of vicarious worldliness in the human sciences, which stretches back to Plato. Hillis Miller names Immanuel Kant as one of Plato's heirs in this regard and offers a powerful example of Kant's condemnation of the "worldliness" of novel-reading. "Novel reading," Miller writes,

> is an example of what Kant, in a word he frequently used, calls *Schwärmerei*. "Fanaticism" is a feeble translation of this wonderful German word. It means also revelry, riotous behavior, enthusiasm, rapture, ecstasy over something, idolization.
>
> (94)

In the experiential nature of *Schwärmerei*, which literature provokes, there is a problem for literary studies—and the human sciences more generally—which is not a problem for the nomological or retrospective sciences.

Here is the problem. The re-thinking of heat not as an experience, but as physical phenomena measured in terms of energy, does not erase the object of study, but situates it in a new intellectual framework or context: heat understood as energy rather than an immediate experience. But when experience itself is the object of study—as in the OED definition of the event of experience as "**2a** .... to feel, suffer, undergo"—a non-experiential abstraction, such as the "energy" by which we may understand heat, is much more complicated. Physics can replace "heat" with "energy" in its systematic development of a new vocabulary "to pick out features of the world of indefinite complexity in ways that transcend our practical understanding," which Platts describes (Moore 1145). But to "transcend" an understanding of "experience" cannot proceed by means of replacement. Rather, a disciplined account of "experience" calls for a double-take on experience itself, both experience and the "same" experience "renewed" (to cite the term we find in Felski, Taylor, Wittgenstein, Austin, and others). Remember my definition of pain as "*by definition a conscious experience*" (*Pain* 10). That is, the absence of the experience of heat lends itself to the explanatory description of—the replacement by—the energy-event of heatedness, while engagements with "experience" in literary studies does not "replace" experience but calls for a double-take on experience, which at once turns literature into something else (psychology? sociology? neuroscience? even Miller's "literary theory"?—all procedures which Clune describes as the subservience of literature to scientific disciplines), even while it *alternatively* allows literary studies to fill a "a particular caesura in the scientific study of human life," namely "experience" itself (Clune 57). To put this in another way, the "object of study" in literary studies, as Said suggests, is *essentially* worldly, and such worldliness shapes the discipline itself in its inability to fully—once and for all—"transcend" immediate experience. According to Samuel Weber, the object of literary studies, namely, literature, "has traditionally been distinguished from other 'objects' of study precisely by a certain *lack* of objectivity .... And such a lack of objectivity has, from Plato onward, confronted the study of literature (or of art in general) with the problem of its *legitimation*, and hence, with its status as, and in regard to, *institution(s)*" (33). By "*lack* of objectivity," Weber means the inability to turn "the immediate sensations of experience" fully inside out (to use Frye's terms) in the discipline of literary studies, since what literary studies focuses upon are experiences—worldly and so-called vicarious experiences—themselves. But, as I said, this is a matter I return to in my final chapter.

4. Improvisation: Discipline as Freedom. Before I turn, in this catalogue of disciplines, to the notions of "discipline" that are the focus of these chapter-lectures—namely the formal intellectual disciplines of professional education, which presents a "worldly" or "institutional" version of the "idea" of intellectual disciplines I just set forth—I want to say a word about the relation of discipline to freedom. The great saxophonist Charlie Parker practiced twelve or fourteen hours a day so that he could have the freedom of improvisation in his performances. In her analysis of Aristotle's notion of *phronesis*—the concept of "practical wisdom" or "practical reasoning," to which I repeatedly return—Martha Nussbaum argues that "theatrical improvisation" is "a favorite ... Aristotelian image for the activity of practical wisdom." "An improvising actress," she notes,

> if she is improvising well, does not feel that she can say just anything at all. She must suit her choice to the evolving story, which has its own form and continuity. Above all, she must preserve the commitments of her character to the other characters .... More, not less, attentive fidelity is required.
>
> (94)

"Attentive fidelity" is disciplined, even if it often seems to be simply "lucky." (An important book by Nussbaum I do not cite is entitled *The Fragility of Goodness: Luck and Ethics in Greek Tragedy and Philosophy*.) It's like a "lucky" shot in tennis: often so-called luck comes after hours of practice. Thus, "attentive fidelity" creates the freedom of choice among *faithful* activities. Such faithfulness is measured, like the disciplines of work, restraint, and explanation, against the goals of active and passive actions: the ability to work toward particular future goals; the ability to resist impulses; and the ability to organize thinking in relation to worldly accomplishments. The freedom of improvising creates itself by means of the discipline of long practice, as Parker knew and as we all know as we get better at things through practice. It is useful to remember that disciplined practice, however, creates a kind of "artificial" (or as Clune says, a "supernatural") instinct, the feeling—and perhaps the fact—of immediate and automatic action created through the mediations of disciplined practice.

In the discipline of "free" improvisation, it might be wise to remember J. L. Austin's assertion, cited at the very beginning of this book, that "'freedom' is not a name for a characteristic of actions, but the name of a dimension in which actions are assessed" (*Papers* 180). Stanley Cavell elucidates some of that dimension *as a verbal dimension* when he compares Austin's categories of illocution and perlocution, which he argues define the opposition between what Austin calls "performative utterances" and what Cavell himself calls "passionate utterances." "A performative utterance," he writes, "is an offer of participation in the order of law," by which he means—as does Austin—the order of convention, institutions, sociality. And he goes on: "And perhaps we can say: A passionate utterance is an invitation to improvisation in the disorders of desire" (185). In *Intangible Materialism*, I used similar language (in a text that antedates Cavell's analysis and follows Erwin Schrödinger's description of biology as tracing the creation of "biological/evolutionary order out of [physical] order") to describe the parallels between the physical sciences, the biological sciences, and semiotics: physics traces the creation of order out of disorder; evolutionary biology traces the creation of order out of (physical) order; and semiotics, I argue, traces the creations of disorder out of order (see *Intangible Materialism* 52–8 and *passim*). But what can the "creation" of disorder out of order possibly mean? A. J. Greimas perhaps best articulates this state of affairs in *Structural Semantics*, when he argues that the "edifice" of language "appears like a construction without plan or clear aim, like a confusion of floors and landings [*paliers*]: derivatives take charge of classes of roots; syntactic 'functions' transform grammatical cases by making them play roles for which they are not appropriate; entire propositions are reduced and described as if they behaved like simple adverbs" (133; see *Intangible Materialism* 52–3). A good example of such a disorderly mix-up of categories of understanding is the sentence "'I like Ike' is my favorite sentence," where a sentence—President Eisenhower's campaign-slogan sentence—becomes the subject-noun of another sentence. Such disorder calls for improvisation and the discipline of improvisation, practicing sentences and nouns over and over again, practicing phrases on the saxophone, practicing backhand and forehand on the tennis court.

What Cavell has taught me is that the "disorder" that I described in *Intangible Materialism* might fruitfully be described as an invitation to improvise in the face of the "disorders of desire." In his analysis, Cavell offers a strong description of improvisation and, in it, he suggests ("insinuates") the nature of the "dimension" of freedom in which actions are assessed. "Perlocutionary acts," he writes,

> make room for, and reward, imagination and virtuosity, unequally distributed capacities among the species. Illocutionary acts do not in general make such room—I do not, except in special circumstances, wonder how I might make a promise or a gift, or apologize, or render a verdict [all actions among Austin's examples of performative utterances (i.e., utterances that "perform" the act they articulate, as when the act of saying "I apologize" renders or enacts an apology)]. But to persuade[, which is a perlocutionary utterance that effects a response in one's interlocutor,] you may well take considerable thought, to insinuate as much as to console may require tact, to seduce or to confuse you may take talent.
>
> (173)

In this catalogue, Cavell is outlining the discipline of improvisation: improvisation takes "considerable thought," the *practices* of thinking and motor coordination, the *training in inferential understanding* that allows one to grasp the "purport" of insinuation. And this discipline helps define the dimension of freedom altogether. Finally, I should note Cavell begins his study of "Performative and Passionate Utterance" by noting that Austin's *How to Do Things with Words*, like Aristotle's texts, which he cites along with Austin, were "a set of lecture notes ... edited and published posthumously" (156). As such, the transformation of lectures into a book might itself call for improvisation, with all the discipline of practice, training, and grasping the purport of insinuation, that the "re-description" and "reordering" *of all writing* calls for (see Felski 85). Surely my repeated, almost Germanic term *lectures-book*—like the various hyphenated terms throughout, which certainly at best are only awkward English—suggests some gesture of improvisation, some disorder of desire, which the accidents of experience call for.

   5. **Worldly Discipline: Historicizing Intellectual Disciplines in the Time of Consumerist Capitalism.** The catalogue of disciplines I am

setting forth here has to do with (a) the discipline of physical work, both toolmaking and the resistance to impulse and (b) non-physical disciplines of intellectual work and the seeming non-physical—or at least non-volitional—outcomes of practiced improvisation engrained to function as if they were instinctual. Such disciplines have always characterized human life: some have even suggested that "toolmaking" and improvising "play" define human beings altogether. But the formal intellectual disciplines of professional education, which I mentioned earlier, are the focus in this chapter. Such formal intellectual disciplines as we know them—the disciplines of Anthropology, Economics, Sociology, even Physics (as opposed to the more "worldly" discipline of Evolutionary Biology), the practical discipline of biomedicine, and of course the discipline of literary study—date back to the late nineteenth century and, more particularly, to the rise of the lower middle class and the necessity for intellectual discipline as well as the discipline of labor in the creation of wealth and well-being in the commercial society of corporate capitalism. That is, if institutions of higher learning create "literature in our modern sense" in the early nineteenth century, then "modern senses" of other disciplines—Anthropology, Sociology, Economics, etc., and even literary studies itself—arise in the late nineteenth century.

Note how precisely we are able to date "Economics," on or about the year 1871. Most historians agree that the modern discipline of "Economics" dates from William Stanley Jevons's development of marginal mathematical economics in *Theory of Political Economy*, first published in 1871. But Economics was not the only new discipline to arise during the time of cultural modernism: notably Anthropology dates itself from Edward Tylor's *Primitive Culture: Researches into the Development of Mythology, Philosophy, Religion, Language, Art, and Custom* (1871), and its appearance creates a "science" of imperialism just as Economics creates a "science" of corporate/business value. Similarly many familiar disciplines are associated with late nineteenth-century figures or particular works: Modern Languages and Literature (cf. Matthew Arnold), Psychology (cf. Wilhelm Wundt, William James), Physics (cf. William Thompson, Lord Kelvin), Sociology (cf. Max Weber, and also Karl Marx), and Semiotics (cf. Ferdinand de Saussure, Charles Sanders Peirce) all found articulation as particular scientific disciplines, usually associated with the work of particular scholars in the late nineteenth century (see Schleifer *Political Economy* 56–7). In explaining why his study of experiential aesthetics focuses of a "clustering" of literary examples after 1800, Clune notes that his focus "undoubtedly has historical causes. Scholars looking for such causes," he suggests, "might start with the consolidation of consumer capitalism, the rise of medical science, or the waning of traditional religion in the educated classes" (16; see Exhibit 3.3).

Exhibit 3.3: Commodity Fetishism and Intellectual Disciplines

Let me take this opportunity to say a word about consumerist capitalism, which is co-incident with the rise of modern disciplines in higher education. In arguing that "literature's power to renew our perception of the world" (68) is particularly pronounced in literary texts that focus on "the addictive object"—his examples are "De Quincey's laudanum [in *Confessions of an Opium Eater* and] Nabokov's nymphet [in *Lolita*]" (70)—Michael Clune offers an extreme example of consumerism and the "experience" that seems to be commodified in the context of the development of capitalism. Thus, he notes how many literary scholars "represent addictive objects [as] in some respects resembl[ing] the way literary critics have traditionally represented commodities," namely as "a mode of commodity fetishism" (71; Ngai also makes the connection between "the gimmick's aesthetic logic and the structure of addiction" 97). He goes on to note that "commodity theory as practiced by writers from Adorno and Lukacs to Jameson and David Harvey is unintelligible without reference to the classical labor theory of value" even though, as he strongly argues, "the consensus about the about the labor theory of value among social scientists is that it is unworkable, and this consensus is nearly a century old" (72). Still, many Marxist literary scholars take commodity fetishism to be a commanding example of capitalist exploitation. Sianne Ngai, for instance, describes such fetishism under the category of "gimmick" and argues that the "aesthetic category [of gimmick] reflects nothing less than the basic laws of capitalist production and its abstractions as these saturate everyday life" (3; see also 202, 228, and *passim*).

Two things are going on here. (i) Clune is describing an economic "theory of value"—whether it bases itself on labor, on price, or even a sense of the economic "margin" that seems to erase the opposition between production and consumption inherent in the opposition of labor and price—as if the discipline of Economics (and especially "marginalist" Economics as articulated by Jevons) figures it out once and for all in the late nineteenth century. A late contemporary of Jevons, Thornstein Veblen, historicizes the labor theory of value, which found an early articulation in John Locke, when he argues that such a focus on labor arises coincidentally with productionist mercantilism where proto-factory handcrafts significantly supplemented value associated with land (*Business* 40–1). In relation to this, in *A Political Economy of Modernism* I have argued that the labor theory of value and its central notion in Marx of "surplus value," based as they are on absolute subsistence wages for workers, are closely tied to Enlightenment positivism, and that when a "culture of abundance" arose with capitalism—a culture which produced a significantly large supply of available goods beyond the necessities of subsistence—Jevons's consumerist/marginalist theory of value superseded a productionist/labor theory of value (see also Birken for this argument). That is, it is possible to historicize the economic theory of value rather than assuming one can discover it once and for all. (It is also possible to historicize a literary theory of value, which I attempt in this Exhibit— and, indeed, throughout this book.)

(ii) The notion of commodity fetishism, in Ngai and many others, suggests that the consumer choices of the emerging lower middle class that accompanies consumerist capitalism, are fully the result of manipulations, which commentators often imagine they understand better than these (still-exploited) white-collar workers do, whose pleasures in commodities (the way that automobiles might make one feel, greeting cards expressing sentiments written by others, a brand of beer which is indistinguishable from other brands of beer) are simply the result of deceptive scams. In such analyses, consumerism, which accompanies "alienated" workers, is, as Ngai says, "cheap and fraudulent" (3) so that "even when the gimmick is an aesthetic experience, it is one that perpetually tarries with the nonaesthetic. For here our dissatisfaction with the form of the object, based on spontaneous appraisals of the labor, time, or value it embodies, quickly morphs into ethical, historical, and economic evaluations of it as fraudulent, untimely, and cheap" (23). In fact, the notion of "aesthetics" that arises from Ngai's *Theory of the*

Gimmick is that aesthetic "experience" itself is built upon "aesthetic judgments," in which "the aesthetic pleasures or displeasures of other people, including strangers, [are] ... accurately felt as part of my own [pleasures or displeasures]" (95), and that such judgments "'recall us to what is shared in our everyday practices,' most often and vividly by first revealing what is *not* shared" (95; Ngai is citing Simon Critchley). It is my contention, as I suggest in Chapter 6, that in the context of healthcare—and of the practical wisdom of *phronesis* more generally—practical engaged aesthetic experience, as tutored by literature and the discipline of literary studies, reinforces empathy rather than judgment.

Martin Jay—while making a different point—catalogues analyses, which implicitly claim the analyzer is in a position to more clearly judge that the value of the experiences and fulfillments of others, usually others in a different and often "lower" social and economic class, is somehow worthless. Thus, many commentators, Jay notes at the beginning of *Songs of Experience*, speak of "a crisis in the very possibility of having experiences in the modern world. Walter Benjamin often deplored what he called the 'poverty of human experience,' Theodor W. Adorno warned that 'the very possibility of experience is in jeopardy,' and Peter Bürger bemoaned 'the loss of opportunities for authentic experience'" (2). At the base of such judgments, I believe, is a kind of nostalgic romanticization of pre-capitalist "experience" as somehow "authentic" and more fully "lived," what Jay describes in discussing the "Marxist humanism" of Raymond Williams and E. P. Thompson as "robust, immediate, and authentic experience" (213) and what Ngai calls "the pre-alienated essence of things" (83), phenomena which the "alienation" of labor under capitalism has removed from possibility. But even Marx and Engels, in *The Communist Manifesto*, understand that much pre-capitalist "experience" presented most laboring human beings—"nine Parts in ten of the whole Race of Mankind" Edmund Burke had noted (cited in *Political Economy* 163)—with, in Burke's term, overwhelming "drudgery," what Marx and Engels describe as "the idiocy of rural life" (17). "The bourgeoisie," they note, in creating capitalism create a situation in which "the cheap prices of commodities are the heavy artillery with which it batters down all Chinese walls" (16): "what earlier century," they conclude, "had even a presentiment that such productive forces slumbered in the lap of social labour?" (17).

Despite their nineteenth-century racism, Marx and Engels are describing significant numbers of people whose lives are organized beyond subsistence (and beyond the "idiocy" subsistence entails) in a nascent world of mass production. Thus, in China, for instance, as one scholar notes, "in the last 22 years of the 20th century"—that is, in little less than a generation—"China transformed itself from a poor, centrally planned economy to a lower-middle-income, emerging market economy .... China's per capita GDP more than quadrupled during this period. The benefits of growth were also shared by the people on a broad basis: the number of people living in absolute poverty was substantially reduced from over 250 million to about 50 million, a decline from a one-third to a twenty-fifth of its population; and life expectancy increased from 64 in the 1970s to over 70 in the late 1990s" (Qian Yingyi 297; cited in Wang and Schleifer 78). Similarly, if not so dramatically (since levels of poverty were not so high), wide-spread increases of well-being characterized the second Industrial Revolution in the United States and Western Europe during the long turn of the twentieth century (see *Political Economy* 79–98; 110–12).

There is something problematic, I believe, in focusing on the oppression created by capitalism and commodity fetishism without noting the benefits of available commodities, the productive power of social labor. That is, as Reginia Gagnier has argued, there is something problematic in the critic's ability to identify and empathize with the oppression of people from a different social class while maintaining significant critical disdain for their pleasures and delights (235–43). This may be compounded in the critic's subtle discriminations of others' expressions of their pleasures, as when Ngai notes Jane Austen's "fascination" with the "slightly cringeworthy performances of aesthetic evaluation" by Marianne in *Sense and Sensibility* (318), which suggests that "we [are] repelled by the style of people's expressions of aesthetic appreciation [and] not by the fact or intensity of their pleasure per se" (42). And it is certainly compounded in the critic's outright disdain, as in L. C. Knight's adjective in describing "labor-saving devices" as similar to "the goods advertised in women's journals … [which leave] the mind free for the more *narcotic* forms of enjoyment" (cited in Ngai 54, italics added). That is, as Marx himself well knew, capitalism created the possibilities of heretofore unimaginable wealth for many people who lived lives of narrow drudgery, and to too-quickly disdain their recently won pleasures—often, I should note, from the vantage of educated leisure—needs careful re-consideration. As I have argued, the two great themes of modernist literature at the time of the advent of consumerist capitalism in the early twentieth century—and especially of modernist fiction—are imperialism and the rise of the lower middle class, both of which presented themselves as particular culture crises to their middle-class literary audience (*Political Economy* 218). In this context, I should add here that while much modernist fiction sets forth (sometimes scathing) implicit political critiques of imperialism, at the same time it also critiques—and often ridicules—people struggling out of the "drudgery" of rural or working-class existence into the lower middle class. In any case, the felt sense of "crises" occasioned by imperialism and the growth of the lower middle class occurred at the very time that the productive power of social labor freed many to pursue disciplined knowledge.

In completing this catalogue of disciplines, which preceded this long Exhibit historicizing value, let me note three aspects of formal professional disciplines in the late nineteenth century as social institutions arising at the same time as the second Industrial Revolution: namely, the *institutional nature* of knowledge (e.g., "literature in the modern sense" conditioned by institutions); the *collaborative nature* of knowledge (e.g., that "truth" is demonstrated by replication conducted by different practitioners); and the *anonymous understanding* of knowledge (e.g., the authority of knowledge was not vested in the authority and reverence of its author but by the institutional collaborative nature of knowledge itself). These three phenomena—institutionalization, collaboration, and anonymity—are part and parcel of the shape and power of emerging corporate capitalism at the end of the nineteenth century as well. That is, they correspond to three defining features of the impersonal corporation. These features are the *institution* of autonomous "legal personhood" of the corporation; the elaborate structural integration of *collaborative/productive* functions in what came to be called the "vertical integration" of corporate production; and "absentee ownership" (Veblen's term) of corporations run by a managerial class rather than entrepreneur-owners.

In *A Political Economy of Modernism*, I argue for the "homology" among cultural institutions such as economic enterprises, aesthetic experiences, and organizations of intellectual disciplines, which I repeat here in drawing parallels between intellectual disciplines and the structure of economic enterprises. (You may remember I have used this term "homology" already several times earlier in this chapter.) "Homology"—a key term in the Victorian science of evolutionary biology—describes phenomena that share the same structure even while they perform different functions: the skeletal structures of the bat's wing and the human hand are homologous, as are, I am arguing, the organizing structures of corporate capitalism and developing professional disciplines in the late nineteenth century. The manner in which homology pursues the investigation of a seeming self-evident (or "immediate") phenomenon into ("mediated") parts for analysis—its distinction between structure and function—characterizes all of the species of discipline I have outlined here: creating tools for anticipated rather than immediate need; understanding impulse as something that can be resisted because it itself is a function rather than an immutable state of affairs; supplementing worldly engagements with ideas; participating in intentional and conscious practice in order to create possibilities of automatic behavior. Finally, the creation of professional disciplines, which pursue systematic and independent frameworks of symbols and procedures in order to understand and engage with phenomena ("the immediate sensations of experience"), also creates possibilities of homological interdisciplinary work.

The Discipline of Literary Studies

Now, then, let me describe my work in relation to the discipline of literary studies. For the past twenty years I have been team-teaching with physician-medical faculty people a course on "Literature and Medicine" for undergraduate pre-med students, second- and fourth-year medical students, exchange students and faculty (mostly from China), and we have also organized lectures and workshops for healthcare professionals (again from America, Europe, and Asia). In the United States, students pursue training in healthcare as postgraduate work after obtaining the bachelor's degree: thus, unlike medical education almost everywhere throughout the world—certainly in China, as I noted in my Harbin lectures—we have large numbers of "pre-med" students in our country. This has been an exhilarating and a sobering experience: exhilarating to see smart and committed young people discover in our classes new ways of engaging with experience and with their future work; and sobering in the assumptions people have—especially people training in the nomological sciences—concerning the relative lack of discipline that governs intellectual engagements within the humanities. Many years ago, the linguist-semiotician Louis Hjelmslev described the governing assumptions about the study of the humanities, assumptions he attempts to refute. In *Prolegomena to the Theory of Language* published in 1943—a systematic exposition of Saussurean linguistics and semiotics—he describes a widespread sense of what he calls the "humanistic tradition." "According to this view," he writes,

> humanistic, as opposed to natural, phenomena are non-recurrent and for that very reason cannot, like natural phenomena, be subject to exact and generalizing treatment. In the field of the humanities, consequently, there would have to be a different method—namely, mere description, which would be nearer to poetry than to exact science—or, at any event, a method that restricts itself to a discursive form of presentation, in which the phenomena pass by, one by one, without being interpreted through a system. In the field of *history* this thesis has been held as doctrine, and it seems in fact to be the very basis of history in its classical form. Accordingly, those disciplines that may perhaps be called the most humanistic—the study of literature and the study of art—have also been historically descriptive rather than systematizing disciplines.
>
> (8–9)

Needless to say, I have also encountered the opposite to Hjelmslev's resistance to this attitude in people committed to the study of the humanities and literature, which is to say people who embrace the fact that the humanities focus on unique experiences—*incommensurable* experiences—which cannot, they believe, be studied systematically in a disciplined fashion. In fact, it could be said that the tradition of "close reading," which Joseph North describes in the work of I. A. Richards and the American New Criticism, offers an example of the singularly *descriptive* nature of literary studies, which Hjelmslev articulates. (However, North's understanding of the *evaluative* nature of "close reading" might modify this judgment.) A notable instance of the opposite of Hjelmslev's project was the response of a student in a class on "Literature and Medicine" I taught a number of years ago at a small liberal arts college in Colorado. After a few weeks of class, the student came to my office almost seething in anger. "I see what you're trying to do," she said: "You're trying to make literature *practical!*"

Phronesis. I bring these judgments together, that of Hjelmslev and that of my student, because they touch upon the practicality of literature, its uses and its value. My working assumption in my teaching and work in the health humanities (but also in my work in literary and cultural studies) is that to be useful—to be humanly practical—requires systematic engagements that, precisely *because* they are systematic, lend themselves to *transferable skills* that can be shared and developed. In *The Chief Concern of Medicine* Jerry Vannatta and I spend some time focusing on Aristotle's notion of *phronesis*, which, as I have already mentioned, is usually translated as "practical reasoning" or "practical wisdom." Aristotle's examples of *phronesis* in *The Nicomachean Ethics* are medicine (his father was a physician) and navigation, and he argues that *phronesis* as such can only be achieved through long first-hand experience. Our argument is different: we argue that experience itself does not simply call for description, which Hjelmslev submits traditional practices of the humanities seem to pursue. Rather, we argue, as I argue in this chapter and throughout this book, that experience lends itself to systematic analysis and practice, and such analysis and practice can be taught and developed in ways that allow the achievement of the practical wisdom of *phronesis* to result from systematic engagements with vicarious (and, as Alvin Goldman has it, "simulated") experience rather than—or more practically, in addition to—long-time life-experiences. This understanding of experience as susceptible to systematic analysis grew out of my study for my book *Pain and Suffering,* which I have already mentioned. My study for that book taught me that the extreme phenomenal *immediacy* of pain, such as we saw represented in Roddy Doyle's novel *The Woman Who Walked into Doors*—which can be taken in its extremity as a defining example of "the immediate sensations of experience" itself—can be understood not as simply *immediate*, but as *mediated* through schemas of experience that govern human "experience" itself (see also "Aesthetics of Pain"). (Note that in my discussions of the language of Doyle's novel, I deploy Greimas's *systematic* semiotic understanding of language, a "system" homologous with Hjelmslev's project.) Here, then, is my thesis concerning the discipline of literary studies:

> Literary studies in a disciplined and systematic fashion—even when that discipline remains implicit in its practice rather than explicitly pursued—analyzes the mediating systems that govern seeming immediately-felt "experience." In this, it studies experience even while it does not take "human experience" to be the structure of literature but rather something, as Northrop Frye notes (44), "to be explained in terms of a conceptual framework different in shape from" human experience itself.

Before I elaborate my argument for this thesis in this chapter, let me return to my angry Colorado student for a moment and fill out the notion of *phronesis*. I understand the source of her anger about our course was the manner in which it worked to demonstrate the ways that literature fosters the practical results of Empathy, Theory of Mind, and Vicarious Experience that has been the focus of in recent experimental work in cognitive psychology (for a review of this work, see Goldman, Schleifer and Vannatta *Literature and Medicine* 3–5, 243–45, and Hester and Schleifer). Her anger, as I understood it, was based upon a sense that the goal of literature—what Jerry and I call in that first chapter of *Literature and Medicine* and elsewhere, "art narrative"—is not to promote practical action in the world, but to enlarge the horizon of experience and understanding altogether, to increase "sensibility" and, I might say, "the breadth of experience." In many ways, this focus on sensibility and experience is at the heart of Kantian Enlightenment aesthetics, which has governed much of Western engagement with the arts for many generations. In *Uses of Literature*, Rita Felski describes this attitude as possessed by those who want to read, not "for knowledge or entertainment" or any "real-world consequences," but simple "to read literature 'as literature'" (5); such readers, she goes on, assume that "literary works can be objects of knowledge but never sources of knowledge" (7).

My work in the health humanities has led me to contrast "art narrative" with "everyday narrative." Healthcare professionals, as we all know—after all, we have all been patients—encounter "everyday narratives" on a daily basis, the stories of suffering, worry, what we call "concern" that people bring to the clinic every day. The goal of everyday narrative, as Brian Boyd argues in his evolutionary analysis of narrative, *On the Origin of Stories: Evolution, Cognition, and Fiction*, is to promote some action—usually collective action—in the world. (I should add that Dr. Vannatta and I offer a "close reading" of Boyd's analysis in order to demonstrate the degree to which there is a "gap" in his conclusions insofar as he does not deploy systematic work in the human sciences [e.g., narratology and semiotics; see *Chief Concern* 77–81].) "Art narrative," however, is different: it seeks not to promote action, but to enlarge the horizon of experience. What I am calling "art narrative" serves, in Felski's metaphor, as "an ideal laboratory for probing ... experiential and aesthetic complexities" (32). The well-known narratologist, James Phelan makes a similar point when he argues that "the attention that literary narrative requires" encourages the discernment of the "cognitive, emotive, and ethical responses" that narrative provokes and the discernment of "the complexity of the relationship between facts, hypotheses, and theories" (14, 15; cited in *Literature and Medicine* 16). More generally, I would argue that what is going on here is something we see throughout human history (and what I mentioned earlier in relation to the neurological study of David Huron), namely the appropriation of "evolutionary" systems organizing human well-being—and, really, the wider well-being of all successful life-forms—that are taken up to new and different ends in expanded strategies of adaptation. Stephen Jay Gould calls this "the triumph of homology," and I suggest throughout this book that homology offers a working strategy for interdisciplinary studies, which takes into account the concerns about interdisciplinary "knowledge" in Kramnick and Davidson.

I have recently argued—as I mentioned already earlier in this chapter—that corporate capitalism at the turn of the twentieth century takes up the forms of entrepreneurial capitalism to new and different ends, and that the modernist arts—in its slogan "make it new!," articulated by Ezra Pound (*Political Economy* 6)—participate in the "action" of *evolutionary homology*, where the "same" evolutionarily developed phenomena are taken up to new functions and purposes. Homology, then, describes the ways that inherited evolutionary structures are re-purposed for new and different functions, as in the bat's wing and the human hand. In *The Genealogy of Morals* (1887), Friedrich Nietzsche declares that "whatever exists, having somehow come into being, is again and again reinterpreted to new ends, taken over, transformed, and redirected by some power superior to it" (77), and the same motto, I am suggesting here, could be taken up as the practical goals of everyday narrative are transformed to the cognitive and affective goals of art narrative. Felski makes a strikingly similar argument about literature and, more generally, about mimesis: she notes that "we are eternally enmeshed within semiotic and social networks of meaning that shape and sustain our being," and that such "semiotic material is ... *configured* by the literary text, which refashions and restructures it, distancing it from its prior uses and remaking its meanings"; and she notes that in literature "we rediscover things as we know them to be, yet reordered and redescribed, shimmering in a transformed light" (85, 102; see also 91, 120). In Chapter 4, I take up this notion of transformation in speech-act theory—the discovery of "aspects" of experience conditioned by value, which "light up," as Wittgenstein says (§118), our engagements with the world.

Purpose and Feedback. Before I turn to a comparison of the discipline of the literary humanities to the seeming stricter disciplines of the law-like or nomological sciences and the retrospective systematic analyses of the social sciences, I want to say something about the manner in which the process of homological transformation can be understood in relation to future-oriented "purpose." In *The Prolegomena to a Theory of Language* Hjelmslev argues that the term "meaning" should be replaced with the term "purport" (see Exhibit 3.4).

Exhibit 3.4: Hjelmslev's "Purport"

For advice on Hjelmslev's Danish text, I consulted Peter Juul Nielsen, who patiently went over the Danish text with me. My conclusions, however, should not be taken to be Professor Nielsen's conclusions. Hjelmslev uses the Danish term *Mening*—translated as the English "purport," which is not the same Danish term translated as "meaning" (i.e., *Betydning*) in the English translation of the *Prolegomena*. *Betydning* is "meaning" apprehended within a particular linguistic system, while *Mening* designates a sense of meaningfulness seemingly "independent" of systematic semantics. It might be understood as connotation or as a species of overtones in musical performance, part of the "experience" of meaning, which is discussed at greater length in Exhibit 4.5: The Qualities of Overtones. (For a thorough-going structuralist/semiotic account of connotation, see Barthes 1968: 89–99.) Hillis Miller describes this sense of *Mening* when he analyzes Walter Benjamin's meditation on translation, in which both original and translation participate in a seemingly antecedent "pure language" (*On Literature* 61–3), again, as I say here, independent of systematic semantics. With this, I want to suggest that *purport* designates the *quality* of meaningfulness, like the quality of *blueness* in English, as distinct from the color-term *glas* in Welsh, which is examined in Chapter 4. The quality of blueness describes the "experience" of blueness: like the "interpretant" in the semiotics of Charles Sanders Peirce, it is an event rather than a "timeless" meaning such as the simple (positive and positivist) measure of blue-light wavelengths mentioned in Chapter 4.

In English, "purport" describes a subtle sense of "meaning": it suggests the ways that a particular meaning is grasped and understood, how meaning is *construed*. The first definition of "purport" as a noun in *The Oxford English Dictionary* is "that which is conveyed or expressed, esp. by a formal document or speech; effect, tenor, import; meaning, substance, sense." And in its definition as a verb, it means "to convey to the mind; … to express, set forth; to signify, imply." In other words, what the word "purport" adds to our sense of "meaning" is the manner in which it is received or grasped: "purport" emphasizes both the temporality of meaning and, perhaps even more importantly, the sociality of meaning. In his study of music, Oliver Sacks articulates the complex temporality of the "grasping" of purport when he notes that "hearing a melody is hearing, having heard, and being about the hear, all at once" (*Musicophilia* 228). And in his semiotic notion of "interpretant"—which designates, as the *Oxford English Dictionary* notes, "the effect of a proposition or a sign-series, upon its interpreter, the person who understands it"—Charles Sanders Peirce nicely captures the sociality of meaning implicit in the English word "purport." (Note, by the way, the functional similarity of Peirce's *interpretant* to Austin's concept of *perlocution*, which I discussed in examining the relation between discipline and freedom. I should also remind you that the work of *purport* is closely connected to the work of *construal* I discuss in Chapter 1.) "Meaning," then, as opposed to "purport," as Hjelmslev suggests, feels monumental and law-like, a species of Ngai's "transcendent concepts" (187), which exist so to speak as truth without a speaker, like the formulas of nomological science I mention in a moment or even the explanations of empiricism in the social sciences I also mention. To use the metaphor Daniel Herwitz sets forth in contrast to the active absorption provoked by impressionist painting, Hjelmslev's "meaning" suggests a "distanced, hermetic image" (Herwitz 184; see Exhibit 3.5).

Exhibit 3.5: A Neurological Examination of Purport

In *Simulating Minds: The Philosophy, Psychology, and Neuroscience of Mindreading*, Alvin Goldman sets forth a neurological account of mirror neurons, which describes how observing the activity of a cohort—in both human and many primates—activates the similar firing of neuronal activity in the observer. "The discovery of mirror neurons and mirroring systems is the product of Giacomo Rizzolatti's laboratory in Parma," Goldman writes. "They first discovered mirror neurons for action in the central premotor cortex (area F5) of macaque monkeys .... Action mirror neurons are cells that discharge both when an acting monkey executes a goal-related action—the initial research dealt with hand actions—and also when an observing monkey watches the same type of hand action performed by someone else (a monkey or a human). Each of several types of goal-related hand actions—such as grasping, holding, or tearing an object—has a distinctive family of associated mirror neurons in the premotor cortex (and also the parietal cortex) .... Because the premotor cortex is mainly responsible for action planning, it was quite surprising that the mere observation of another's action should involve some of the same neuronal activity as the planning or representation of one's own action .... Each family of mirror neurons comprises the substrate of a distinctive type of (nonconscious) mental representation, something like a *plan* to achieve a certain behavioral goal (grasping or tearing, for example). In the case of the observer, however, the plan is not executed" (134). In this neuroscientific account, Goldman sets forth the equally surprising phenomenon of the *automatic* physiological reaction to "goal-related" actions. This observation—though, needless to say, Goldman doesn't make this point—suggests that there might well be some neurological or material basis for the goal-related activities of *purport*.

In Hjelmslev's distinction between meaning and purport, "purport" renders "meaning" necessary but not sufficient; it indicates a further—a future—"effect, tenor, import" grasped after pronouncement. Moreover, such an analysis of meaning/purport could profitably be related to the feedback systems of complexity theory, in which feedback expands the time of meaning by making what takes place after an event or after a pronouncement transform (in a feedback "loop") that original event/pronouncement itself. This is the import of Nietzsche's pronouncement in *On the Genealogy of Morals* I cited in relation to biological homology. In this, I am suggesting the ways that complexity theory in its feedback systems offers an example of a discipline that, like the discipline of literary studies I focus on in this chapter, offers necessary but not sufficient criteria for understanding. (I hope this enigmatic expression becomes clear later in this presentation. See also the study I did with Jonathan Stalling for an account of complex feedback in linguistic translation—in our case, translation from Chinese to English.) Towards the end of Chapter 6, I note—following David Chalmers—the connection between experience and the complex/feedback phenomena that information theory examines.

In analyzing Paul Ricoeur's masterful investigations of the nature of narrative, the Canadian philosopher Charles Taylor describes the workings of language in a manner than can help us understand how important the temporality of feedback is to the discipline of literary studies. I hardly need to add that the working of language—and its work to provoke "experience"—after all, is the object of study organizing the discipline of literary studies. In his analysis, Taylor nicely defines "nomological" science, what I describe here as seeking "formulaic" understanding. Nomological science, he argues, "concerns a form of explanation whereby the phenomenon to be explained is completely absorbed by the law or structure which constitutes its explanation" ("Discussion" 175). In this mode of explanation, any "event" is explained by its "subsumption" (to use Taylor's word) by atemporal structures and laws that exist once and for all. Against this nomological schema, Taylor posits "a very different type of relation between structure and event" whose "paradigmatic example is that of *langue-parole*" (176). In mentioning *langue-parole*, Taylor is citing a central distinction in the linguistics of Ferdinand de Saussure. "*Langue*," in Saussure, is the system or structure of language: it is distinct from particular language-utterances, what he calls "*parole*," and as in nomological science, it seems to be the structure or the law that governs and explains the event-utterances of language.

But unlike the formulas of nomological science, *langue* is necessary but not sufficient in organizing and/or explaining linguistic phenomena.

Offering another example of the "creation" of disorder out of order I discussed earlier in this chapter, Taylor argues that

> a language may be viewed as a structure of rules, or of possible formations and transformations. But this structure has purchase on the real only by virtue of *parole*. It is only through repeated acts of communication by members of a linguistic community that a structure has real existence. But 'events' or 'particular cases', which are speech-acts, are not in a simple relation of subsumption with the rule to which they are submitted. They may be in conformity with it, or they may deviate. This renewal is not however dictated by the nature of things; it is not a mere example, nor is it a particular case of a regularity .…
>
> For it is a matter of human acts aiming (in principle) at the realization of a structure, which may, however, not succeed or which may even be directed against the structures which must (in principle) rule them. Languages live only through successive renewals, each of which is a risk, for it runs the risk of not coming through this renewal unharmed.
>
> (176)

The "human acts" he describes are not necessarily intentional insofar as their "aim" or "purport" can be a function not simply of conscious intentional meaning, but of the organization of communal understandings (habits of thought), which condition the apprehension of those who receive its meaning/purport (see the Great Vowel Shift in early modern English). Thus, if nomological explanation seeks the hermetic "certainty" of atemporal and universal law (e.g., $e = mc^2$), then the model of language Taylor is describing focuses on the community out of which knowledge arises *at a particular time*. Most of all, it suggests communal and temporal aspects of knowledge rather than its monumental self-evidence. It suggests the "worldliness" of intergenerational knowledge and care: what better describes intergenerational relationships than "renewal"?

In his description of the evolution of the brain, Sam Harris offers a simile that illuminates, I believe, Taylor's description of the "renewals" of language. "No region of the brain," Harris writes,

> evolved in a neural vacuum or in isolation from the other mutations simultaneously occurring within the genome. The human mind, therefore, is like a ship that has been built and rebuilt, plank by plank,

on the open sea. Changes have been made to her sails, keel, and rudder even as the waves battered every inch of her hull …. We are, in every cell, the products of nature—but we have also been born again and again through culture.

(155–6)

This is particularly apposite because language is both a "natural" part of human life and also a major constituent element of "culture." As I note in Chapter 6—and really throughout this book—language shapes as well as represents and provokes experience. (Remember as well, in the context of Taylor's sense of renewal, the philosophical notion of "semantic depth" mentioned earlier in this chapter.)

As I noted, in describing "human acts aiming (in principle)" at particular ends, Taylor is describing the "purport" of action and/or speech acts, whose fulfilments succeed or fail *after* the event-action takes place. Thus, in this analysis, Taylor is describing the evolution of language, not by natural selection but by the artificial selection of language users. By "successive renewals" Taylor posits the way that any particular speech act (i.e., "*parole*"), including the objects of literary study (such as any particular novel that is defined by the overarching and "subsuming" category of the literary genre "novel"), does not simply instantiate a literary form but has the ability to "renew" literary forms. One such example of this is the manner in which Toni Morrison "renews" the genre of slave narrative in creating a new or "renewed" genre of the neo-slave narrative in her novel *Beloved* (see Jacobs and Schleifer). The "structure of rules or of possible formations and transformations" (Taylor "Discussion" 176) that constitutes language does this all the time—Taylor is right in this—in such ordinary examples as metaphors ossifying into literal expressions or, in our consumer society, proper names of objects (such as the American brand names "Scotch Tape" or "Frigidaire") becoming common nouns. Such phenomena are creatures of feedback loops that disturb or, more kindly, renew the hierarchical relation of subsumption between grammatical categories and particular speech-act utterances or literary genre and particular literary examples of that genre. In this way the necessary structures or rules and transformations are themselves transformed, "again and again," as Nietzsche says, "reinterpreted to new ends, taken over, transformed." (Notice how I am doing just this to Nietzsche's citation: taking it over for new ends.) In particular speech acts, then—including of course in literary speech acts—"we rediscover," as

Felski says, "things as we know them to be, yet reordered and redescribed, shimmering in a transformed light" (102). Such a discovery is the goal of the organizing discipline of literary studies.

The Nomological, Social, and Human Sciences

Now, though, I want to turn to the particular workings of intellectual disciplines to help situate and flesh-out this discussion of feedback renewals in literary studies. As I hope this small discussion of the renewals of literary studies begins to suggest, we can—and in the human sciences and literary studies we do—marshal tools of systematic analysis, however implicit they are, to the ends of cognitive, affective, and practical understanding. Such "marshalling," I am suggesting, describes both the practical and the cognitive "uses" of literature. But in order to begin to substantiate this, I'd like to spend the rest of this chapter drawing structural parallels ("homologies") among the nomological sciences, the social sciences, and what I like to call the human sciences. As you might imagine, teaching with physicians and biomedical students for many years has made me particularly sensitive to understanding our work in literary studies to be as systematically disciplined as the sciences in which they are trained. In Chapter 6 I outline thirteen features of narrative analysis that are set forth in *Literature and Medicine* with the aim of making literature "useful"—as in Rita Felski's *Uses of Literature*—in the development of *phronesis* in healthcare pedagogy specifically and in moral education more generally.

Nomological science, since the time of René Descartes and Isaac Newton in the seventeenth and eighteenth centuries, has pursued "certainty," as Descartes described it, and discovered certainty in mathematical representations of facts and events. That is, science, at this extreme, aims at discovering the *necessary and sufficient conditions* that govern the existence of phenomena and their behaviors, which is to say facts and events; it aims, at this extreme, to articulate universal laws, which in their universality are "timeless." This is the purport of Errol Morris's notion of "scientific realism" (see Exhibit 1.4: Scientific Realism) and his critique of Thomas Kuhn's historical paradigms. More generally, it is the meaning of "nomological" or "law-like" science, and its chief representative example can be seen in the universal formulas of mathematical physics that describe the necessary and sufficient conditions governing physical facts and events. For such sciences, empirical facts and events are "commensurable" across different particular cases, which means that different instances can be taken as equal: *any* falling object will behave like any other, or any neuron like any other. Thus, in her philosophical analysis of pain, Valerie Grey Hardcastle argues that "the neurons that make up the brain are essentially identical across all animals in the kingdom"; and throughout her book, *The Myth of Pain*, she repeatedly notes that all pain is the "same": "all pains are physical and localizable and ... all are created equal" (63, 7).

Along with the nomological sciences, there are also other scientific pursuits that are less logically rigorous in their goals, empirical and explanatory sciences such as epidemiology, evolutionary biology, or the social sciences in general. Like evolution, most of these social studies pursue retrospective science since, as Stephen Jay Gould has argued, they cannot *predict*, as nomological science can, future facts and events ("Triumph," *Wonderful Life*). Nomological science can do this because its formulas (for instance, $e = mc^2$ or $f = ma$) *universally* apply so that if we are given the mass (m) and acceleration (a) of an object, we can always calculate and predict its force (f). In distinction to such nomological science, evolution and, in a different register, other social sciences, are historical sciences, which make sense of facts and events in retrospect; this is true whether a social science pursues "holistic" accounts (i.e., focuses on social phenomena) or "individualistic" accounts (i.e., individual responses to social phenomena; see Zahle). This is clear in the explanations of evolution, but even in the statistical analyses of sociology we see retrospective explanations—which is to say, explanations after the fact, which do not aspire to the predictive power of nomological formulas. In this, the social sciences describe *sufficient but not necessary conditions* governing facts and events. That is, evolution pursues not universal formulas but *retrospective explanation*: it is not "necessary" that the mammalian eye evolved—one can imagine a different kind of sensory-perceptual system—but having come into existence, one can explain it, retrospectively, as the product of a long history of "sufficient" advantageous adaptations. In a sense, this is still, weakly conceived, a law-like science insofar as it is governed by the "law" of natural selection—itself clearly discernable in precise empirical study (see Weiner 1995 for a fine empirical study of natural selection)—just as other social sciences are governed by the "laws" of statistical analyses. But in the social sciences such laws are the *basis* rather than the *goal* of their scientific endeavor.

Against these scientific projects, the work of the human sciences and literary studies is different. Literary studies and other studies of the arts do not seek the *necessary and sufficient* formulas of nomological science governing facts and events or the *sufficient but not necessary explanations* of facts and events in evolutionary or epidemiological science. Rather, they focus on *experience* rather than seeming self-evident *facts and events*; or, better, they focus on facts and events as apprehended and mediated through *structures of experience*. As I mentioned in Chapter 2, I am modelling this concept on Raymond Williams's notion of "structures of feeling." Let me return to Williams's formulation. He notes that "structures of feeling" are

> concerned with meanings and values as they are actively lived and felt .... An alternative definition would be structures of experience: in one sense the better and wider word, but with the difficulty that one of its senses has that past tense which is the most important obstacle to recognition of the area of social experience which is being defined. We are talking about characteristic elements of impulse, restraint, and tone; specifically affective elements of consciousness and relationships: not feeling against thought, but thought as felt and feeling as thought: practical consciousness of a present kind, in a living and inter-relating continuity.
>
> (132)

The nomological sciences focus on facts and events as apprehended and mediated through the abstractions of *mathematical formulas*, and the social sciences focus on facts and events as apprehended and mediated through *statistical analyses*, and, more generally as in the case of evolutionary biology, through *functional analyses*. But the human sciences focus on *structures*—in *Pain and Suffering* I deploy the term *schemas*—of experience, which allow us to comprehend seeming "unique" facts and events as conditioned by a worldly "space of meaning," what Thorstein Veblen calls historical "habits of thought," which I examine closely in Chapter 4.

In developing disciplinary "frameworks" (to return to Frye's vocabulary) of *structures of experience*, literary studies and other studies of the arts can be understood as the discipline that articulates the *necessary but not sufficient* conditions governing facts and events. In this, experience itself is analyzable in terms of complex feedback systems. Thus, a grammatical subject or a narrative Hero is necessary for a sentence or a narrative, but what would sufficiently fulfill that necessity—what Felski describes as "embedded and embodied agents" (91)—is not formulaically or retrospectively comprehended. Rather, as in complex systems, the ("sufficient") characteristics of this "necessary" element—the Hero of a narrative or a grammatical subject of a sentence—*emerge* within the worldly activity of both adhering to and contesting the disciplinary rules of narrative or grammar. (We have seen this is using Eisenhower's campaign slogan as the subject of a sentence: "'I like Ike' is my favorite sentence.") That is, the feedback—the artificial selection—of language systems allows a particular instance of an entity to be "sufficient" to function as a Hero. And doing so, it transforms and "renews" (in Taylor's language) the category of "Hero" altogether. This is different from the sufficient explanations of the social sciences. In accounting for the mammalian eye I mentioned a moment ago, evolutionary biology *begins* with an example of "sufficiency"—namely, the functioning eye—which comes about through historical accident (mutation and/or environmental changes). In the human sciences, however, the fulfillment of a sufficient condition comes about through the "artificial selection" of speakers, which does not need to be consciously pursued in the manner in which dog breeding is consciously pursued (e.g., the Great Vowel Shift was not purposeful artificial selection, but it nevertheless notably "renewed" the English language).

Here is an example. In a passage that directly contradicts Hardcastle's assertion that "all pains ... are created equal" (7), David Morris argues in his historical and cultural study of pain that "what we feel today when we are in pain ... *cannot* be the same changeless sensations that have tormented humankind ever since our ancestors crawled out of their caves" (4). Here, pain is a necessary condition of human life, but the *quality* of pain that is sufficient to realize it as pain is neither *self-evident* nor measured by simple *functionality*. To make this argument, Morris focuses on particular timely *experiences* of pain—including the "change-of-quality" of pain—which he suggests are not always commensurable with other experiences of pain. In *Pain and Suffering*, I try to bring together these two arguments by focusing on both the "fact" and the "experience" of pain. I attempt to do so by describing the ways that the schemas of experience condition both facts and experience. More generally, in the human sciences when we study the style of the French post-impressionist painter Vincent Van Gogh, or the style of discursive strategies of the American Nobel Prize novelist Toni Morrison, or the abstract economic patterns of historical behavior, or the characteristic musical patterns of Wolfgang Amadeus Mozart, we focus on experience. More precisely, in the human sciences we study the structures or schemas that govern our experiences of paintings, novels, ideas, and music, the regular patterns of *attention and expectation* that constitute experience. (One important feature of literary narrative I return to in Chapter 6 is the seeming ephemeral feature of "style"; it is a feature that makes a "double-take" discussion of "the exposition in short" as important as the "thesis in short" set forth in the Thesis chapter at the beginning of this lectures-book.) Articulating such schemas is the work of much of the social sciences, but in the human sciences phenomena do not simply offer examples of schematic elements but can modify and even transform, as Taylor notes, the governing schemas themselves. (See Exhibit 3.6.)

Exhibit 3.6: A Note on Necessity and Sufficiency

Throughout *The Ashtray*, Errol Morris focuses on "necessity" in relation to nomological science. He does so because the focus of his critique of the *social constructionism* of Thomas Kuhn (to return to Patricia Waugh's distinction between "constructionism" and "constructivism" [108]) is the "denial," as he calls it, of reference to facts and events separate from systems of meaning in Kuhn's paradigmatic account of the history of science. Throughout his critique, Morris discusses particular explanations of empirical phenomena that are "necessary" in order to isolate the essences of phenomena. He does not use the phrase "necessary and sufficient," by which I am describing intellectual disciplines. Morris neglects to do so, I suspect, because he believes that essences by definition describe conditions that are both necessary and sufficient. Still, his extended example of a "necessary" understanding is the *glyptodont*, what *Wikipedia* describes as "an extinct subfamily of large, heavily armored relatives of armadillos …. The best-known genus within the subfamily is *Glyptodon*." The glyptodont weighed more than two tons. Morris asks: "how can we distinguish it from other armadillos and armadillo-like creatures? Are there necessary properties that define a glyptodont and distinguish glyptodonts from all other living things?" (135; this locution—i.e., "necessary" and "distinct"—is a version of "necessary and sufficient"). He goes on to note that "very recently, in 2015, glyptodont DNA was recovered and analyzed" (135), and he concludes that "molecular biology affords us the opportunity to identify necessary properties, but it does something more. It helps us discoverer not just the idea of what a glyptodont is, but also how it has evolved, what it has evolved from, and how it is related to current species. Call it *progress* in scientific understanding. (Even though Kuhn would argue there is no such thing)" (141).

In his argument, Morris interviews Ross MacPhee, a co-author of a paper analyzing glyptodont DNA, who says that "you could take a completely reductionist point of view and say, if it is a [glyptodont] genetically [i.e., by virtue of its DNA], ... then by definition it is a [glyptodont] .... But you only get so far in life being a reductionist .... Just because you've got data doesn't mean you understand anything at all" (141).

Thus, when I talk about the "sufficiency" of evolutionary accounts of the mammalian eye—an example of social-scientific accounts—I point out that "sufficient" evolutionary adaptations are *historical*: this is Stephen Jay Gould's emphatic argument in "The Triumph of Homology," which I discuss in Chapter 6. It is also the case when I suggest that the labor theory of value arose *historically* in conjunction with mercantile economics (see Exhibit 3.3: Commodity Fetishism and Intellectual Disciplines). Thus, as distinct from the nomological and social sciences, the human sciences, I contend, focus on what is necessary but not sufficient, and that particular ("historical") instances of narrative and sentential descriptions supply "sufficient" embodiments of abstract necessities (e.g., Heathcliff in *Wuthering Heights* is a peculiar kind of Hero) in order to fulfill or complete the necessity of a grammatical subject for a sentence or a Hero for a narrative.

One critique of Kuhn, which Morris sets forth, focuses on Kuhn's account of Aristotle's theory of motion. (Patricia Waugh takes up this account not as a critique of Kuhn, but as an instance of "the double coding of history at the level of the paradigm," a very "Eureka moment" in Kuhn's intellectual life [102–3].) Kuhn as a young scholar was perplexed by the "absurdity" of Aristotle's theory of motion. Then one day, Kuhn notes, "for the first time I gave due weight to the fact that Aristotle's subject was change-of-quality in general, including both the fall of a stone and the growth of a child to adulthood." He calls this "a new way to read a set of texts," and notes that "after I achieved this one [new way of reading], strained metaphors often became naturalistic reports, and much apparent absurdity vanished" (cited in Morris 153). Morris mocks Kuhn's "strained metaphors": thus, he asks "how about Aristotle's claim ... that the brain was a radiator for cooling the blood?" (153). But in Kuhn's own account, as Waugh suggests, he is noting that Aristotle is not analyzing facts and events—the existence of actual, "referential" facts and events in the world—but the *quality* of events, which, as I argue throughout this book, is both the locus of experience and the object of the discipline of literary studies. That is, "a new [or renewed!] way to read a set of texts" offers a "sufficient" way of fulfilling the "necessity" of reading a set of texts, while beforehand Kuhn imagined there was only one "way of reading." The discovery or articulation of this kind of "sufficiency" is the disciplined work of the human sciences, the disciplined "unpacking" of philology. It is "experiential" and "qualitative" sufficiency insofar as it isolates features of a world of indefinite complexity—in this case, myriad different ways of reading, different ways of engaging discourse, different armadillo-like creatures—which allow us to more fully comprehend experience itself.

Before this lengthy Exhibit on necessity, I had mentioned "attention and expectation," a topic I return to in Chapter 4. (I also practically deployed the phrase "attention and expectation" in reading *The Woman Who Walked into Doors* in Chapter 2.) Other sciences study attention in different ways from the human sciences. Let me return to the eye—this time the human rather than the mammalian eye. Sam Harris notes that

certain biological traits appear to have been shaped by, and to have further enhanced, the human capacity for cooperation. For instance, unlike the rest of the earth's creatures, including our fellow primates, the sclera of our eyes (the region surrounding the colored iris) is white and exposed. This makes the direction of the human gaze very easy to detect, allowing us to notice even the subtlest shifts in one another's visual attention.

This "biological trait," Harris goes on, suggests that "I must be in a social environment full of others who are not often inclined to take advantage of this [ability to discern my visual attention] to my detriment," an environment in which I am "benefited" by "shared social attention" (79–80). Here, sufficient explanation—qualitative purposeful explanation—comes after the fact and, most importantly, is imbricated with *future* action and understanding, imbricated with *inference* and *purport*. The discernment (or discovery) of structures and schemas of experience offers necessary features of explanation that *anticipate* their "sufficient" instantiation. Goldman sets forth a thorough discussion of psychological and neurological data substantiating gaze-following beginning very early in human life, and he notes that autistic children—who seem unable "to establish normal relationships with peers" such that "many researchers have concluded that the core of autism is a brain dysfunction that impairs mentalizing [i.e., simulation]" (200; see also 203)—are "deficient in the development of both joint visual attention … and proto-declarative pointing" (193).

Both Taylor's sensitivity to transformation and Harris's sensitivity to cooperation bring together the very notions of "fact" and "event" under the category of experience. The nomological sciences focus on "fact"—even, or particularly, when they take "events" to be facts themselves and simply understand events, like "things" in the world, to be positive "facts": such analysis is particularly notable in mathematical formulas. The social sciences focus on "events" of social behavior—even when they analyze events as if they were facts: such analysis is particularly notable in the statistical analyses of "trends" that govern much work in the social sciences. But the human sciences, I am arguing, imbricate fact and event; they involve fact and event with one another: surely the involvement of fact and event—which we might fruitfully take to be a working definition of *experience* as change-of-quality—is what Taylor means when he talks about the possible and future-oriented "transformational" renewal of linguistic and discursive schemas, and it is certainly what J. L. Austin means when he asks "whether flames are things or events" (179).

Shoshana Felman makes such imbrication clear when she notes the relationship between the "facts" attended to by referential language and the "events" (i.e., "acts") of speech-act theory: "the referential knowledge of language," she writes, "is not knowledge *about* reality (about a separate and distinct entity), but knowledge that *has to do with reality*, that acts within reality, since it is itself—at least in part—what reality is made of. The referent is no longer simply a preexisting *substance*, but an *act*, that is a dynamic movement of modification of reality" (51). Discursive allusion—Benjamin's citation without quotation marks—which I repeatedly mention and simply enact throughout this book, is a striking example of reference being no longer simply a substance, but an act within a particular context. In this, "reference" is a qualitative act, the experiential "active absorption" I mention in Chapters 1 and 6. In his "Presidential Address" to the Modern Language Association in 1986, Hillis Miller offers terms that clarify Felman's argument. In his address, he defines "literary theory" as

> the displacement in literary studies from a focus on the meaning of texts to a focus on the ways meaning is conveyed. Put another way,

theory is the use of language to talk about language. Put yet another way, theory is a focus on referentiality as a problem rather than as something that reliably and unambiguously relates a reader to the "real world" of history, of society, and of people acting within society on the stage of history.

(283)

The problematization of reference—which is to say, the imbrication of reference and qualitative judgment—turns the immediate sensations of experience "inside out."

I will talk more about the "problem" of reference in Chapter 4 when I focus on the relation of value to facts and events. But even here I should say a few words about the concept of "event," which is at once self-evident and also obscure. Enlightenment Modernity took as self-evident that the comprehension of phenomena created an economy of "things" in the world in such a manner that a significant part of our Cartesian/Enlightenment inheritance assumes that both knowledge and events are phenomena that function, mechanically, like worldly objects that can be embodied and accumulated; such an assumption nicely comports with Said's analysis of the notion of knowledge as a "simple additive or mechanical notion of what is or is not factual" (159; see also Schleifer *Analogical Thinking* 181). In *Gulliver's Travels* Jonathan Swift mocks this attitude when he has "projectors" at the academy of Lagado work to replace language with a sack of "things" carried by servants. In arguing that, since the late nineteenth century, the similarities of analogy (or "homologies," "aspects," "overtones," "acts of allusions") have come more and more to replace the strict positivism of identities inherited from the Western Enlightenment, I note that within the mechanical sense of the world Descartes subscribes to—a world in which all forces are reduced to momentary collisions that specifically exclude actions at a distance—event is always secondary to existence: the "duration" of a thing (i.e., its historical instantiation), Descartes asserts, "always remains unmodified," so that, like numbers, it is best conceived as what he calls a "universal" of knowledge and thinking. The goal of Enlightenment understanding—the goal of nomological science and its apprehension of "commensurable" data—results from and in the parsimonious reason of Descartes's mechanistic world, the easy transformation of similarity to identity (see *Analogical Thinking* 182). The apprehension of similarity as identity grasps the "commensurability" of phenomena. That is, the mechanistic science of the Enlightenment—in Newton as well as Descartes—creates what Max Horkheimer and Theodor

Adorno call in *Dialectic of Enlightenment* "the conversion of enlightenment into positivism, into the myth of that which is the case" (xii; an earlier translation renders this "the myth [of things] as they actually are" [Cumming translation (x)]). Elsewhere I have argued, as I mentioned earlier, that such positivism—namely the transformation of "political economy" to the positivism of "economic science" in the late nineteenth century—was "an attempt to squeeze experience out of understanding" (*Political* Economy 59), which is to say, to squeeze the apprehensions—the "feel"—of qualitative evaluation out of understanding.

The imbrication of "fact and event"—a compound term I repeatedly deploy in this book—nicely arranges itself in relation to literature. This might be clear if I unpack the "hybrid" simulation theory for "mindreading"—his term for Theory of Mind—that Alvin Goldman sets forth in *Stimulating Minds*. ("Theory of Mind" is a disciplinary "term of art" in psychology that isolates and defines the phenomenon, which experimental psychology has demonstrated begins in humans around the age of four, of attributing to others different thoughts, beliefs, feelings, and so on from those one possesses oneself.) More specifically, in the course of developing a hybrid model based upon an enormous number of experiments and studies in psychology, neuroscience, and philosophy, he emphasizes simulation (i.e., the "replication" of experience). Simulation—and especially the imaginative simulation Goldman emphasizes—is, as I note more fully in my final chapter, closely related to the vicarious experience, which literature provokes and often represents.

Thus, Goldman constructs a hybrid account of the human ability to grasp a sense that one can understand that another "creature"—a member of a cohort or simply a purportedly sentient creature (e.g., a dog or a magical stone)—possesses or experiences thoughts, beliefs, and feelings different from one's own. Goldman's "hybrid" model includes the necessity of "information" as well as "experience" in these phenomena, where "naïve psychological theories," circulating in what Owen Flanagan calls a cultural "space of meaning," are objects of cognitive understanding while "simulation" focuses on experience. In this, Goldman distinguishes between *cognitively* "supposing" some state of affairs might be true for someone else (e.g., "information" such as attributing a belief to someone else that one does not hold) and "enactment imagination" (which he designates as "E-imagination" [48]), where one *imaginatively* (i.e., by means simulated experience) is able to accomplish "the crucial role [of] putting oneself in others' shoes" (3).

In discussing a psychological experiment in which subjects are asked to "suppose" they own a mug displaying a college insignia, he argues that

> one mistake lurking here is the possible confusion of E-imagination with supposition. Sure, it's easy to *suppose* one owns a mug. But supposition isn't E-imagination, or re-creation. Merely supposing one owns a mug doesn't re-create the psychological circumstances operative in a decision-making task. Analogously, I can easily suppose that I am now living in ancient Troy and observing Helen [of Troy]. What is not so easy is to create an accurate visualization of her. The requisite visual information isn't stored in my head. So although I can *try* to visualize Helen, I can't make the visualization faithful to a genuine seeing of her. This doesn't mean that my powers of visualization are *never*, or *rarely*, up to a simulative challenge. The powers are fine if they are accompanied by suitable knowledge or experience to guide the visualizing act ....
>
> This line of explanation critically appeals to information: Missing information often prevents an accurate (enough) simulation .... [Still,] acknowledging that accuracy of inputs requires information guidance doesn't undercut the simulational aspect of the cognitive performances in question; the inputs are inputs *for simulation*.
>
> (175)

In this account—replete with the disciplinary vocabulary of abbreviation ("E-imagination"), the "head" as a place of "storage," the language of "inputs" and (implicitly) "outputs"—one can discern (if one approaches it *homologically* from the discipline of literary studies) the combination in literary texts of both *factual* "information" and *experiential* "simulation," the "facts and events" I repeatedly note throughout these chapters, which give rise to and are the objects of the "double-take" of literature. Such discernment, I should add in passing, takes up "knowledge" in psychology not as facts about the world, clear and simple, but "features of the world of indefinite complexity" that have been "picked out" by the discipline of psychology (Platts in Moore 1145) to be taken up, homologically for different purposes, by the discipline of literary studies.

The Experience of Meaning and the Experience of Sensation

Here, then, let me repeat my thesis: the discipline of literary studies pursues the systematic analysis of experience, even when such "experience" imbricates information and qualities. I began this chapter with Hjelmslev's articulation and rejection of the traditional assumption of the incommensurability of the objects of the humanities, which therefore could only be described rather than systematically engaged with. Such a traditional view suggests that rather than analyzing phenomena in ways that focus on their exact and generalizing treatment, literary studies focus on phenomena as they are *simply* (which is to say, uniquely and unmediatedly) experienced. There is good reason to disagree with this conclusion because there is good evidence that it is possible to treat human experience in exact and generalizing ways by studying the *schemas of experience* (as Jerry Vannatta and I try to do in *Literature and Medicine*, which surveys recent work in cognitive psychology measuring, in statistical analyses, responses to literary texts). That is, I am arguing that it is mistaken to understand the humanities as simply "mere description." Rather, the *experience* that the human sciences study—and, in fact, human experience more generally—is not immediate and unique, even if it feels itself to be so, but rather is the combination of fact and event, which lends itself to systematic disciplined analysis. (Moreover, in Chapter 6 I also offer another alternative to "mere description" in Stephen Jay Gould's systematic inferential analysis of historical homologies.)

In the humanities, unlike the social sciences, we focus on meaning and purport. Ludwig Wittgenstein nicely argues for this when he contends that *meaning* itself—Hjelmslev's *purport*—is best understood as an experience rather than as a cognitive apprehension of a meaningful "fact." Thus, he questions:

"What would you be missing if you did not *experience* the meaning of a word?"
What would you be missing, for instance, if you did not understand the request to pronounce the word "till" and to mean it as a verb,—or if you did not feel that a word lost its meaning and became a mere sound if it was repeated ten times over? (§261; see Exhibit 3.7). (Notice Wittgenstein's philological "unpacking" of *till*, which contextualizes the word as verb [to till the soil], noun [cash register], and adverb [of time: "until"]: I'm filled with wonder at the sensitivity and acuity—the affect and knowledge—of Wittgenstein's translators.)

Exhibit 3.7: Religious Experience

Long before Wittgenstein, the "experience of meaning" was noted in religion and theology. Thus, in his history of the term *experience*—as I mentioned earlier, a fully philological history—Martin Jay notes that "Luther's reliance on scripture alone—*sola scriptura*—was premised on the claim, as B. A. Gerrish puts it, that 'we must feel the words of Scripture in the heart. Experience is necessary for understanding the Word, which must be lived and felt.' Adopting the Stoic doctrine of *katalepsis*, which trusted in the power of clear and unerring impressions of the world on our sense organs, Luther sought to answer Erasmus's skeptical probabilism by appealing to the overpowering compulsion of self-evident experience" (82).

In his analysis, Wittgenstein goes on to discuss reading "a poem or a narrative with feeling," and he observes that "when I pronounce this word while reading with expression it is completely filled with its meaning." But then he questions this: "How can this be, if meaning is the use of the word?" (§265). The answer his observation suggests—he does not answer his own question—is that language is experienced as well as "used," and precisely the "uses" of literature encompass these wider understandings of "meaning," "comprehension," and "experience" itself. In this, I am suggesting that the *felt-immediacy* of perception and experience—including the extreme defining cases of the perception and experience of human pain and of literary meanings, which I took up in Chapter 2—can be understood as *mediated*.

In his book, *Sweet Anticipation: Music and the Psychology of Expectation*, neuroscientist David Huron examines what he argues are three basic human experiences that are provoked by the aesthetic organizations of sounds and systems of sound-meanings in music, namely laughter, awe, and what he calls frisson. I return to these particular responses to experience in a moment—and, in fact, I return to them more fully in Chapter 5—but first I want to set forth Huron's larger argument. "School children," he writes,

are commonly taught that there are five senses—taste, touch, smell, sight, and hearing. Over the last century, physiologists have established that in fact there exist many more than five. For example, we have a sense of balance (equilibrium), and a sense of body position (proprioception). Even our sense of touch turns out to entail four distinct sensory systems for heat, cold, pressure, and pain.

In many ways, *expectation* can be regarded as yet another sense: a *sense of future*. In the same way that the sense of vision provides the mind with information about the world of light energy, the sense of future provides the mind with information about upcoming events. Compared with the other senses, the sense of future is the closest biology comes to magic. It tells us not about how the world is, but how the world will be. It arose through natural selection's myriad efforts over millions of years to produce organisms capable of clairvoyance and prophecy. A stockbroker might value the ability to predict the future as a way to becoming rich. But for Nature, the value of predicting the future is the more precious gift of living longer.

(355)

The ability to anticipate what might happen is clearly a life-prolonging evolutionary adaptation. Thus, we can note how a rustle in the grass might portend—or "purport" or occasion the "inference" of (see Davidson 247)—a snake attack, for instance. But equally important, Huron is suggesting that the opposition between sensation and cognition—the sensation of "light energy" and the cognition "information about upcoming events"—may well be too strict. This is of particular moment because, as I am arguing, while experience (even *vicarious* experience) seems essentially *sensational* and ethics and morality (upon which I focus in Chapter 6) seem essentially *cognitive*, a *moral education* in its nature is experiential and cognitive at the same time. It is so because ethics evaluates and judges behavior, and evaluation is a cognitive process and behavior an experiential event.

This is why, in Huron's study, the *expectations* provoked by music are so important. He argues that the experience of music is closely tied to the phenomena of more or less automatic responses of flight/fight/freeze of most animate living creatures when faced with the surprise of purported predatory attack. Music, he argues, provokes feelings/experiences of laughter, frisson (a "fighting" reaction, which he calls "thrills from chills" [33]), and awe. These feelings, he argues, are conditioned by different and distinct neurological systems associated with reactions, respectively, of flight, fight, and freeze. In an elegant and elaborate argument he describes "the sense of future," a system whose purpose is to avoid surprise, to reasonably predict future occurrences so that there are *no* surprises. But surprise in the relative safety of the music hall brings its own pleasures, and it is precisely the ability to create safe surprises, he argues, that is the source of pleasure in music. If I had more time in this already long chapter, I'd examine the ways that the arts—and particularly music, perhaps the most sensational art (see "Aesthetics of Pain")—take up existing sensory and cognitive systems in order to provoke particular emotional and cognitive responses rather than to do work in the world. (I begin to take up this in Chapter 4.) Doing work in the world not only entails the protection and propagation of individuals and their gene lines—the "gift of living longer" Huron describes—it also entails the protection and propagation of communities of individuals.

But if music might be the most sensational of the arts, aesthetic literary discourses—fiction, poetry, drama—are, I believe, the most future-oriented. That is, the discursive arts present explicit and implicit narrative formations, whose purport is to build to a future "end" that seemingly resolves contradiction and provokes, like music, a kind of safe surprise. This phenomenon is of particular importance in relation to ethics precisely because ethics is a science of the future, of how we shall behave in the future: thus, Owen Flanagan observes that "[John] Dewey says the moral problem concerns the future" (35). The future-oriented focus—I might even say the "purport"—of both discourse and ethics might become clearer when we focus on the science of discursive meaning, namely semiotics. Thus, Charles Sanders Peirce—who in the United States, about the same time as Ferdinand de Saussure in Paris, coined the term *semiotics*—argues throughout his career that his description of the "symbol" (as opposed to "icon" or "index") is best understood as the "law that will govern the future" (I, 23). As we have seen, a generation later, another semiotician, Louis Hjelmslev working in the Saussurean tradition significantly different from Peirce's American semiotics, redefines "meaning" as future-oriented "purport" (55).

In his *disciplined* study of signification—pursuing a systematic framework of symbols and procedures that Northrop Frye calls for in literary studies—Peirce sets forth intellectual categories to systematically analyze what *always* takes place in the experience "of whatever is ... before the mind." "My view," Peirce wrote early in his career,

is that there are three modes of being, and [I] hold that we can directly observe them in elements of whatever is at any time before the mind in any way. They are the being of positive qualitative possibility, the being of actual fact, and the being of law that will govern the future.

(I, 23)

The "qualitative possibility" he describes is the sheer sensation of phenomena—the seeming "brute fact" of immediate experience as such— the "redness" of experience before it is associated with an object or a meaning, the "force" or "dynamism" of the musical tone: the *icon* (his term for this mode of experience), he says, excites "analogous sensations in the mind" (II, 299). The "being of actual fact" is apprehended by the *indexical* nature of signs (his term for a second mode of experience): the fact that signs "point" or refer to objects in the world. "No matter of fact," he writes, "can be stated without the use of some sign serving as an index" (II, 305); an index, he says, stands "unequivocally for this or that existing thing" (II, 531); "anything which focuses the attention is an index" (II, 285). The Periodic Table is such an index, focusing the attention on features of the world of indefinite complexity, which it picks out. The difference between *index* and *icon*, then, is related, I suspect, to Wittgenstein's observation that "pointing to the shape" of an object is different from "pointing to [its] color" (§33). Peirce's third modality, "law that will govern the future," is the modality of *symbolism*, and it nicely comports with Hjelmslev's redefinition of meaning as "purport" (55): future-oriented signaling, marking (literally? figuratively?) periodicity itself. Such "periodicity" is not only expressed in the Periodic Table of chemical elements, it is expressed in the periodicity of grammar, of literary genres, of *Wen* (文), patterns or markings in natural objects, in inherited cultural traditions, and in the order of the cosmos. For Peirce, a *symbol* is "a sign which refers to the object that it denotes by virtue of a law, usually an association of general ideas, which operates to cause the symbol to be interpreted as referring to that object" (II, 249). Moreover, Peirce makes clear that all signs—and experience and understanding themselves I am contending—participate in all three of these modalities, even if one of these aspects of signs seems to dominate in any particular case. It is because of this, that the seeming "brute fact" of immediate experience is almost always "immediately" absorbed into simultaneous participation in Peirce's semiotic mediating systems. Redness, almost immediately, is absorbed into the experience of a red apple (both fact and event), which itself comes to symbolize, in our Western Judeo-Christian tradition, temptation. As Felski says, "we are eternally enmeshed within semiotic and social networks of meaning that shape and sustain our being" (85).

Another neurologist, Oliver Sacks, describes the neurological breakdown of this simultaneous participation of Peirce's three modalities. Sacks describes the breakdown of their simultaneous interaction—the technical term for this breakdown is "simultagnosia"—in relation to a composer-patient who, after brain injury, could not integrate the sounds of musical pieces. In a note, Sacks says that "something analogous to a transient simultagnosia may occur with intoxication from cannabis or hallucinogens. One may find oneself in a kaleidoscope of intense sensations, with isolated colors, shapes, smells, sounds, textures, and tastes standing out with starling distinctness, their connections with each other diminished or lost" (*Musicophilia* 115; others, I should add, suggest the opposite: that hallucinogens *promote* the integration of modalities of experience). In any case, Sacks's neurological analysis of the experience of music nicely corroborates Peirce's disciplined argument that experiences of consciousness "of whatever is at any time before the mind in any way" are mediated by the simultaneous apprehension of the facts and events of differing modalities that can be systematically classified by the science—the discipline—of semiotics (for further elaboration see Schleifer *Intangible* 26-7, 179).

Structures of Experience

It is no accident that I begin and end my examination of the discipline of literary studies with two semioticians, Hjelmslev/Saussure and Peirce, because they focus on the ways in which the seeming *immediate* experiences of meaning, feeling, cognition, and sensation can be understood to be *mediated* by neurological and semiotics structures or schemas. (This formulation might also help us understand Frye's argument that physics becomes a disciplined science when it takes "the immediate sensations of experience" and questions and analyzes those seeming "immediate sensations" themselves [44].) A future-oriented understanding of meaning and signification, perhaps more fully than music taking up flight/fight/freeze impulses, offers the kind of protection and propagation of communities and individuals Huron describes. Such wider protection and propagation is, as I suggest in Chapter 6, the work of the ethical judgment of behavior.

Francis Steen, a scholar of film narrative, suggests that the "testing out" of future scenarios—as noted in Chapter 1, he describes it as the ability to "construe" possible outcomes of action in the world—is the evolutionary-adaptive function of narrative, and he argues that adaptive narrative structures are recognizable in the "playfights" of rhesus monkeys (97–100), which serve to teach the younger monkeys to "construe" possible ends of their actions. In their play, he argues, the monkeys exhibit "the development of proto-narratives in the form of multiple ... strategies with an underlying structural design" so that "rhesus playfighting ... has the *structure* of fictive narratives" (98). The adaptive function of such playfights, he argues, is intergenerational: to teach younger monkeys what to expect from action in the world by means of simulated "playfighting" with older cohorts that exhibits predictable structures of action. In Steen's description of rhesus playfighting, "rhesus macaques occupy a first-person role in an exciting and aboriginal drama. By fighting with a larger and more experienced individual, younger monkeys are challenged to anticipate their opponent's moves. To master this task, they must construe these moves in narrative terms and grasp the underlying plot" (98). In his analysis, he demonstrates the parallel structure of the "plot" of playfighting to the plot of "Little Red Riding Hood." This analysis of primate activity in relation to the structures of narrative discourse distinguishes the temporality of the discursive arts from other arts in the purport of language but also in the global intergenerational impulse of the discursive arts themselves, even though Huron—and, for that matter, Walter Pater—emphasizes the temporal nature of music. As we have seen, Huron emphasizes the temporality of music—the "psychology of expectation" of his title— under the category of *experience* as such even while the discursive arts of literature, drama, and to some extent cinema provoke, more fully, kinds of *making sense* and *construing* of the meaning and value of experience both as simulation (e.g., being in "others' shoes" Goldman notes [3]) and as inheriting from an older generation practical wisdom (*phronesis*).

Steen's key term, which he italicizes, is the "*structure* of fictive narrative" (98), because such structures allow for the isolation of forms of mediation—structures, schemas, grammars, even periodic tables—that underlie seeming immediate experience. The isolation of these "forms of mediation"—perhaps most notably in periodic tables—picks out features of the world of indefinite complexity. Sacks offers a wider sense of what is going on in this. "Language and thought, for us," he says,

> are always personal—our utterances express ourselves, as does our inner speech. Language often feels to us, therefore, like an effusion, a sort of spontaneous transmission of self. It does not occur to us at first that it must have a *structure*, a structure of an immensely intricate and formal kind. We are unconscious of this structure; we do not see it, any more than we see the tissues, the organs, the architectural make-up of

our own bodies. But the enormous, unique freedom of language would not be possible without the most extreme grammatical constraints.

(*Seeing Voices* 74–5; note Sacks's connection between discipline and freedom)

There is a pretty good consensus that there are a small number of features of narrative that allows even very young children to distinguish between well-formed and ill-formed stories (see Polkinghorne 20). In Chapter 6 I spell out these aspects of narrative discourse, which allow us to examine immensely intricate and formal structures found in everyday and literary narratives.

My point here, however, is that this *kind* of analysis pursues the work that Frye outlines, that of a disciplined science, which takes "the immediate sensations of experience" and questions and analyzes those seeming "immediate sensations" themselves (44), in this case meanings and feelings—in a word, *experiences*—provoked by narrative. Both meanings and feeling—cognition and affect—can and should be understood in relation to judgments of value as well as assertions of fact. (In this assertion, you might hear the influence of speech-act theory on my discussion in this chapter, which I examine more closely in Chapter 4 and to which I return in Chapter 6.) Both cognition and affect understood in relation to judgments of value as well as assertions of fact underline the manner in which the discipline of literary studies complements the formulaic cognition of the disciplined nomological sciences and the retrospective cognitions of the social sciences. It does so by allowing us to comprehend the systematic provocation of experience, value, and understanding discernable in our disciplined encounters with literature (see Exhibit 3.8).

Exhibit 3.8: Structures of Experience

Experience *is* value, and value—like meaning/purport—comprehends or grasps the future in the present, promise inhabiting the immediate moment. As such, among other things, structures of experience are—which is to say, structures of experience *organize*—possibilities of good health and well-being in their immediate force of ongoingness. A fine analogy (or instantiation) is Oliver Sacks' description of melody: "hearing a melody," he notes, "is hearing, having heard, and being about the hear, all at once" (*Musicophilia* 228).

CHAPTER 4
THE NATURE OF VALUE AND
THE NATURE OF LANGUAGE

In Chapter 3, in analyzing the discipline of literary studies I focused some attention on the relationship between facts and events. There, I argued that the nomological (or "law-like") sciences, such as mathematical physics or chemistry, focus on "facts"—even, or particularly, when they take "events" to be facts themselves and simply understand events, like "things" in the world, to be positive "facts": such analysis is particularly notable in mathematical formulas. The social sciences focus on "events" of social behavior—even when they analyze events as if they were facts: such analysis is particularly notable in the statistical analyses that govern much work in the social sciences. Both of these intellectual discipline groups grow out of the more or less linear understandings of mechanics, which were the driving force of Enlightenment science in the seventeenth and eighteenth centuries. In the search for "certainty"—which René Descartes described as the goal of philosophy—Enlightenment science sought to distinguish, absolutely, between the "true" and the "false"; it sought to articulate linear approximations for nonlinear phenomena. Linear thinking pursues the certainty of identity: the formula $X = Y$ presents itself as a "linear" straight line in a Cartesian coordinate system. Such a system *identifies*—absolutely and numerically—points on the system. It allows for the algebraic analysis of geometry, which one might understand as the mathematical analysis of a world that remains independent of any observer. It pursues such a goal of "objective" truth even though, as David Huron argues, "our senses are not transparent windows onto the world. Instead, our senses are adaptations that select, distill, augment, and (sometimes) deceive. We tend to accept our sensations as truthful reflections of reality. But in fact, our senses evolved not to decipher the truth, but to enhance our chances of survival and procreation" (355).

In any case, against these "factual" sciences, I argued in Chapter 3, the human sciences imbricate fact and event, which is to say they involve fact and event with one another. *Imbricate,* in its "family of meanings" (Wittgenstein §77), as I noted in Chapter 1, is a technical term that nicely spans the natural world of things (e.g., scales on an animal), the social world of work (e.g., tiles on a roof), and the creation of artifice in human affairs (e.g., organizing layers of tissue in surgery). Surely the imbrication of fact and event—which we might fruitfully take to be a working definition of *experience*—is what Charles Taylor means when he talks about the possible "transformational" renewal of linguistic and discursive schemas. Shoshana Felman makes this clear when she notes the relationship between the "facts" attended to by referential language and the "events" (i.e., the "acts") of speech-act theory: she notes, as I mentioned in the Chapter 3, that "the referential knowledge of language is not knowledge *about* reality (about a separate and distinct entity), but knowledge that *has to do with reality,* that acts within reality .... The referent is no longer simply a preexisting *substance,* but an *act,* that is a dynamic movement of modification of reality" (51).

Here, then, is the thesis of this chapter: the "dynamic movement of modification of reality" is closely related to what J. L. Austin calls the "force" of a linguistic speech act. With these terms, "dynamism" and "force," both Felman and Austin identify the linguistic/semiotic system of meaning as *a system of value,* which creates what Thorstein Veblen and John Searle call "institutional facts." The philosopher of music, Viktor Zuckerkandl, as we shall see, also brings together the terms "force" and "tonal dynamic qualities" (63) when he describes the quality that allows sound to be apprehended as music. The category of "institutional fact"—Searle opposes it to "brute fact"—helps us to see how *value modifies reality*: it allows us to more fully comprehend the indefinite complexity of seeming self-evident phenomena such as "fact," "event," and even "experience" itself. I should note that I am not being arbitrary when I bring together Veblen, a scholar studying political economy, and Searle, a scholar studying speech acts (however shortsightedly, I should add): bringing them together suggests how both political economy and speech-act theory are systems that focus on value (see Exhibit 4.1).

Exhibit 4.1: Searle's Short-Sightedness

I mention that Searle's analysis is "short-sighted" because he consistently too-quickly assumes that complicated phenomena are simply "self-evident" facts. One such assumption is his contention that pain is a simple "fact." He notes in *Speech Acts* that "institutional facts" are the result of conventional rules, like the moves in a game of chess. But he notes that "there is no rule to the effect that [a loud noise] *counts as* causing pain; one can feel pain whether or not one knows the conventions" (39). In *Pain and Suffering* I argue to the contrary that there is persuasive historical and psychological evidence that demonstrates that the experience of pain is conditioned by social and neurological "schemas," which, in the case of cultural differences in the phenomenal experience of pain, is, in fact, a function of conventions (*Pain and Suffering* Part I) and what Veblen calls "habits of thought."

Searle's work, like that of Felman, is unpacking the speech-act theory developed by J. L. Austin in the 1950s. So before I begin the examination of how we might understand the "nature" of value in discourse and language, whose analysis the discipline of literary studies pursues, let me set forth a quick summary of Austin's inaugural understanding of the nature of language. Here is my quick summary: Austin asserts that language can be understood as (i) "reporting" or describing a state of affairs and, as such can be judged to be true or false. Austin describes such use of language as "statement" or— later in his discussion of speech-act theory—as "constative." And language can also be understood as (ii) "performing" an action rather than stating a proposition. Austin describes such use of language as "performative." Philosophers contemporaneous with Austin (i.e., in mid-twentieth century) took understanding (i) as the proper understanding of any statement/ proposition, and designated language uses not capable of being judged true or false as "nonsense." Rather than dismissing nonpropositional language in this way, however, Austin distinguishes between propositional language (language organized to convey information, which is either true or false) and nonpropositional language (language, I suggest, organized to establish social relationships) in order to recognize and attend to what he calls the "force" and "felicity" of language that does not convey information that is true or false, but that *enacts* social relationships among people who talk to one another. Such enactments, like action in general, can be successful or unsuccessful (felicitous or infelicitous), judged by their outcomes. Towards the end of *How to Do Things with Words*, Austin rethinks the opposition of performative and constative in terms of three "aspects" of any utterance: *locution*, which conveys propositions; *illocution*, which perform speech-acts; and *perlocution*, which effects a response in one's interlocutor. Earlier I set forth Stanley Cavell's argument that helps us understanding improvisatory freedom by reconceiving perlocution as "passionate utterance." I should add here a structural homology: just as a sign in Charles Sanders Peirce's analysis of language can alternatively be grasped as predominantly iconic, indexical, or symbolic, so an utterance in Austin's understanding can be alternatively grasped as a proposition, an enactment of value, or a gesture of interested (i.e., "passionate") interpersonal persuasion.

Interdisciplinary Studies and the Aesthetics of Experience

Before I turn to a closer look at facts and events in language and discourse, I should touch upon the ways that recent literary criticism—often focused on form, on "surface meaning," and on a new interest in aesthetics more generally—has taken up studies in psychological, neuroscientific, and philosophical examinations of the nature of experience altogether. A good example—one that I have already brought up—is Alvin Goldman's monumental synthetic study, *Simulating Minds: The Philosophy, Psychology, and Neuroscience of Mindreading*. There is good reason for this interdisciplinary interest. In his analysis of what I might call "the aesthetics of experience"—his study of "Romantic and post-Romantic writers" (9)— Michael Clune pursues, as I have in my work in the health humanities, the ways in which everyday events and literary narrative attempt to grasp and prolong experience itself. Thus, he begins *Writing against Time* by focusing on experience in everyday life and in literature. "Is art different from life?", he begins. And answers:

> According to an emerging consensus, our experience of a description of a house, person, or landscape in a novel or poem, and our experience of an actual house, person, or landscape, are not essentially different. Critics and philosophers have drawn on recent neuroscientific research to argue that the brain processes the images prompted by literature in much the same way as it processes any other image.
>
> (1)

I have made and will continue to make a similar claim throughout this book. As might be readily apparent, any project to heighten and widen caretakers' engagements with patients by means of engagements with literature will take the continuity of everyday experience and aesthetic experience as an important starting point. However, it is notable that Clune historicizes the literary aesthetics he focuses upon as Romantic and post-Romantic. More specifically, he argues, as we have seen, that the most robust and enduring "experience" comes with first impressions: "since in everyday life," he writes, "the most vivid perception of a thing tends to be the first impression, the persistence of the qualities of the first impression across the second, tenth, and hundredth impressions signals a countering of time's effect on the feeling of life. And in fact, as we shall see, a central criterion for artistic success within this tradition is the extent to which a work produces and preserves the effect of a first impression" (9).

One discursive strategy for producing first impressions is "defamiliarization." This is a term that was coined by literary scholars in Russia in the early twentieth century, the "Russian Formalists"—and most specifically by Viktor Shklovsky—and it is a strategy Clune repeatedly focuses upon throughout his study. Thus, he repeatedly cites Shklovsky: "'In order to make us feel objects,' declares Viktor Shklovsky, 'to make a stone feel stony, man has been given the tool of art.' Shklovsky," Clune continues, "writes that habit, the operation of time in the human sensorium, tends irresistibly to destroy the surface of the world" (89). The Russian Formalists, more generally, were attempting, as I am in *Literary Studies and Well-Being*, to define the object of study in literary studies as precisely as possible in order to distinguish literary discourse from non-literary ("everyday") discourse, although unlike the Russian Formalists—but like Mikhail Bakhtin and his analysis of everyday speech-genres examined in Chapter 5—I am anxious to note the continuity between the semiotics of everyday language uses and aesthetic deployments of language. To make this distinction, the Russian Formalists focused on particular discursive strategies that counteract habitual "non-experience," such as describing familiar objects in unfamiliar ways (hence "defamiliarization"). In one example, Shklovsky notes:

> Tolstoy makes the familiar seem strange by not naming the familiar object. He describes an object as if he were seeing it for the first time, an event as if it were happening for the first time. In describing something he avoids the accepted names of its parts and instead names corresponding parts of other objects ... [so that] the familiar ... is made unfamiliar both by the description and by the proposal to change its form without changing its nature.
>
> (59; see Exhibit 4.2)

Exhibit 4.2: Historicizing Experience

It is notable that Clune makes clear his focus on Romantic and post-Romantic aesthetics, since these literary traditions, coinciding with the first and second Industrial Revolutions beginning around the start of the nineteenth century, are increasingly caught up in a consumerist culture, in which "experience" rather than the satisfactions of needs is a context in which value is apprehended. (See Exhibit 5.6: A Well-Being Theory of Value.) The discursive strategy for producing and preserving first impressions is that of *defamiliarization*, as Clune notes, developed in the early twentieth century. Thus, Ezra Pound's slogan for cultural modernism, "Make it New!," is also a slogan for consumerist capitalism: it powerfully describes homological structures of desire in economic consumption, aesthetics, and sociality in the early twentieth century (see the footnote about the complicated provenance of this slogan in my *Political Economy* 6). Thus, in *Literature and Medicine*, "Defamiliarization and Style" is one of the "features" of literary narrative, which Dr. Vannatta and I have found is particularly useful in engaging healthcare students with literature (25–6). I discuss this at some length in Chapter 6.

Still, the curious fact of defamiliarization is that the "experience" of recovering a first impression requires or manifests itself in a double-take, a "redescription" of a habitual response as if it were a "first" response. Clune makes a similar argument when he notes in Proust that the "experience" focused upon is that of "a weakly imagined wall together with the equally weak, dreamlike image of magic lantern light," which taken together "combine to create an image of surprising solidity" (2); and Clune goes on to note the manner in which "two feeble images are folded on top of one another to give an effect of solidity" (2). The creation of "an effect of solidity," which is, in fact, the creation of "simulated" vicarious experience, results, I am suggesting, both from and in the double-take of literature: that of power and knowledge I discuss in Chapter 1, but also the "two kinds of facts" I examine in the present chapter; and, more generally, that of the "double-take" of "homologous" interdisciplinary studies, the "two general approaches to the relation of literature and science" in recent years, which

Clune describes as the dependence in some literary studies on scientific models in "applying" those models to literary texts; and as the project in other literary studies to fill a "gap in scientific knowledge" (Clune 57; see Exhibit 1.10: The Hard Problem of Experience for a detailed exposition of these two general approaches).

Facts and Events

Linear "scientific" understanding in the nomological and social sciences, as I have suggested, traffics in "facts," where "a fact," to cite a popular definition found on *Wikipedia,*

> is a thing that is known to be consistent with objective reality and can be proven to be true with evidence. For example, "this sentence contains words" is a linguistic fact, and "the sun is a star" is a cosmological fact. Further, "Abraham Lincoln was the 16th President of the United States" and "Abraham Lincoln was assassinated" are also both facts, of the historical type. All of these statements have the *epistemic quality* of being "ontologically superior" to opinion or interpretation—they are either categorically necessary or supported by adequate historical documentation.
>
> Conversely, while it may be both consistent and true that "most cats are cute," it is not a fact (although in cases of opinion there is an argument for the acceptance of popular opinion as a statement of common wisdom, particularly if ascertained by scientific polling). Generally speaking, facts transcend belief and serve as concrete descriptions of a state of affairs on which beliefs can later be assigned. ("Fact")

This definition sets forth two *kinds* of facts: (1) the first kind are facts that are "categorically necessary" or "supported by adequate documentation" (i.e., adequate "evidence"): such necessary or documented facts are traditionally described respectively as "analytic" and "synthetic" propositions; and (2) the second kind are facts that present themselves as statements "of common wisdom, particularly if ascertained by scientific polling." These two kinds of facts track onto the distinction between nomological science and social science I make in Chapter 3.

Because "facts" are measured to be true or false independent of any observer, Enlightenment thinkers—Descartes, Galileo, and most systematically John Locke—distinguished between "primary qualities" of objects, which are independent of any observer, such as solidity, extension, motion, number, and figure; and "secondary qualities" of objects, which were thought to produce sensations in observers, such as color, taste, smell, and sound. Such "secondary qualities," as this list suggests, occupy the realm of experience rather than fact, while the primary quality of "extension," for example, can be seen to be simply a "matter of fact." In Chapter 2, I have already touched upon the reason that I replace the traditional notion of "sensation" by "experience" in this assertion, and my reasoning should become clearer in the course of my discussion in the present chapter. In fact, part of my argument about value here focuses on the very limited domain where the "brute facts" of sensation—Charles Sander Peirce's abstract *icon*, the seeming "brute fact" of immediate experience I described Chapter 3—are independent of the "institutional facts" of experience. (Peirce, I argued, finds the brute fact of the icon, the empirical fact of the index, and the meaningful fact of the symbol imbricated with one another.) Finally, I should also add that the seeming absolute distinction between primary and secondary qualities—like the distinction between the physical and the psychic Viktor Zuckerkandl makes, which I cite later in this chapter—is subject to the complications of feedback and information theories, what Patricia Waugh describes as the "complex systems which are entangled, unpredictable at different scalar levels, emergent and uncertain" (108).

Facts, in the common-sense popular understandings found in *Wikipedia*, are *transcendentally* true, by which I mean the truth (or falseness) of a factual proposition or a statistical tendency is true for all time, once and for all: primary qualities in this understanding, even the numerical primary quality set forth by a statistic for a particular moment, are *atemporally true*. The truth of the historical "fact" of Abraham Lincoln's assassination is no less atemporal than the ("analytic") propositions of linguistic fact and cosmological fact (e.g., "this sentence contains words"; "the sun is a star") found in the *Wikipedia* definition of fact: in this account, no events in time can modify the factual veracity of what *Wikipedia* calls "objective reality." In this way, then, as I suggested in the previous chapter, in Enlightenment understanding an "event" is apprehended as an "ontological" fact, by which I mean that an event, so understood, exists (ontologically) once and for all, rather than being determined or modified by temporal considerations. Moreover, the assumption of the "ontological superiority" of fact over opinion or interpretation—its "superiority" over the temporal nature of opinion and interpretation, which, subject to "ontological" correction, can only be understood as *temporal events* rather than *timeless facts*—underlines the certainty of matters of facts. Thus, the exclusive focus on matters of fact in Enlightenment science attempted, as I noted in Chapter 3, to apprehend empirical facts and events as "commensurable" across different particular cases, to transform similarity into identity. In *Analogical Thinking: Post-Enlightenment Understanding in Language, Collaboration, and Interpretation,* what I took to be "post-Enlightenment" in its title was the manner in which analogies—a form of understanding emphasized in the re-evaluation of Enlightenment canons of truth undertaken in recent times—focus on similarity rather than identity. What I didn't know when I wrote that book was that there was a better way to discuss "similarity"—the similitudes or "likenesses" of analogy—namely, in relation to the notion of "aspect" developed by Ludwig Wittgenstein. I elaborate on the notion of "aspect" later in this chapter.

The "facts" I have been describing—bolstered by the "common wisdom" of the *Wikipedia* definition—are what John Searle calls "brute facts" in his discussion of speech act theory (50–3). "Brute fact" is a version of the positive facts of philosophical positivism I mentioned in Chapter 3, where I cited Max Horkheimer and Theodor Adorno. The *Oxford English Dictionary* defines "positivism" (in part) as "any of various philosophical systems or views based on an empiricist understanding of science, particularly those associated with the belief that every cognitively meaningful proposition can be scientifically verified or falsified, and that the (chief) function of philosophy is the analysis of the language used to express such propositions." Philosophical positivism was developed in the early nineteenth century by Auguste Comte—he coined the term "positive philosophy"—but it is implicit in the mathematical physics of Descartes and Newton, the mechanics of Galileo, and the analysis of political economy in Adam Smith and its critique in Karl Marx. It is also a central tenet of the well-known biologist E. O. Wilson in his defense of twentieth-century science in his book *Consilience.* (Comte is also credited with founding the discipline of sociology.) Positivism is based upon three major assumptions, which I have already touched upon: that the phenomena of the world are ultimately *simple,* such that the whole of any phenomenon is made up of the sum of its parts; that phenomena of the world are basically value-free, such that whoever seeks knowledge encounters, *accurately,* phenomena that are not affected by the attitudes, presuppositions, or even the sensory apparatus of the knower; and that the phenomena of the world behave in a law-like way and such laws are universal and, *generalizing*, and because of this can predict the future. (For further analysis of positivism and its significance in Enlightenment Modernity, see Wang and Schleifer, Ch. 1 and 59–61.)

Against such positivism, which came to inhabit mathematical economics beginning around 1871, Thorstein Veblen in the early twentieth century argued that we should understand that most (if not all) phenomena we experience are "institutional" facts rather than positive "brute" facts. "Institutional facts," he suggests, are based on institutions, which he defines as governed by "habits of thought" held by members of a community: "institutions," he writes, "are settled habits of thought common to the generality of men" (*Modern Civilization* 239). One can reasonably think Veblen is describing "ideology," which underlies—not necessarily with full conscious awareness—the shared values and actions of a community. In his study of "meaning in a material world," Owen Flanagan describes what Veblen calls "habits of thought," a term Veblen learned from his teacher Charles Sanders Peirce and one, as far as I know, Flanagan is not familiar with. Instead of "habits of thought," Flannigan attempts to capture the layered complex alternative to the simplicities of positivism with a phrase containing an odd superscript: "The Space of Meaning[Early 21st century]." In deploying this term, he means a "sextet (art, science, technology, ethics, politics, spirituality)" *at a particular historical moment* (i.e., the "Early 21st century"), which contributes "to the constitution of our worlds. A world, or the multiplicity of worlds, in the relevant sense, is not the world in the sense of Earth, but the way ... individuals live and conceive of their lives on Earth." It is "the Space of Meaning for some social group ... that some group uses to make meaning and sense of things" (11). In Chapter 3, I mentioned an idea similar to Veblen's "habits of thought" and Flanagan's "Space of Meaning" in Rita Felski's observation that "we are eternally enmeshed within semiotic and social networks of meaning that shape and sustain our being" (85). Felski adds, importantly I believe, that such "semiotic material is ... *configured* by the literary text, which refashions and restructures it, distancing it from its prior uses and remaking its meanings" (102). It is important, of course, because she makes clear—as does Hillis Miller in his study *On Literature* I note in Chapter 2—the force and power of literary texts in contributing to "habits of thought," "Space of Meaning," and "semiotic and social networks of meaning."

It is also important to note, as Felipe Almeida argues in discussing the role of vicarious experience in Institutional Economics—the school of economics that Veblen founded—that "habits are performed by people but they are not just personal. They are inputs and outputs of institutions so they can be performed by, or be a part of the performance of, a single individual—although habits are also outcomes of social learning" (841). More extensively, Veblen explicitly defines "institutions" as:

> principles of action which underlie the current, business-like scheme of economic life, and as such, as practical grounds of conduct, they are not to be called in question without questioning the existence of law and order. As a matter of course, men order their lives by these principles and, practically, entertain no question of their stability and finality. That is what is meant by calling them institutions; they are settled habits of thought common to the generality of men. But it would be mere absentmindedness in any student of civilization therefore to admit that these or any other human institutions have this stability which is currently imputed to them or that they are in this way intrinsic to the nature of things.
>
> (*Modern Civilization* 239)

Such imputation, he says elsewhere, is simply "conventional finality" (*Modern Civilization* 273). He also argues that "institutions are of the nature of prevalent habits of thought, and ... therefore the force which shapes institutions is the force or forces which shape the habits of thought prevalent in the community" (*Modern Civilization* 314; see also *Absentee* 101).

Almost a century later John Searle repeats the term "institutional fact" in his analysis of the "performativity" of language in speech-act theory— without any indication he is aware of Veblen's use. In his book *Speech Acts*, he develops the distinction between "brute facts"—he also calls them "natural physical facts" (37)—and "institutional facts." In discussing "institutional facts" Searle notes that:

> a marriage ceremony, a baseball game, a trial, and a legislative action involve a variety of physical movements, states, and raw feels, but a specification of one of these events only in such terms is not so far a specification of it as a marriage ceremony, a baseball game, a trial, or a legislative action. The physical events and raw feels only count as parts of such events given certain other conditions and against a background of certain kinds of institutions. Such facts,... I propose to call *institutional facts*. They are indeed facts; but their existence, unlike the existence of brute facts, presuppose the existence of certain human institutions.
>
> (51)

By way of example, he goes on to describe "an American football game in statements only of brute facts": he describes the "periodic clustering" of men on the field, their "like-colored shirts," and various statistical laws one might abstract from these phenomena. He goes on to assert, however, that "no matter how much data of this sort ... and no matter how many inductive generalizations we ... make from the data," football still has not been described since the *meaning*—the "semantics" as Searle articulates it—has not been grasped (52–3).

What is striking about Searle's analysis is that although he describes these "institutions" as "facts," all of his examples describe complex events rather than simple facts: a ceremony, a game, a trial. In Chapter 6 I return to this issue, where I examine the nature of an "act" or an "event" beyond the rarefied notion of "event" in contemporary philosophy as "a happening that we do not foresee" (see Currie 225). But here I might jump ahead with a bald assertion: occurrences in the world designated by the "ordinary" usage of "event" to describe an easily "foreseen" event such as meeting with a friend (i.e., the "ordinary language" notion of "event" rather than the extra-ordinary sense of "event" Currie traces in "the work of Deleuze, Lyotard or Derrida" [and Žižek as well: 226, 227–9]) are complicated phenomena; they are, as I have repeatedly noted, "of indefinite complexity." And to designate and delimit a cluster of occurrences as a particular "event" (such as the Battle of New Orleans I discuss in Chapter 6)—or, in Austin's language, as a singular "act"—creates that designation or assertion by means of implicit value judgments. But I will talk about this more later. Here, in his analysis—and implicitly in Veblen's—what Searle understands as the "semantics" of this state of affairs is, in fact, the very sense of *value*. Ferdinand de Saussure, in offering a systematic analysis of language, distinguishes between "meaning" of an element of language and the "value" inherent in linguistic systems. Value, for Saussure, is a *relational* category opposed to self-evident meaning insofar as value designates signifying differences. (In this, his "value" is akin to—it is *similar to*—Hjelmslev's notion of "purport.") Saussure's example is the different value of "mutton" in English, as opposed to the French *mouton* in that the English term exists in relation to another English term, "sheep" which does not independently exist in French (114). That Saussure uses an example related to "taste"— "mutton" in English, after all, is sheep under the category of food—is not accidental in discussing value.

But perhaps a better example of an analysis of the seemingly "immediate" and uniquely idiosyncratic nature of taste can be found in

Viktor Zuckerkandl's discussion the felt "value"—the *aesthetics*—of music. "Suppose," Zuckerkandl speculates,

> we hear the tone 𝄞≡ ["e-natural"], just the single tone, and ask ourselves whether it is a usable concluding tone. The question would have little meaning. Listen to the tone as intensely as we will, we shall discover nothing in it that could either especially qualify it or disqualify it as a concluding tone. The situation is, however, basically changed if we heard the same tone at the end of the first phrase of our melody and then ask ourselves the same question. The tone we hear is the same; everything that we heard before, we hear now. But we hear something more, something new, of which there was not even a trace in the single tone. A new quality has accrued to it—we must call it a dynamic quality.
>
> (19; see Exhibit 4.3)

Exhibit 4.3: Zuckerkandl's Typeface

Zuckerkandl uses an image of musical notion in this paragraph rather than spelling out "e-natural," as I have done in brackets. I suspect he does so to indicate what I am calling the "brute-fact" nature of the isolated sound—the "brute fact" of the sonic "event"—although he does not use this terminology.

Moreover—and this, I think, is of the utmost importance—Zuckerkandl wants to insist upon the "reality," which is to say the *factuality*, of the phenomena he is describing, the *institutional factuality* of what he calls a "third thing." "What we experience in music," he argues, requires "a third thing, which belongs to neither the physical nor the psychic context. [This is] pure dynamism," which he later calls "the external psychic" or "force." This phenomenon, he concludes, "would then prove to be something purely dynamic, not feeling but force—a force for which the physical would be as it were transparent, which would work through the physical without touching it" (63). In making this argument—it is an argument about the nature or the "event" of the *experience* of music—Zuckerkandl argues that "every tone of a melody, as it sounds, directly announces at what place in the system we find ourselves with it. Hearing music does not mean hearing tones, but hearing, in the tones and through them, the places where they sound in the seven-tone system" (35).

To corroborate his contention, he cites psychological studies of the manner in which dogs respond to "single tones" but not the seemingly "same" tone in a melody. "Experiments with animals," he notes, "reveal the extent to which musical tone is not ... [merely] an acoustical phenomenon. Conditioned reflexes, which are otherwise infallibly produced when a certain tone sounds, are not produced when the tone appears in the context of a melody" (35). That is, dogs can be trained, as the Russian physiologist Ivan Pavlov trained them, to salivate when they hear e-natural (165HZ), but when e-natural is part of a melody (e.g., in a D-major version of "Twinkle, Twinkle Little Star," in which e-natural appears as a passing tone leading to the final d-natural), they do not respond with that conditioned response. The "third thing" he describes in his analysis of music, although he does not use the term, is what I am describing as the *institutional fact of value* that inheres in language, a fact (or "event") in the world, but different from the positive fact of nomological science and the statistical fact of social science, just as it is different from a physical "fact" and a psychological "effect," which correspond to primary qualities and secondary qualities. Such institutional facts—namely *facts of experience*—are, I am arguing, the objects of study of the human sciences.

A phenomenon not directly associated with music that might clarify Zuckerkandl's argument is the phoneme of language. The phoneme in language, which is the smallest independent unit in language that functions as a mechanism of attention by allowing the distinction of one meaning from another, "works through the physical" without being reducible to the physical. That is, when we are fluent in a language, we "notice" or "register" a phoneme without *experiencing* its particular—and often idiosyncratic—pronunciation. This is true because a phoneme does not function as a "positive" entity—a simple positive *fact* in language—but rather as a differentiating "entity," marking its difference from other phonemes. So in English we distinguish the difference—we seemingly automatically and seemingly *immediately* register the difference—between the words *to* and *do* whether they are pronounced in a high pitch or a low pitch, in a southern or northern accent, by a child or an adult. On the other hand, we register different sound productions of the word *take* as the "same" word, even when one person aspirates the /tʰ/ while another does not /t/. In phonetics—the study of sound rather than phonemics, which studies signifying elements of language—aspiration is the strong burst of breath accompanying the pronunciation of some consonants. In English such sounding does not distinguish one consonant from another consonant and therefore does not register as a signifying contrast, while in other languages, notably most Indian and East Asian languages, aspiration is a "distinctive feature" in some phonemes that marks them as different from others, just as the phonemes /t/ and /d/ register different meanings in English. Phonemes work "through" the physical—phonetics can measure the sound of phonemes—without being reducible to the physical insofar as phonemes are more or less unique to particular languages rather than being "ontological" facts, true and false once and for all. In this, phonemes are clear—and ubiquitous—instances of institutional facts.

Many scholars who systematically study language contend that the organization of bundles of distinctive features, which are the mechanics, so to speak, of speech-sound production such as the engagement of the vocal cords, the placement of the tongue, unblocked air flow, etc., work in tandem (i.e., in "bundles") to produce phonemes. The difference between /t/ and /d/ in English I just mentioned can be seen in the difference between engaging the vocal cords in the phoneme /d/ as opposed to the non-engagement of the vocal cords in /t/, the "distinctive feature" of "voiced" versus "unvoiced." Particular distinctive features can be present, absent, or "unmarked" in the production of any particular phoneme. Some argue that these basic organizing principles of presence and absence (+/-) and marked and unmarked govern all levels of discourse: the systematic organization of bundles of morphemes (syllables) that comprise words, and the systematic bundles of words that comprise sentences. And others, who study extra-sentential language—in the basic elements of narrative organization, in the systematic oppositions governing ideology (and consequently the "habits of thought" of cultural studies), and in systematic patterns of discourse we recognize as style—also find these organizing structures in the discursive phenomena they examine. This, then, is one of the ways of describing how the discipline of literary study turns the "immediate sensations of experience" in engagements with language and semiotic systems "inside out," as Frye says (44), by picking out "features of the world ... that transcend our practical understanding" (Platts cited in Moore 1145). Frye himself does so in the systematic analysis of the modes, symbols, archetypal myths, and genres of literature in *Anatomy of Criticism*. All these linguistic and extra-sentential phenomena work through the physical without being reducible to the physical. (See Exhibit 4.4.)

Exhibit 4.4: Northrop Frye

In his "Foreword" to the 2020 edition of Frye's book, David Damrosch notes that "*Anatomy of Criticism* is probably the single most influential work of literary theory ever written by a North American critic, and it set the stage for the rise to prominence of ... the theory boom that begin in the late 1960s. With more than 150,000 copies sold to date, *Anatomy's* influence has spread far beyond the rarefied precincts of a good deal of theoretical discourse .... *Anatomy* has had direct literary repercussions. David Lodge's novel *Small World* is built on quest romance motifs, and Lodge actually has his characters discuss Frye's theory of romance; Margaret Atwood would probably never have written *The Handmaid's Tale* or *The Penelopiad* without her deep engagement with Frye's theory of myths and archetypes. With his extensive outreach on behalf of Canadian literature, Frye became a household name in Canada. He is likely the only North American literary critic ever to have been featured on a postage stamp" (ix). Novels organized in relation—a "feedback" relation—to literary studies are fine examples of the "renewals" of language that Charles Taylor describes.

Philosophical Performance: Aspect as a Temporal Event

Wittgenstein's "Aspects." I can elaborate on Zuckerkandl's analysis of the force and dynamics of music if I turn to another man from Vienna, three years younger that Zuckerkandl, whom we already encountered, Ludwig Wittgenstein. (Both are younger contemporaries of another person from Vienna, Sigmund Freud, whose work in the science of value is at the heart of Shoshana Felman's analysis of speech-act theory.) As we have seen, in *Philosophical Investigations* Wittgenstein seems to reiterate the opposition between primary and secondary qualities I mentioned earlier when he notes that "pointing to the shape" of an object is different from "pointing to [its] color" (§33). This distinction between primary (physical) and secondary (psychic) is not the same distinction Zuckerkandl makes between presentation of "the single tone" e-natural and the apprehension of that tone in a melody because a tone in a melody is not "psychic" but rather part of a system of meaning, like the phonemes of language and the elements of literary discourse. Were the color Wittgenstein mentions to exist within a *system* of colors, then it would be the "third thing" that Zuckerkandl describes. Still, in Wittgenstein's analysis—as in Zuckerkandl's "third thing"—we can discern the difference between similarity and identity I mentioned earlier. (See Exhibit 4.5.)

Exhibit 4.5: The Qualities of Overtones

In a passage from his famous essay, "The Chinese Written Character as a Medium for Poetry," which Ezra Pound left out of the version he published in 1916, Ernest Fenollosa argues that "all arts follow the same law; refined harmony lies in the delicate balance of the overtones." Overtones determine the *quality* of sound in musical instruments: oboes and flutes can play the "same" sound e-natural (165HZ), but all except tone-deaf people can hear a difference. "In painting," Fenollosa goes on to say, "great color beauty springs not from the main color masses, but from the refined modifications or overtones which each throws into the other, just as tints are etherealized in a flower by reflection from petal to petal" (cited in Wang and Schleifer 175). Here Fenollosa is describing the *system* of color—most noticeable in complementary colors—both in nature and in the plastic arts rather than "color masses," which I believe Wittgenstein is describing when he asks us to point to an object's color (and Zuckerkandl is describing when he asks us to attend to the sonic "event" of "the tone ♮ " [19]). That the color system of flowers, "petal to petal," participates in "information theory" I describe in a moment—attracting pollinators, such as bees—suggests that it is a "third thing."

Wittgenstein seems to repeat the distinction between primary and secondary qualities in distinguishing between identity and similarity in his analysis of two different "uses of the word 'see,'" but as I note in a moment he really does not. Rather, in distinguishing between two "uses of the word 'see,'" he explores the apprehension of likenesses, which are explicitly articulated in discursive similes. Thus, before I turn to Wittgenstein's analysis, let me set forth the manner in which the Chinese novelist and scholar, Qian

Zhongshu, describes the function of discursive similes in philosophy. (In China—and probably worldwide—Qian is best known from his great novel, *Fortress Besieged* [*Wei Cheng* 围城].) "The use of multiple similes to convey a single idea," he writes,

> is a technique philosophers use in an attempt to prevent the reader from becoming fixated on a particular analogy and clinging to it rather than the idea …. When analogies and illustrations are presented *en masse*, each vying to be the most apt or alluring, the insights keep shifting and according themselves to different vehicles. In this way, each analogy gives way to the next and none lingers, the writing flows and does not dwell on a single notion, and the thought penetrates to all aspects of the subject and does not guard a single corner.
>
> (cited in Wang and Schleifer 143–4)

In arguing for "the triumph of homology," Stephen Jay Gould focuses on similarity and inference as the essence of the historical sciences. He notes that "the sciences of organic diversity do not usually seek identity in repeated experiment, but work by comparing the similarities among objects of nature as given. Kind, extent, and amount of similarity provide the primary data of historical science" (66). But in Gould, as in Qian, the work of analogy is not so much to convey knowledge as it is to provoke attention. Donald Davidson makes this clear in his analysis of metaphors, where, like Gould and Qian—and even Wittgenstein—he pursues what I am calling "philological philosophy." Davidson argues that "we must give up the idea that a metaphor carries a message, that it has content or meaning" (cited in Clune 104). Instead, metaphor—and the analogical thinking implicit in the language of both metaphor and simile, I would add—does not ask, as Clune notes in discussing Davidson, "what artistic language means," but instead "we should ask what it 'brings to our attention, what it makes us notice'" (104); and such a notion of "attention" emphasizes the imbrication of fact and event. Clune concludes by noting that "Davidson accounts for the fact that some metaphors elicit a wide range of different interpretations, not by making a claim about the indeterminacy of meaning or by trying to rule some interpretations out …, but by arguing that metaphor isn't about meaning at all. For Davidson, metaphor is about attention, experience, noticing" (105). I must likewise add that the explicit comparisons of analogy are also about attention, experience, noticing.

Now, then, let me return to Wittgenstein's philological analysis of two "uses of the word 'see'," in which he does not so much multiply similarities but rather enlarges experience under the usual category of perception.

Two uses of the word "see".

The one: "What do you see there?"—"I see *this*" (and then a description, a drawing, a copy). The other: "I see a likeness between these two faces"—let the man I tell this to be seeing the faces as clearly as I do myself.

What is important is the categorical difference between the two "objects" of sight.

The one man might make an accurate drawing of the two faces, and the other notice in the drawing the likeness which the former did not see.

I observe a face, and then suddenly notice its likeness to another. I *see* that it has not changed; and yet I see it differently. I call this experience "noticing an aspect." (§111, §112, §113)

* * *

The "aspect-blind" will have an altogether different attitude to pictures from ours .... Aspect-blindness will be *akin* to the lack of a "musical ear."

The importance of this concept lies in the connection between the concepts of seeing an aspect and experiencing the meaning of a word. (§258, §260, §261)

In analogizing "aspect blind" and "the lack of a musical ear"—what we call in English someone who is "tone deaf"—Wittgenstein is describing someone who can hear the single note "e-natural" as a particular wavelength of vibrating air (a nomological description of the "fact"—the audio frequency— of "e-natural" as 165HZ) but who cannot grasp and experience the "event" of a melody, a complex relationship of so-called events of sound that stretches over time, and cannot grasp and experience the timbre/overtone in music or intonation in language, the qualities of "style." But more importantly, in making this distinction between a visual fact and an apprehension of a relationship (one face "looks like" another face), Wittgenstein is attempting to isolate what I might call "the fact/event of value."

Let me expand upon this for a moment. In the 2000 US presidential election, many people compared two "objects of sight," the image of George W. Bush and that of a cartoon character of *Mad Magazine*, Alfred E. Neuman:

(see Exhibit 4.6).

The Stanford chemist Carl Djerassi swore that he had seen the face in Vienna after the Anschluss, with the caption 'Tod den Juden' ('Kill the Jews')" (website, n.p.). For a full image of *Mad Magazine*'s image, see *Wikipedia* "Alfred E. Neuman."

"During George W. Bush's reign," Sweet notes, there were "a spate of appearances" of Alfred E. Neuman, and many people "clearly" saw the likeness of one to the other, including likenesses in value and insight beyond the visual likeness that Wittgenstein describes. That is, the "likeness" was discernable to some people in the simple-mindedness of the cartoon character—with *Mad Magazine*'s expanded motto "What, me worry?"—and what many took to be Bush's simple-minded approach to politics. This is clear in the liberal (i.e., anti-Bush) publication *The Nation*, which rendered a version of candidate Bush's face drawn to call up the face of Alfred E. Neuman; in the image Bush wears a multi-colored button that simply says "Worry" (see https://www.marklives.com/2008/11/george-w-bush-a-retrospective-in-magazine-covers/).

In this comparison, as one can see in the two images I set forth, one can discern value apprehended as fact. In the same way—here is my own similitude—the "likenesses" Wittgenstein isolates, the "aspects" of phenomena, are *values apprehended in the experience-perception of "facts."* Now, when Qian discusses the multiple use of similes in philosophy—as you can see, his analysis is a version of philological philosophy I mentioned at the beginning of this book—he is demonstrating the way that philosophy provokes attention and "noticing" so that we can apprehend the way that so-called facts embody value.

Another political example might make Wittgenstein's notion of "aspects" even more clear. In the 2020 election year in the United States, President Trump compared Democrat Pete Buttigieg to Alfred E. Neuman. At the time, a news story noted that

President Donald Trump is fond of using unflattering comparisons and backhanded nicknames to describe his political rivals. Jeb Bush was "low-energy," Marco Rubio became "Little Marco," Joe Biden was called "Sleepy Joe," and so on.

On Friday, South Bend, Indiana, Mayor Pete Buttigieg became "Alfred E. Neuman."

In an interview with *Politico* [an American political journalism company], Trump said "Alfred E. Neuman cannot become president of the United States," referring to Buttigieg. Alfred E. Neuman is the longtime wispy haired boy mascot of MAD magazine.

When asked, Buttigieg told *Politico*, "I'll be honest. I had to Google that," he said. "I guess it's just a generational thing. I didn't get the reference." (Wu "Trump")

In these instances of "noticing an aspect"—Bush and the postcard; the cover of *The Nation*; Trump's calling up the image in relation to a rival—it is important to see that the aspect-likeness that is pointed out is not simply a matter of isolated fact or event, like the "single note" Zuckerkandl describes, but it is a value-judgment that exists in a network of relationships—the very kind of feedback relationships I discussed in Chapter 3—which Qian contends is articulated through the discursive-literary figure of simile. It is notable in this last Buttigieg example that we encounter a relationship of intergenerational knowledge, which Google, like the dictionary and *Wikipedia*, addresses. Moreover, such a judgment-fact is an act of appraisal as I describe it in a moment, and also—especially in the context of Wittgenstein's notion of "aspect blindness"—it is an *experience* that can, infelicitously, fail to take place. Such failure is possible because an "aspect" exists within a network of relationships, as do the institutional facts Veblen describes, and not simply reducible to a "positive" fact or an individual psychological state.

The relational-experiential nature of this phenomenon is particularly important to my argument because, as I mention throughout this book, the discipline of literary studies analyzes the mediating systems that govern seeming immediate felt "experience." That is, as I have already suggested, experience itself is always the experience of *qualities*, where such qualities are not "subjective"—a term my friends in the biomedical sciences like to use to describe the humanities, and a term I should add that they consistently use as a negative descriptor. Such qualities, as I said, are not "subjective," but rather they are institutional facts—as Felipe Almeida says, "habits are performed by people but they are not just personal" (841)—and the grasping or engagement with institutional (and instituted) qualities of phenomena is the grasping and engagement with value beyond idiosyncratic and "subjective" taste. One way to understand the institutional fact of qualities is to look at the seeming self-evident experience of color. Such experience seems individual, unmediated, a simple matter of fact. But as Louis Hjelmslev argues in *The Prolegomena to a Theory of Language*—a book I mention in Chapter 3—it is possible and, in describing the discipline of literary studies, it is necessary to understand the seeming self-evident (or even "subjective") experience of color qualities as mediated by social institutional facts—Veblen's "habits of thought"—governing the forms of attention within a community.

Forms of Attention. Before I turn to the experience of color, however, I should look at the notion of "forms of attention." The notion of attention is crucial here, as it is in any "close reading" (see my discussion of Roddy Doyle in Chapter 2). In Chapter 3, I began focusing on Huron's analysis of anticipation and expectation in tracing the working of aesthetic experience, and now I focus on attention. Our automatic—*habitual*—registering of the meaningfulness of phonemes is such attentiveness. And the fact that we apprehend even severely mis-pronounced phonemes as belonging to a particular class of phonemic sounds is testimony to the power of expectation. In my study of "The Aesthetics of Pain," which compares ordinary experiences, such as pain and other "sensate" experiences, with what I might call the "extraordinary" and "unnatural" (Clune's "supernatural" [59]) aesthetic experiences of music and literature, I argue, following a strong consensus in cognitive psychology, that experience in general is conditioned by schemas of experience that direct *attention and expectation* ("Aesthetics" 471; see Exhibit 4.7).

Exhibit 4.7: Attention and Expectation as Structured Phenomena

Remember Oliver Sacks' observation in the Chapter 3 about how language "must have a *structure* … of an immensely intricate and formal kind" (74). Both David Huron and Francis Steen (among many others [see Goldman, Hardcastle, etc.]) focus on the ways that schemas condition experience. Just as we saw in Chapter 3 that Huron notes that there are many more than five senses, which function as evolutionary protective strategies, so Steen argues that "our conscious perceptual experience is the fine-tuned product of hundreds of millions of years of mammalian evolution, presenting an orderly world of objects, agents, and events" (95). In other words, attention and expectation are institutional "habits of thought" because they are organized by means of structures or schemas, which can be inherited or acquired.

Nothing commands attention as much as pain—that is the burden of my essay "The Aesthetics of Pain," in which I note (as I did in Chapter 3) that "attention" is closely related to Charles Sanders Peirce's semiotic category of "index": it points to objects in the world. One biological function of pain— marked by particular nociceptive nerve cells—is to call attention to pain even faster than its conscious cognition (see *Pain and Suffering* 30–7 for an account of physiological reactions to pain, which consistently *precede* the feeling or conscious experience of pain). It is the larger argument in "The Aesthetics of Pain" that excruciating pain collapses the opposition between attention and expectation (485).

More specifically, excruciating pain erases the distinction between two well-defined neurological systems by collapsing, so to speak, the second into the first. The first of these is "implicit memory," which allows us to remember patterns of behavior, like the kind of complex "patterned" motor and cognitive processing that takes place, automatically or "implicitly," in riding a bike or driving an automobile or even simply reading this page. As I mentioned in relation to Charlie Parker, we train ourselves for such "automatic" activities through disciplined practice. The processes of these activities might be described as forms of attention without experience: hence we can drive an automobile without *experiencing* driving as such; we can read a billboard without having the *experience* of reading; we apprehend (i.e., "attend to") a particular phoneme in English without *experiencing* its particular—and often idiosyncratic—pronunciation; we transform a musical phrase into another phrase by means of automatic improvisation. These examples suggest that "implicit memory" is hardly memory at all, but precisely motor and cognitive activities that are performed *without* remembering them as activities as such. In fact, the burden of Michael Clune's analysis of aesthetic experience— dependent as it is on "defamiliarization"—precisely argues that literary art works to counter the forgetful non-experience of implicit memory. The second well-defined neurological system is "explicit memory," which allows us to remember particular occurrences (such as having read a particular poem or particular genres of poetry) and to remember, so to speak, things that are "expected." Thus, in the experience of pain, attention so overwhelms expectation that pain obliterates any possibility of expectation, any possibility of imagining a future alternative: instead, "pain—," in Emily Dickenson's metaphor, "has an Element of Blank—" (cited in *Literature and Medicine* 169). The "Blank" she describes is the overwhelming self-evident positive *facticity* of pain and suffering, which is inherent in the fact that *expectation*—including the "purport" of meaning—is overwhelmed by the insistent *attention* that pain and suffering command (for this psychological and physiological distinction between implicit and explicit memory, see *Intangible Materialism* 138–9).

The Experience of Color. But in an examination of color we can return to what I have called "a solid balancing of attention and expectation" ("Aesthetics" 477). In the *Prolegomena*, Hjelmslev specifically compares terms for color in English and Welsh—language systems from contiguous areas in the British Isles. In the chart Hjelmslev presents (rendered below) the vertical line is the wave-length color spectrum, while the horizontal lines describe the manners in which these two contiguous language systems divide the color spectrum and, in so doing, condition the attention and expectation of members of these language communities. This division "picks out"—that is to say, calls attention to—"features of the world of indefinite complexity" (Platts cited by Moore 1145), in a description I have repeatedly called to your attention in this book. Look at Hjelmslev's chart.

Green	Gwyrdd
Blue	Glas
Gray	
Brown	Llwyd

(adapted from Hjelmslev 53)

Members of the Welsh language community apprehend three separate English "colors," green blue, and gray, as shades of the "same" color *glas*. While light-sensitive photon receptors in the human eye respond to "identical" wavelengths, the qualities of those experiences are conditioned by "habits of thought" shared within a community. (For a fine account of the neurology of color reception, see Sacks "Colorblind." For a discussion of the experience of color as "part of everyday common sense," see Ngai 226.) Members of these language communities—inhabitants of a shared "space

141

of meaning" (Flanagan 11)—attend to different aspects of these colors, just as they attend to contrastive aspects of phonemes and fail to attend to non-contrastive phones (such as /t/ vs /tʰ/ in English), and their attention is conditioned by expectations set up by habit and community understanding. I should add here, that when Sianne Ngai asserts that *aesthetic* categories name "a relationship between a relatively codified way of seeing and a way of speaking that the former compels"—and she adds in a note that by "seeing" she also means ways of "hearing, smelling, or touching" as well (5)—she is also describing Hjelmslev's *non-aesthetic* semiotic account of the experience of meaning altogether (see Exhibit 4.8).

Exhibit 4.8: The Experience of the Color Spectrum

For an illuminating account of the intense experience of color, see Martin Jay's account of Walter Benjamin's "speculation" that "children have the ability to see [colors] prior to forms"—which is to say, before colors are abstracted from "objects that exist in time and space," children experience color "with pure eyes" (318). (At the end of Chapter 6, I note that, in a similar fashion, numbers, originally modifying "objects that exist in time and space" [e.g., "three apples"] are "abstracted" to seemingly signify an abstract concept [e.g., the abstract number "three"].) Then, Jay goes on, in commenting on Benjamin, to offer what seems to me a neat account of Hjelmslev's semiotic analysis. "The rainbow," he notes, "serves as a figure of life because the gradations shifting from one hue to another are infinitesimally small and defy the attempt to impose a categorical structure with clear borders on them. Colors are relationally entangled, defining themselves by what they are not, rather than discrete and self-sufficient. The child is intuitively immersed in this chromatic world rather than standing apart from it and judging it reflectively" (318). Needless to say, the fact that we name both colors and color-experiences in our languages, as Hjelmslev notes, demonstrates that colors (and experiences more generally) do not successfully "defy" categorical structures, even if they define themselves (as does semiotics in general, as Saussure argues), differentially, "by what they are not." (This is an instance of "negative science" I examine in Chapter 6.)

Michael Moore nicely summarizes philosophical refutations of the self-evidence of positivism with another example of the perception of color, in his case the "common sense position" that "factual beliefs … can be known to be true just by looking." (This describes "self-evident" truth of positivism mentioned earlier.) His example is the sentence-observation "this thing is brown" (1109). He goes on to argue that "much of the work of the psychology of perception of the last forty years has shown the inferential nature of perception" so that "one infers that it is brown because that is the best explanation for it appearing brown" (1110). He is following "inference to the best explanation," a modern version of Charles Sanders Peirce's logic of "abduction." Such explanations are implicit in a community's habits of thought (see Exhibit 4.9).

Exhibit 4.9: Abduction

In *The Chief Concern of Medicine* (Chapter 4), Jerry Vannatta and I argue that the logic of abduction—inference to the best explanation—offers a *systematic* account of strategies of diagnosis, which are usually modelled but not methodically analyzed in medical training. Such apprentice "modelling" offers the immediate sensations of experience without turning them inside out to create a disciplined science of their understanding. In an influential essay, Gilbert Harman argued that "inference to the best explanation" more fully characterizes knowledge and the process/experience of knowing than "enumerative induction." "Enumerative induction," he writes, "is supposed to be a kind of inference that exemplifies the following form. From the fact that all observed *A*'s are *B*'s we may infer that all *A*'s are *B*'s (or we may infer that at least the next *A* will probably be a *B*). Now, in practice we always know more about a situation than that all observed *A*'s are *B*'s, and before we make the inference, it is good inductive practice for us to consider the total evidence. Sometimes, in the light of the total evidence, we are warranted in making our induction, at other times not" (90). Thus, we might "know" and experience light stimulus (*A*) as the color blue (*B*). But we always know more: for example, that "blue" exists on a linguistic color-name spectrum shared by our neighbors as a "habit of thought" so that the next *A* we encounter, we will experience, inferentially, as blue (*B*).

In the final chapter I return to Hjelmslev's colors and note that my wife and I have argued over whether a pair of my pants were blue or gray. I suggest, as you will see in Chapter 6, that had we lived in Wales, there would be no need of making a conscious judgment at all concerning whether my pants were blue or gray and no need of conjugal dispute; our Welsh language would have made it clear that my pants were *glas*—a Welsh color designation that encompasses the line of distinction between blue and gray in English—rather than *llwyd*, a color akin to (e.g., "homologous with") our English brown.

The Temporal Aspect of Experience. Wittgenstein doesn't fully engage with the qualitative and on-going experiential qualities and appraisals I describe in this chapter, but he does fully engage with the temporal aspect of experience in his example of visual aspects, which can be discerned in optical illusions. This temporality, marked by the adverb "suddenly," is clear when he notes that "I contemplate a face, and then suddenly notice its likeness to another. I *see* that it has not changed; and yet I see it differently" (§113). And later when he discusses the optical illusion of the duck-rabbit,

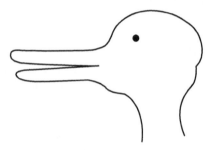

he asserts that "I must distinguish between the 'continuous seeing' of an aspect and an aspect's 'lighting up'" (§118) at a particular moment when we *see* the resemblance of a rabbit as well as a duck (or the other way around). (Note how the duck-rabbit works: the indentation on the right side is a "distinctive feature"—homologous to the distinctive features of phonemes—insofar as it distinguishes a rabbit's mouth and, *alternatively*, a "non-distinctive" bump on the back of the duck's head—homologous to the non-distinctive pronunciations of phones.) That is, optical illusions always call attention to the temporality of the grasping of signification, the temporality of the experience of meaning in *alternative* comprehensions of signification: in this case, the fact that one can "see" the duck or the rabbit, but never at the same time. The experience of the optical illusion and—more generally (and less obviously)—the grasping of the aspect of a phenomenon such as George Bush's face do not and cannot erase the temporality of meaning (or better: as I mentioned in Chapter 3, the temporality built into the notion of "purport") and the temporality of experience. After all, the seeming immediate sensations of experience are temporal events. It is for this reason that I have called this section "Philosophical Performance": the appraisals and judgments of aspects and even the alternating apprehensions of an optical illusion have to be performed in time.

The Appraisals of Language

Toward the end of Chapter 3, I quoted part of Wittgenstein's description of the "*experience* of meaning" when one reads a poem or a narrative "with feeling." Let me return to that passage from Wittgenstein and cite it more fully so that we might more fully notice an aspect of its signification:

> "When I read a poem or narrative with feeling, surely something goes on in me which does not go on when I merely skim the lines for information." —What processes am I alluding to? —The sentences have a different *ring*. I pay careful attention to intonation. Sometimes a word has the wrong intonation, stands out too much or too little. I notice this, and my face shows it. I might later talk about my reading in detail: for example about the mistakes of intonation ....
>
> When I pronounce this word while reading expressively, it is completely filled with its meaning. —"How can this be, if meaning is the use of the word?" Well, what I 1said was intended figuratively. Not that I chose the figure: it forced itself on me. —But the figurative employment of the word can't come into conflict with the original one.
>
> (§264, §265)

In Chapter 3, I answered Wittgenstein's question, how can expressive recitation be filled with meaning "if meaning is the use of the word" in the first place, by noting that language is experienced as well as "used," and precisely the "uses" of literature encompass these wider understandings of "meaning," "comprehension," and "experience" itself. In this, I am suggesting that the *felt immediacy* of perception and experience—including the defining cases of the perception and experience of human pain and the perception and meaning of literary meanings, but even, I can add here, the experiences of color, sound, and the intonations of language—can be understood as *mediated*.

In his essay "Performative Utterances," Austin answers Wittgenstein's question better than I do. "The more you think about truth and falsity," he notes,

> the more you find that very few statements that we ever utter are just true or just false. Usually there is the question are they fair or are they not fair, are they adequate or not adequate, are they exaggerated or not exaggerated? Are they too rough, or are they perfectly precise, accurate, and so on? 'True' and 'false' are just general labels for a whole dimension of different appraisals which have something or other to do with the relation between what we say and the facts. If, then, we loosen up our ideas of truth and falsity we shall see that statements, when assessed in relation to the facts, are not so very different after all from pieces of advice, warnings, verdicts, and so on [all examples of "speech acts"].
>
> We see then that stating something is performing an act just as much as is giving an order or giving a warning; and we see, on the other hand, that, when we give an order or a warning or a piece of advice, there is a question about how this is related to fact which is not perhaps so very different from the kind of question that arises when we discuss how a statement is related to fact.
>
> (*Papers* 250–1)

Here, Austin is explaining the rationale behind his replacing the strict opposition between constative and performative utterances with comprehending *aspects* of all utterances: *locutionary* meaning (as opposed to "purport"), *illocutionary* speech acts, and *perlocutionary* effects on interlocutors, which we encountered in Stanley Cavell's analysis of passionate utterances. The import of this passage, however, is more global than its discrimination among "features" of phenomena. In addition, it suggests that the act that is accomplished in "stating something" is an act of judgment, the discernment of value. In this essay ("Performative Utterances"), Austin also catalogues the functions of nonpropositional language, which his contemporaries dismissed: nonpropositional language (non-"constative" language) "influences people" (234); attends to "the circumstances in which the utterance is being made" (235); it "indulges" in actions (235); it is not a report of "some internal spiritual act" (236). He also suggests some examples of non-propositional language: cursing, including (something he does not mention) the non-intentional coprolalia (the blurting out of obscenities) of Tourette Syndrome, which is hardly true or false; the passionate (or "feeling," as Wittgenstein calls it) language of poetry; all kinds of religious, social, political ritual-languages; and, although Austin hardly mentions it explicitly, the language of jokes.

I say Austin hardly mentions jokes explicitly because Shoshana Felman's wonderful analysis of speech-act theory, *The Scandal of the Speaking Body* (whose original English translation replaced Felman's title with *The Literary Speech Act*), offers a sustained meditation of Austin's "dry" British wit, which she claims Jacques Derrida fails to "get"—in a manifestation of what we might call "aspect-blindness"—in his critique of Austin. Whenever I teach speech-act theory, I begin by asking all my students to bring a joke to class. I do so because I want to demonstrate the ways that the discursive—almost always narrative—language of jokes can provoke bodily responses. Such bodily responsiveness—like the bodily responses to danger and death I described in the next chapter on the neurological bases of narrative genres—offers a strong example the power of language, what Austin calls the "force" of language. "Saying anything at all," he argues,

> is always doing a good many different things. And one thing that emerges when we [say anything] is that, besides the question that has been very much studied in the past as to what a certain utterance means, there is a further question distinct from this as to what was the *force,* as we may call it, of the utterance. We may be quite clear what 'Shut the door' means, but not yet at all clear on the further point as to whether as uttered at a certain time it was an order, an entreaty or whatnot. What we need besides the old doctrine about meanings is a new doctrine about all the possible forces of utterances, towards the discovery of which our proposed list of explicit performative verbs would be a very great help.
>
> (*Papers* 251)

One clear example of such force is the laughter language can provoke, or for that matter the tears, the anger, even, alas, the boredom, or confusion that language also often provokes. In this—it is the work of appraisal—we can see that the quality of boredom, for example, is not simply a fact of the matter—an immediate sensation—to be noticed and judged to be true or false, but a quality of experience, an instituted fact or "force" of value. In "The Storyteller," Walter Benjamin notes that "boredom is the dream bird that hatches the egg of experience" (*Illuminations* 91), and in doing so he suggests that the nondescript dullness of boredom might reveal—or better, "enact" and "embody"—qualities and *force* by which we can understand the degree to which "the referential knowledge of language," as Felman says, "*has to do with reality*, that acts within reality" (51). (Needless to say, both in class and on the lecture stage, I find it somewhat worrisome to bring up the issue of boredom.)

But jokes are a particularly good example of forceful, nonpropositional language because, more clearly than many other linguistic or speech acts, they explicitly lend themselves to appraisal. We are accustomed to talk about a "good" joke or a "bad" joke in ways we do not explicitly respond to the force of an informational description, such as the discussion of "fact" in *Wikipedia*, or an itemized list of historical facts ("events")—or the "force" of boredom, for that matter. We do use this explicit language of appraisal, however, when we talk about a political speech, an advertisement, a poem, or even the "elegance" of a logical argument. But even in advertisements this is complicated. We might go out and buy *Nike* shoes we don't really need, but the nonpropositional strength of the advertisement—the fact that it attempts to provoke an attitude toward experience rather than setting forth the persuasive qualities of a commodity in its slogan "Just do it!"—doesn't call attention to the commodity to be purchased but rather to the experience associated with it. Perhaps the *Coca-Cola* slogan, "Taste the Feeling," makes this clearer. It might well be, as I suggested earlier, that renewed attention to experience—in literary studies, speech-act theory, even semiotics—is a function of the trafficking in experience (commodifying experience) in the consumption-beyond-need promoted by the culture of consumerist capitalism, that was concomitant with the late nineteenth-century emergence of intellectual disciplines I described in Chapter 3 (and more fully in *A Political Economy of Modernism* and with my colleague Tiao Wang in *Modernist Poetics in China*). Attention to the experience of meaning might be particularly clear in the emergence of the intellectual discipline of semiotics.

The function of jokes is different from advertisements' commodification of experience. The work of jokes, like that of many instances of laughter, is to dissipate a fearful situation (see Wang and Schleifer, Ch. 4), and standup comedy functions in the same manner that "art narratives" transform the function of everyday narratives: that is, standup comedy functions to aestheticize and privatize the social work of joking. Everyday jokes, I believe, function to dissipate antagonism, usually between men. It allows strangers who might come to blows share in laughter instead. (This is a corollary to the laughter of playfighting I examine in Chapter 5.) But in the formal setting of joke-telling—on stage, at a party, even jokes in a classroom or a lecture—while a so-called bad joke might provoke a groan and a different kind of laughter, in the everyday setting of joking between antagonists a "bad" joke—tasteless, misunderstanding its audience, hurtful—often exacerbates anger. This is clear in the opposite, when purposeful hurtfulness is excused as being "just a joke" (see Exhibit 4.10).

Exhibit 4.10: The Dismissal of Experience in Literary Studies

Such dismissal of experience that we find in the excuse "I was just joking" might also be clear in the way literary scholarship often works to avoid charged engagements. Thus, Yeats's poem "Leda and the Swan" might prompt feelings of fear and awe—and even the outraged anger I have encountered in women students, responding to Yeats's taking up violence against women to make some other point—when one listens to or reads the poem. (I discussed such feelings of fear and awe in relation to "blank tragedies" in the next chapter and also in relation to Yeats's poem itself in Chapter 6.) But in literary criticism focused on Yeats, more often than not literary scholars often struggle against the violent force of Yeats's poem by pursuing more propositionally-comfortable "meanings" abstracted from its violent "purport." Again, this is clear in the ways that Vivian Bearing in the play *Wit*, which I discuss in Chapter 5, has spent her life as a literary scholar analyzing rather than confronting the power of death in John Donne's poetry. And it is precisely this attention to—rather than dismissal of—"experience" that engagements with the "practical reasoning" of healthcare brings to literary studies. Patients bring emotions to the clinic—fear, anger, sadness (see Chief Concern 196–200)—and part of the work of healthcare workers is to bring into focus the experience of emotion in their clinical work.

What is important here—and central to this chapter—is the work of appraisal, which is, after all, the measure of value and "moral" meaning as seemingly opposed to factual meaning. Michael Moore's extended meditation on the "reality" of value—his thorough analysis of "Moral Reality"—focuses on refuting the common-sense opposition between "objective" fact and "subjective" value, an opposition articulated in

Wikipedia. Moore nicely reviews a vast number of philosophical analyses of this opposition. "There are no analytically necessary and sufficient conditions for the correct use of a word in natural languages," he writes, "nor are there paradigmatic examples of the things within the extension of such words" so that the purport of such words cannot be simply a matter of fact. "Justification of factual judgments," he continues, "cannot thus be different … from justification of moral judgments. Any belief, moral or factual, is justified only by showing that it coheres well with everything else one believes" (1112–13). He concludes that "in no sense are factual beliefs any more secure in their justification [by means of self-evident positivism] than are moral beliefs. Justification of any belief, factual or moral, is not the locating of undubitable particular ['positive'] judgments from which all else can be known by induction…. Justification of any belief is a matter of its coherence with all the other propositions that we believe to be true" (1116). Thus, he argues, quite persuasively I judge, that "factual judgments," like moral judgments, exist within a network of beliefs, a network of inferences to the best explanation, where what makes one explanation "better" than another is a function of social habits of thought and spaces of shared meaning/experience, a "third thing" beyond the physical and the psychic: "of course those pants are simply, 'self-evidently,' the combination of blueness and grayness captured in the Welsh word *glas*." As Moore suggests, such a network of beliefs is not simply "personal." Rather, it exists within a world of "habits of thought," a space of meaning, in which "habits are also outcomes of social learning" (Almeida 841). Buttigieg's aspect blindness in relation to Alfred E. Neuman was a function of the community in which he grew up and not simply a congenital tone deafness, which Wittgenstein suggests in his analogy between aspect blindness and the lack of a musical ear. (Yeats, strangely enough, is reported to have been tone-deaf despite the lyricism of his poems.)

Still, Wittgenstein does suggest a sense of a community of values in his analysis of the experience of apprehending aspects. We have seen Wittgenstein describe the apprehension of an "aspect" of an image this way: "I contemplate a face, and then suddenly notice its likeness to another. I *see* that it has not changed; and yet I see it differently" (§113). Austin uses remarkably similar language, even while he takes up literature rather than visual images in his example. "In moral or practical affairs," he writes in "A Plea for Excuses," we can know the facts and yet look at them mistakenly or perversely, or not fully realise or appreciate something, or even be under a total misconception. Many expressions of excuse indicate failure at this particularly tricky stage: even thoughtlessness, inconsiderateness, lack of imagination, are perhaps less matters of failure in intelligence or planning than might be supposed, and more matters of failure to appreciate the situation. A course of E. M. Forster and we see things differently: yet perhaps we know no more and are no cleverer.

(*Papers* 194)

A course of E. M. Forster is, of course, an academic class focused on early twentieth-century literature, which I'd like to remind you is the period in literary history I study as an English Professor. But in any case, to see things differently without any change in the facts of the matter is to appraise and feel the value of a text rather than—or along with—its meaning. And when Austin focuses on adverbs, as he does in "A Plea for Excuses," he is working to find the place of value within the workings of language.

That working does not exclude meaning, even as value allows us to "see things differently" in the language of both Wittgenstein and Austin by allowing us to see how language can be meaningful and evaluative; it can be grasped as propositional statements of matters of fact and performative utterances alternatively, like the duck and the rabbit. Thus in "Performative Utterances" Austin notes that

if we look back for a moment at our contrast between statements and performative utterances, we realize that we were taking statements very much on trust from, as we said, the traditional treatment. Statements, we had it, were to be true or false; performative utterances on the other hand were to be felicitous or infelicitous. They were the doing of something, whereas for all we said making statements was not doing something. Now this contrast surely, if we look back at it, is unsatisfactory. Of course statements are liable to be assessed in this matter of their correspondence or failure to correspond with the facts, that is, being true or false. But they are also liable to infelicity every bit as much as are performative utterances.

(*Papers* 247–8: note Austin's "also" reiterates
the alternation—the double-take—of the duck-rabbit)

In other words—these are Freud's words—the nature of a language use, alternating between proposition or speech act, statement or utterance, is "overdetermined": it is not so much true or false as it is one thing or another, a duck or a rabbit; or as both Wittgenstein and Austin say, it can be grasped and experienced by an interlocutor to be one thing or another. In this distinction, I am trafficking in "purport" rather than "meaning," as I described the difference in my earlier chapter. In fact, Wittgenstein's notion of "aspect" itself traffics in overdetermination: that George W. Bush may (or may not) seem similar to Alfred E. Neuman allows us to understand that the Freudian notion of "overdetermination" is the determination of value in experience (including the experience of meaning). It is the experience of "aspect," where aspect itself describes experience, whether it is uninflected everyday meaning—"Oh, that's George Bush"—or a pronounced "aha!" apprehension—"He looks like Alfred E. Neuman!" Uninflected, "dull" experience—like the dullness of boredom—gives rise to the punctuations of insight.

In other words, the "value" I have been discussing in this chapter is, above all, "informational" in the sense of information theory, which describes institutional facts of value in-forming (which is to say *constituting*) experience. (Do not confuse complexity of "information theory" I am describing here with simple "information" as matters of fact I mentioned earlier in the oppositions between "factual 'information' and experiential 'simulation'" and between "information and qualities" [see p. 108 above].) This suggests that the "information" of "information theory" is essentially social and essentially complex in the manner in which Brian Arthur describes the dynamism of the economy as essentially complex in his book *Complexity and the Economy* (see *Political Economy* 159). Many years ago, Norbert Wiener argued that "information is information, not matter or energy. No materialism which does not admit this can survive at the present day" (132). More recently, David Chalmers makes a similar argument: "it may even be," he writes, "that a theory of consciousness could eventually be consolidated into a single grander theory of information" ("Puzzle" 86). Chalmers goes on to suggest that

> we might bite the bullet and allow that all information has an experiential aspect—where there is complex information processing, there is complex experience, and where there is simple information processing, there is simple experience. If this is so, then even a thermostat might have experiences, although they would be much

simpler than even a basic color experience, and there would certainly be no accompanying emotions or thoughts. This seems odd at first, but if experience is truly fundamental, we might expect it to be widespread. In any case, the choice between these alternatives should depend on which can be integrated into the most powerful theory.

(86)

As I have noted in this chapter, it is not altogether clear as Chalmers assumes that color experience is a "basic" brute fact. But in any case, in their arguments, Wiener and Chalmers are suggesting that information/experience is the "third thing" that Zuckerkandl describes in music, the "force" that Austin describes in language, the "purport" I have been arguing is discoverable in discourse. The discernment of these phenomena can be pursued in a disciplined and systematic fashion, which is the discipline of literary studies.

* * *

In my next chapter-lecture of this series, I turn to the interdisciplinary study of these phenomena—in literature, of course, but also in related areas of rhetoric, pedagogy, psychology, economics, and other areas—in order to offer hands-on disciplined analyses. As I have mentioned repeatedly over the years, interdisciplinary study necessarily presents a "home" discipline from which to understand the objects of analysis in other disciplines. As I have argued in these chapters so far, a "home" discipline *homologically* takes up and "renews" the work of other disciplines. In my next chapter, then, I pursue some examples of this homological work, which initiates itself in our "home" discipline of literary studies.

CHAPTER 5
THE DISCIPLINE OF DEATH: PRIMARY EMOTIONS, AESTHETICS, AND THE NEUROLOGICAL BASIS OF GENRE

Before turning to the practical nature of value described in relation to literature in the final chapter, in Chapter 5 I focus on the overwhelming "brute fact" of death itself—what Martin Jay describes as "that impossible topic" and a "limit experience" (389, 390)—and the ways in which literature and literary narrative genres engage with death. I end this chapter by suggesting how the relationship between perhaps the largest element in the discipline of literary studies, namely the genres of language and discourse, and perhaps its most fine-grained element, namely aesthetics in general, which etymologically and in fact grows out of the particularities of material human experience, helps shape the discipline of literary studies.

The Aesthetics of Experience

If death, as Jay notes, is a "limit experience," perhaps it is best to begin with what it limits, namely everyday experience and aesthetic experience. The term *aesthetics*, of course, is derived from a Greek term for experience: Wlad Godzich talks of the *aesthesis* of "the individual citizen [in ancient Greece], indeed even women, slaves, and children [all of whom] were capable of aesthesis, that is perception" (1986: xv). Jay adds semantic depth to this understanding when he notes that "the Greek *aiesthesis*, the origin of the Latin word *aesthetica* ... implied gratifying corporeal sensation, the subjective sensual response to objects rather than objects themselves" (138), and he goes on to note that "from the beginning [the term *aesthetics*] contained an ambiguous emphasis ... on both 'sensation' and 'perception,'" the former of which "foregrounds pleasure and emotional response in the subject; the latter ... stresses cognitive values of form and proportion and thus draws attention back to the object" (138 n.26). From the beginning, then, *aesthetics* seems to have called for a double-take.

Godzich of course, but Jay as well—and, as we have seen, Michael Clune, Sianne Ngai, Jonathan Kramnick, and the twenty-first-century "turn" or return to aesthetics more generally—have emphasized the continuity between everyday experience and aesthetic experience. There are two important ways to think about the continuity of aesthetics and experience. First, as Joseph North vigorously argues, the continuity of experience in general and of aesthetics as it relates to the "experience" presented and provoked by artworks is crucial in replacing the Kantian idealization of art with a material sense of the work of art in the world. Such continuity emphasizes the kind of "worldliness" described by Edward Said, which I discussed earlier in relation to philological philosophy. Moreover, implicit in the "fine-grain" of experience is the formal structures of attention and expectation that "aesthetics" shares with "genres." Second, the continuity of everyday experience and aesthetics underlines the social/communal nature of experience and aesthetics, the "habits of thought" that govern the social experience of members of a community as well as the experience of individuals in such a manner that Raymond Williams's notion of "structures of experience," like "structures of feeling," must recognize, as he says, "the area of social experience" (132). When Godzich talks about *aesthetics* and *aesthesis*, he does so in unpacking, philologically, the word *theory* in literary studies. He describes the way that the term was applied to the *theoros*, who was a person sent by a particular Greek city to public celebrations in other city-states as its representative. The role of the *theoros* was *theoria*, "looking on," but his ultimate goal was to report back to the home polity. "Between the event and its entry into public discourse," Godzich concludes, "there is a mediating instance invested with undeniable authority by the polity. This authority effects the passage from the seen to the told" (1986: xv).

The passage from the seen to the told is the passage from the seeming immediacy of sensation/perception to the full-blown mediacy of discourse. "Telling," after all—that is, rendering *experience*—is the worldly and social work of literature and also, in the clinic, the worldly and social work of healthcare. This is so even when—especially when—healthcare professionals and general readers come up against the "limit experience" of death itself. The passage from the seen to the told—or more specifically, the fact that "ways of speaking [are] tethered to specific ways of perceiving" (Ngai 21)— is the focus of Sianne Ngai's "aesthetics," where she suggests that the "verbal dimension" of "judgment's performative dimension" is central to aesthetic experience altogether. Thus, "the passage from the seen to the told" is less a sequence of events than a duck-rabbit double-take in aesthetics, and as such it entails semiotic structures—"structures of experience," as I am contending—so that, as we have seen, what Oliver Sacks describes as the basis of the seeming "effusion, a sort of spontaneous transmission of self," which is the "feel" of spontaneous language-use, is the fact that language—and *experience* as well—"must have a *structure*, a structure of an immensely intricate and formal kind" (*Seeing Voices* 75; see Exhibit 3.8: Structures of Experience).

What makes death a "limit experience" for aesthetics, then, is the fact that it seems to be—that is to say, it is *experienced* to be—structure-less, a blank abyss, a vertiginous "plain sense" without the features that anchor us to the world. It seems simply a "brute fact" that marks, as I will quote Regina Barreca asserting in a moment, the seeming absolute difference between representation and reality. In Chapter 4—perhaps I did so in my first two chapter-lectures taken together (Chapters 3 and 4)—I offered a strong sense of "institutional fact" as the opposite to the positivism of "brute fact." In those chapters, I probably created the impression that brute facts occupy a very small corner of the world, just as Bertrand Russell, speaking about mathematics, noticed in the early twentieth century that "in former days it was supposed (and philosophers are still apt to suppose) that quantity was the fundamental notion of mathematics. But nowadays," he continues, "quantity is banished altogether, except from one little corner of Geometry, while order more and more reigns supreme" (87). Russell is marking what I have recently described as the "post-positivism" that inhabits cultural modernism; post-positivism pursues what Gaston Bachelard describes in his studies of twentieth-century literature and twentieth-century physics as "the *complexification* of what appeared to be simple" (cited in Wang and Schleifer 81; see also 61–71). But even if semiotics and speech-act theory suggest the irreducible complexity of our experience, it is well to remember that there *are* some "brute" facts, borne of necessity rather than desire, which, precisely because of their stark "brutality," cannot be easily grasped as "institutional." Chief among these, of course, is mortality and death, but we should also remember that the act of counting in traditional mathematics, which Russell seems to disdain, grounds itself on the necessity of keeping track of things in the face of the brute fact that for many people many necessities of life are simply in short supply. In this chapter, then, I want to examine the relationship of the discipline of literary studies—and the study of experience in the human sciences more generally—with the brute facticity and the "limit experience" of death itself.

Before I begin, let me call attention to the fact of how quickly what I just said turns away from death to talk about Russell and mathematics, the limits of positivism and complex matters, things very different from the "plain sense" of death and mortality. Part of what we do, as members of disciplines of study and institutions of higher education, is to deploy wit as a cover for the limit experience of death. In "Aubade," Philip Larkin provokes and spells out that limit experience:

> ... the dread
> Of dying, and being dead
> Flashes afresh to hold and horrify.
> The mind blanks at the glare.

> (Larkin; see Exhibit 5.1)

Exhibit 5.1: Uncle George

My book *Rhetoric and Death* begins with a meditation on Philip Larkin's "Aubade," which, as the excerpt I just quoted suggests, represents and provokes the terrifying experience—the "limit experience"—of contemplating death. When the book came out, I visited my uncle George to give him a copy. He read through Larkin's poem and gave the book back to me. "Ron," he said, "I'm too old to read this book."

The Nature of Genre

The notion of literary genre situates itself within the complexities of the discussions in my first two chapter-lectures (Chapters 3 and 4). In "The Function of Criticism at the Present Time"—and in *Anatomy of Criticism*—Northrop Frye makes clear that the notion of genre is one way literary studies can create a systematic framework of symbols and procedures, which are fundamentally different from the worldly phenomena they seek to explain, as I put it in Chapter 3. Frye notes in his 1949 essay that "criticism, incredible as it may seem, has as yet no coherent conception of genres. The very word sticks out in an English sentence as the unpronounceable and alien thing it is" (45). (I should say that when I was editor of the journal *Genre*, one day

I got a note from our office manager informing me that someone named "John Ray" had left a message for me.) Along with this harsh assessment, however, Frye also mentions in this passage that "in Joyce's *Portrait* there is an interesting and suggestive attempt made to re-define" the terms "lyric," "epic," and "dramatic" (45). In a moment, I return to Joyce. But in his essay, and in *Anatomy of Criticism* as well, Frye contends that there is something basic about genre, both literary genre and what Mikhail Bakhtin calls "speech genres." (Frye makes no reference to Bakhtin, the translations of whose work appeared many years after *Anatomy of Criticism*.) Bakhtin's assumption of the basic function of speech genres—their basic sociality—can be discerned, as I argue in this chapter, in the "protocols" of mourning; his assumption, I argue, demonstrates the link between the discursive force of genre and brute facts, just as evolutionary explanations of behavior and phenomena—events and facts—organize themselves around the brute fact of life-and-death struggle. Genre, then, like death, is curiously complex as both an abstract notion and a positive material fact: Maurice Blanchot describes the complexity of dying, a phenomenon, he notes, "which, though unsharable, I have in common with all" (23). Genre makes the "unsharable" individual encounter with brute fact something we have in common as well. I should add that even though I discussed the brute-fact nature of death as I began this chapter, even death calls for a double-take: as both a brute fact, it is "unsharable," unique, experience beyond the domestications of systematic understanding; and also something a person has "in common with all," experience that lends itself to rendering in ("generic") telling and social caring. (Think of the semantic depth of *rendering* itself: socially/ systematically "spelling out" but also, as Herman Melville shows us in *Moby-Dick*, the material boiling down of whale blubber.)

That is, genre seems clearly to be an institutional fact, which, like all institutions facts, is shared; in fact, discursive genres are woven into the basic organization of communication: recall my observation in Chapter 4, which describes the range of meaningful distinctions in discourse ranging from the "distinctive features" of phonemes, based on the physiology of the human speech organ (the glottis, pharynx, nose, tongue, lips, and vocal cords), to genres, which organize everyday and literary discourses. As I said, genres are institutional facts, but they are institutional facts of a special sort in that they form the basis of human communication altogether—including inter-cultural, inter-disciplinary, and inter-generational communications. In this we can discern that the sociality of communication—Sam Harris calls it the basic "human capacity for cooperation" (79)—is less an institution than the basis for the creation of human institutions, which, focusing attention and expectation for communities of individuals (as well as individuals themselves), *shape* experience and, with experience, seem to shape "reality" itself.

Moreover, as I suggested in Chapter 4, if the "distinctive features" of phonemes are the "smallest," perhaps most elementary units of discourse, then genres might be taken to be its "largest," most encompassing units: this is suggested by the fact that Frye ends *Anatomy of Criticism* with his essay on genre. In *The Chief Concern of Medicine*, Jerry Vannatta and I argue for this global nature of genre and the usefulness of understanding genre—in a disciplined fashion—in clinical medicine. In our book, we contend that narrative is defined by the fact that it presents a "meaningful whole," by means of which one can grasp a global sense of a narrative in the same way one grasps the meaning of a sentence that is not reducible to any single element or even any linear combination of elements of that sentence. The semiotician A. J. Greimas describes such wholeness as "the still very vague, yet necessary concept of the meaningful whole [*totalité de signification*] set forth by a message" (*Semantics* 59). Such a "meaningful whole" is the overall sense or point of a story—its "thought," its "aboutness." It is the meaning we take away from the story, its "purport," the "moral" of the tale, and/or even the sense of overall "genre" I describe in this chapter. Thus we say *Hamlet*, *Oedipus*, and even the death of John Kennedy are all "tragedies," despite the fact that they are so different. We make this judgment (or simply have a more or less unarticulated sense of their similarity) because each of these very different narratives of *Hamlet*, *Oedipus*, and Kennedy configures and "grasps" a series of events—intellectual promise, prominent political power, more-or-less unfortunate character flaws, unforeseen yet recognizable violence—in a manner that conveys or provokes particular cognitive and emotional responses. In this way, a "vague" sense of a whole unified meaning emerges from the elements of narrative; this unified meaning, as I said, presents and, in fact, *shapes* our experience of "reality" (see Exhibit 5.2).

Exhibit 5.2: Genre and the Logic of Diagnosis

In *The Chief Concern of Medicine* Jerry Vannatta and I pursue a similar discussion of genre in examining "the logic of diagnosis." We do so in order to examine how crucial for practical reasoning in healthcare generic understanding can be. We argue that the "crucial element" in diagnosis is the framework of understanding that allows a fact or event (that is to say, a symptom) to be configured and comprehended as a Case of a particular illness in the same way that a literary text or a particular interpersonal linguistic exchange can be understood to be an instance of a literary or speech genre. The "thought" or "point" or genre of a story, which I mention above, is such a framework of comprehension, picking out "features" of experience in order to achieve an inference to the best explanation. In medicine, such an inferential comprehension is the diagnosis, the "explanation" of the symptom, which suggests both cause and treatment of an illness or condition (see *The Chief Concern* 118–21).

Keyings of the Real: Genre and Reality

With this in mind, in this chapter I organize a discussion of genre—and especially a consideration of genre in relation to what Stephen Dedalus describes in Joyce's *Portrait of the Artist as a Young Man* as "whatsoever is grave and constant in human sufferings" (204)—with two passages examining literary texts in relation to what each calls "reality," one from John Frow and one from Regina Barreca. Let us look at these two passages. In his book in the Routledge "New Critical Idiom" series entitled *Genre*—a fine and lucid account of literary genre—Frow notes that

> one definition of aesthetic practices is that they are keyings of the real: representations of real acts or thoughts or feelings which are not themselves, in quite the same sense, real. Shifting texts to another generic context has that kind of effect: it suspends the primary *force* of the text, but not its generic *structure*.
>
> (50)

"*Keying,*" Frow notes earlier, "is one of the ways animals play by pretending to fight: what looks like hurtful and aggressive behavior is in fact, bracketed, suspended, so that 'bitinglike behavior occurs, but no one is seriously bitten'" (49; Frow is citing Goffman 41). The rhesus playfighting discussed in Chapter 3 is an example of "keying." Notice also that Frow's description of the maintenance of generic structure while the force of a text is suspended nicely approximates the way evolutionary homology distinguishes between physiological structure and life-world function.

In what might be taken to be an answer to Frow's powerful theorization of genre as an institutional fact, Barreca argues in her essay "Writing as Voodoo: Sorcery, Hysteria, and Art" that

> just in case you thought there was no distinction between representation and reality, there is death. Just in case you thought experience and the representation of experience melted into one another, death provides a structural principle separating the two. See the difference, death asks, see the way language and vision differ from the actual, the irrevocable, the real?

> (174)

Barreca's bringing up death in discussing the power of literary genres is perhaps as shocking as the Bradshaws, in Virginia Woolf's *Mrs. Dalloway*, excusing their lateness to the party by talking about the death of a young man: "Oh! thought Clarissa, in the middle of my party, here's death, she thought"; and "what business had the Bradshaws to talk of death at her party?" (279, 280). In a similar fashion, one may ask: what business is there to talk of death in relation to the ways that literary genres help us to "key"— which is to say, to "ground" and "reground"—comprehensible ongoing experience? How do the "moorings" of literary genres, to use a metaphor I take up later, imbricate themselves in the blank bewilderment of the absolute facticity of death?

These two passages, as I have said, examine literary texts in relation to what each calls "reality," which might—but not necessarily—tie "reality" itself to death. Reality, Frow argues, can be "keyed," and by this term— adapted by both himself and Erving Goffman from anthropology—he is describing the ways that "human behavior is rich in analogous forms of bracketing: make-believe and fantasy, aesthetic activity more generally, contests and ceremonials, ... and the 'regrounding' of an activity in a context where it means something quite different" (*Genre* 49–50; such "make-believe" bracketing is closely related to the neurological "imagination response" designated by David Huron [16] I describe later; it is also related to the "make-believe, make-desire, and so forth," by which Alvin Goldman describes simulated experience [48]). Here Frow is arguing the ways that verbal/narrative genres, as he describes them throughout his study, should be understood as discursive structures that "create effects of reality and truth, authority and plausibility" (2). Barreca argues, however, that in the face of the *irrevocable* reality of death the "reality-effects" of genre, which Frow analyzes, give way to what I might call "non-reality effects" or "supernatural-effects" of hysteria, sorcery, and art (as Barreca has it in her title, "Writing as Voodoo: Sorcery, Hysteria, and Art"), which do not create effects of "regrounding," but rather those of "un-grounding," where meaning isn't so much transformed by means of genre, but where meaning is unmoored, detached in what I describe in this chapter as emotion in the face of the "limit experience" of death: hysterical laughter that unmoors comedy, sorcery violence that unmoors melodrama, and overwhelming sublimity that unmoors tragedy.

In this chapter, then, I closely examine the relation of death—and particularly the irresistible facticity of death—to the literary or, more generally, to the aesthetic genres of irony, melodrama, tragedy. I do so by focusing on Samuel Shem's novel, *The House of God*, which portrays medical students encountering death and dying on a daily basis for the first time in their lives; the melodrama of John Donne and Dylan Thomas heroically confronting death; and the awe-inspiring tragedy of Margaret Edson's drama *Wit* about a Professor of English dying more-or-less alone in a hospital. In this, I examine what I am calling the "affective comprehension" accomplished by the discursive forms of literary genres in relation to evolutionarily developed defense mechanisms. To do so, I take a step back from—but hardly repudiate—Frow's socio-historical analysis of genres as institutional facts. Here, I might simply note that in his discussion of genre a number of years ago—before his publication of the second edition of his "new idiom" study of *Genre* I am citing in this chapter—Frow explicitly suggests that future examinations of genre should situation themselves in relation to what he calls "The New Rhetoric"—by which he means the turn or return to aesthetics in literary studies I have discussed throughout this book—and "Cognitive Poetics" ("Reproducibles" 1630-1), particularly neurological and narrative schemas of cognitive poetics I also discuss throughout this book. I pursue both of these approaches to genre in the present chapter. More specifically, I deploy in my argument a text I mentioned in earlier chapters, David Huron's meticulous neurological study of the power of music, *Sweet Anticipation: Music and the Psychology of Expectation*, to examine the ways literary genres and the aesthetics of music and literature call upon and reground primal emotions of fear, anger, and surprise—emotions which respond to life-threatening situations—as the laughter, triumph, and awe that constitute, in basic ways, the affective comprehension of literary genres. These emotions—fear, anger, surprise—take their place among six primary human emotions that a number of psychologists, often following the work of Paul Ekman, have isolated (the others are disgust, happiness, and sadness); Ruth Leys calls Ekman's catalogue the "Basic Emotions" paradigm (439). And in the present chapter I also focus in my argument on the intergenerational caring of healthcare and, I suggest, the intergenerational caring of aesthetics as well, which offers, I believe, one response—hardly an answer—to the "blank" limit-experience of death itself.

Genre as Etiquette, Language, and a Natural Fact

For many years I edited the journal *Genre*, whose subtitle we changed toward the beginning of the 1990s to *Forms of Discourse and Culture*. We made that change because in the late twentieth century, after the advent and success of continental literary theory in literary studies—namely, structuralism and post-structuralism (where structuralism was curiously akin to Frye's attempt to create a discipline of literary studies in *Anatomy of Criticism*, a version of what Hillis Miller calls "literary theory")—there was the notable turn toward the historicism of cultural studies, in reaction, I think, to the latent formalism and, as Joseph North suggests, idealism in many of the practices of literary theory. This is the turn to the "historicist/contextualist" approach to literary studies, which North traces in his concise history of literary criticism. In any case, this turn to cultural studies certainly inflected the ways in which we study and comprehend the genres that inhabit and, I believe, shape (that is to say, "reground") our experiences of the arts and even the ordinary everyday genres (i.e., Bakhtin's "speech genres"), which shape the experiences of our social lives.

As I have already suggested, this rethinking of the historical situation of literary and other art genres is nicely articulated in John Frow's useful study of genre. His "book's central argument," Frow notes,

> is that far from being merely 'stylistic' devices, genres create effects
> of reality and truth, authority and plausibility, which are central to
> the different ways the world is understood .... These effects are not,
> however, fixed and stable, since texts—even the simplest and most
> formulaic—do not 'belong' to genres but are, rather, uses of them;

they refer not to 'a' genre but to a field or economy of genres, and their complexity derives from the complexity of that relation.

(Genre 2)

In this argument, then—which is close to Charles Taylor's notion of the relation between structure and event I mentioned in Chapter 3—Frow suggests that texts do not "belong" to an abstract generic category, which subsumes them, but rather they participate in a complex relationship between categorical "forms" and historical "manifestations" of phenomena, an "economy," as he calls it (see my *Political Economy of Modernism* for a sustained analysis of such a comparable performative understanding of "economy"). Making this suggestion, Frow situates genre within history and culture—within "habits of thought" and "spaces of meaning"—rather than as "transcendental" formal categories by which phenomenal experience, such as the particular literary and narrative texts examined in the present chapter, might be explained, understood, apprehended.

Still, in making his argument he also posits a comprehensive account of genres in everyday language and literary texts and suggests that there have been four general approaches to understanding and comprehending genre, namely "as a fact of language, as a sociological fact, as a matter of social etiquette, or as something like the natural organism." "In each case," he concludes, "the metaphor provides a way of thinking systematically about a form of ordering that is in many ways resistant to system" (57). Let us look at Frow's categories.

Genre as Etiquette: Everyday Speech Genres. Frow himself focuses on genre as "a sociological fact," but in this chapter I would like to touch upon his other categories as well. A good discussion of genre as etiquette is Amy Olberding's fine account of the Confucian notion of *li* (礼), something I imagined that my Chinese friends in Harbin were much more familiar with than I am. While *li* is usually is translated as "ritual," Olberding translates it as "manners" or "etiquette" in such a way that, I might suggest, it could also be translated as "genre" insofar as she describes etiquette as social forms that "script" patterns of behavior. Such etiquette, she notes,

> would, for example, script patterns of human interaction or choreograph the protocols of formal mourning ... [and] represent an effort to lend efficacious and beneficial order to commonplace and recurrent human experiences. [Such protocols] arise in sensitivity

to human need, be it the need to acknowledge each other as social partners or to organize expression of naturally arising yet perilous emotions such as grief.

(425–6)

Here Olberding relates the "scripts" of etiquette to what Stephen Dedalus describes as "whatsoever is grave and constant in human sufferings" (Joyce *Portrait* 204). I mentioned early in this chapter that genre attends to constants in human experience in order to link genre more clearly with the brute facts of danger and death. Olberding's focus on mourning and grief does the same with "etiquette."

As her description of everyday "protocols" of linguistic behavior suggests, discursive genres are not simply literary, such as the formal literary genres I spell out in the next section of this chapter. The Russian literary critic Mikhail Bakhtin argues that everyday "speech genres" are ubiquitous and more "primary" than literary genres; he argues that all forms of discourse are social and thereby generic so that "speech genres" organize understanding and experience altogether. They are concrete manifestations of "habits of thought." "Even in the most free, the most unconstrained conversation," he writes,

we cast our speech in definite generic forms, sometimes rigid and trite ones, sometimes more flexible, plastic, and creative ones .... We are given these speech genres in almost the same way that we are given our native language, which we master fluently long before we begin to study grammar. We know our native language—its lexical composition and grammatical structure—not from dictionaries and grammars but from concrete utterances that we hear and that we ourselves reproduce in live speech communication with people around us .... Speech genres organize our speech in almost the same way as grammatical (syntactical) forms do.

(78–9)

This might be clear in the particular manner in which we talk with healthcare workers—physicians, nurses, and the like—with whom we observe certain forms and constraints of language. Thus, our doctors usually address us by our first names even while we address them by their titles, and there are certain "forms" of discursive interchange we follow with them, as we do with people inhabiting different social roles, our teachers, our parents, and grandparents, the mechanics who service our automobiles, the police we might encounter, even our intimate friends.

Narrative Genres as a Fact of Language. In this chapter, however, I focus on Frow's description of genre as a category of "something like the natural organism," though first I will also touch upon his categorical description "genre as a fact of language." In my work with the semiotics of A. J. Greimas, I have tried to demonstrate that Greimas argued that narrative genres—along with what he calls "narrative grammar"—can be understood as strictly parallel to—strictly homologous with—the structure of the sentence. Thus, he describes four agents of narrative—he calls them "actants" to allow for nonhuman agency, such as the ring in *Lord of the Rings*—that correspond to parts of speech in the sentence. His model suggests that one can define four narrative genres in terms of the relationships among these narrative agents (see Schleifer et al. *Culture and Cognition* 64–95). The agents he identifies are the Hero (corresponding to the subject of a sentence), the Wished-For Good or Heroine (corresponding the object of a sentence), and the Helper and Opponent (each corresponding to adverbs of a sentence). In the context of these chapter-lectures, I might point out the parallel between Greimas's focus on adverbs—his assumption of the particular importance of syntactical adverbs—and J. L. Austin's focus on adverbs because they articulate the qualities of actions. This parallel suggests the implicit focus on narrative in speech-act theory. In any case, in *The Chief Concern of Medicine*, Jerry Vannatta and I describe a system of narrative genres based upon Greimas's narrative "grammar" (383–4, modified below):

> *Heroic Melodrama (Epic):* a heroic narrative, where the Hero receives the wished-for goods (in myth and tradition, the bride and the kingdom). The Hero conquers the Opponent in the process. Sherlock Holmes is such a Hero.
>
> *Tragedy:* a tragic narrative, where the Helper receives the wished-for goods (both the storied knowledge of what has taken place on the level of the individual destruction of the Hero and the promised reconstruction of the community on the brink of collapse with the destruction of the Hero; this reconstruction is often accomplished by the Helper). Creon in *Oedipus* and Horatio in *Hamlet* are such Helpers.
>
> *Comedy:* a comic narrative, where the Heroine receives the Wished-For Goods (in myth and tradition: the Hero as husband

and the estate of marriage). Elizabeth Bennet in *Pride and Prejudice* is such a Heroine.

Irony: a more-or-less "modern" narrative, where the Opponent receives the Wished-For Goods (to destroy them on the level of the individual and to transform them on the level of general value). War-wounded Jake Barnes in *The Sun Also Rises* is such an Opponent, as is the actant Death in Boswell's *Life of Samuel Johnson* (see Exhibit 5.3).

Exhibit 5.3: Irony Genre

We call this final narrative genre "more-or-less modern" because traditional cultural narratives, which are often anonymous folktales or myths arising within social formations, rarely exhibit the kind of ironic reversal of traditional forms this genre embodies. The existence of this genre is a good example of Charles Taylor's sense of the "successive renewals" of language formations that do not leave the language formations "unharmed" (see also *Literature and Medicine* 176).

This schema of four basic narrative genres, then, follows from a sense of conceiving of genre as, in Frow's terms, "a fact of language."

Genre as "Something like a Natural Organism." Frow, however, takes the biological metaphor for genre as the most robust metaphorical analogue for genre, even more robust than the "sociological fact" he pursues: "it has been above all the model of the biological species, building on the organic concepts of 'kind' and 'genre', that has been used to bring the authority of a scientific discourse to genre theory." And even while he concludes that "none of this is particularly useful for thinking about the literary or other kinds [of genre], for the good reason that genres are facts of culture which can only with difficulty be mapped onto facts of nature" (*Genre* 57), nevertheless he goes on to note that such seemingly "scientific" categorization builds upon the notion of "prototype" in cognitive psychology, which allows categorizations that enable us "to work from what we know best in a sort of concrete and ad hoc negotiation of unfamiliar experiences" (60).

It is my argument in examining the discipline of literary studies that it is useful to think of genres as "facts of nature"—both in terms of responses to "common and recurrent human experiences" and in terms of conceptions of genre in relation to the equally "natural" notion of "facts of language." That is, one function of genre—perhaps a "basic" function, as I will be suggesting—does not aim at incorporating the unfamiliar into systems of familiar conceptual prototypes, but rather builds upon what is most familiar, namely affective responses to experience that are evolutionarily adaptive and thereby both ubiquitous and, in fact, "facts of nature." Such building upon what I and others have called "impersonal" feelings (see Jacobs and Schleifer) might allow us to complicate Frow's contention that genres, as "facts of culture," do not *solely* realize themselves in relation to organic concepts. While Frow's emphasis that genres are cultural institutions may well be useful in tracing the work of genres, nevertheless we can also understand (in another double-take) that the "realization" of a narrative genre can be understood as fruitfully *beginning* with conceiving of genre "as something like [a] natural organism" (Frow *Genre* 57).

The Affective Comprehension of Genre

In a study of the power of affect in literature and politics, Lee Spinks articulates what I am calling "impersonal feelings" in the much more severe designation of "inhuman or pre-subjective forces and intensities" (24). In a similar fashion, Eric Shouse calls these affective phenomena "affective resonances independent of content or meaning" (paragraph 14). As such, they take affect to be simply "brute facts." Summarizing these and other scholars focusing on affect across various disciplines, Ruth Leys notes that:

> they suggest that the affects must be viewed as independent of, and in an important sense prior to, ideology—that is, prior to intentions, meanings, reasons, and beliefs—because they are nonsignifying, autonomic processes that take place below the threshold of conscious awareness and meaning. For the theorists in question, affects are "inhuman," "pre-subjective," "visceral" forces and intensities that influence our thinking and judgments but are separate from these. Whatever else may be meant by the terms *affect* and *emotion* ... it seems from the remarks quoted above that the affects must be noncognitive, corporeal processes or states. For such theorists, affect is, as [Brian] Massumi asserts, "irreducibly bodily and autonomic."
>
> (437; quoting Massumi 28)

In her analysis, however, Leys correctly contends I believe that (in my metaphor: see Exhibit 3.3: Commodity Fetishism and Intellectual Disciplines) the "romanticization" of the noncognitive in these arguments is misdirected (see Leys 456–7 and 458n43). That is, her critique of the "immanent naturalism" in many of these discussions [459] suggests what I am calling the "romanticism" of these arguments, their deployment of a prelapsarian state of affairs (comparable to what has been called "the pre-alienated essence of things" [Ngai 83], which is discussed in Exhibit 3.3: Commodity Fetishism and Intellectual Disciplines). In a strange way, these conceptions of "irreducibly bodily and autonomic" affect drain any sense of *experience* from phenomena that have traditionally defined experience. To use Northrop Frye's metaphor, they turn experience itself "inside out" the way that physics turns heat and moisture inside out, rather than taking experience, as I have tried to do throughout this book, as "an explanatory feature rather than an object of study in its own right" (Jameson 33). That is, if, as many have noted, pain is "*by definition a conscious experience*" (*Pain* 10), then surely the more general category of affect must be "by definition" a conscious experience as well.

In this way, it is my sense, tutored by semiotics as I note earlier, that such "noncognitive" phenomena, which may be "irreducibly bodily and autonomic," are taken up almost immediately, almost universally in human experience by semiotic systems and deployed to new and different ends, different purposes—the ends of the "explanatory feature" of experience. Many scholars focused on "noncognitive" affect theory emphasize the temporal "gap between the subject's affects and their cognition or appraisal" (Leys 443)—a gap measured in tenths of seconds (453)—yet, as Leys nicely demonstrates, such a focus reduces the richness of human experience to the poverty of (an unnecessary) positivism. That is, the notion of "impersonal feelings" I describe here is clearly distinct from the notion of "affects as nonintentional states" that Leys critiques (466n56). Rather, it is useful to comprehend such "impersonal feelings" with qualifications similar to those Jacques Derrida brings to the notion of "intention" in speech acts. In the "typology" of iteration, he writes,

> the category of intention [or, in my argument, the category of the brute fact of "noncognitive affect"] will not disappear: it will have its place, but from that place it will no longer be able to govern the entire scene and system of utterance [or of "feeling"] …. The first consequence of this will be the following: given that structure of iteration, the

intention [or the brute fact of "noncognitive affect"] animating that utterance [or animating that "feeling"] will never be through and through present to itself and to its content.

(192; cited in Culler 341)

By "through and through present to itself," Derrida means it will never be *simply* a "self-evident" positive ("brute") fact, but always already (in Derrida's recurring phrase) be mediated by systems of meaning, always already a double-take. Finally, to return to Leys, what is also apposite in her systematic critique of "the turn to [noncognitive] affect" in relation to my discussion of particular genres in this chapter is that, in developing her critique, she focuses on three experiments, which themselves analyze the laughter (459–61), "the emotion of fear" (463–4, n54), and perhaps—in her examination of Massumi's reference to the "snowman" television experiment (444–52)—the awe, three generic "experiences" I examine, which are all connected to the facticity of death at the base of literary genres.

In his early poetry, W. B. Yeats identifies what he called the "immortal moods" that he pursues in his poetry, which nicely approximates the "impersonal feelings" I am describing here. Yeats describes the "immortal moods" as emotional states one passes through rather than personal emotional states idiosyncratically associated with one's individual self, that one simply expresses. Olberding nicely describes the etiquette-ritual behavior of *li* in similar *impersonal* terms: "the exchanges and experiences of ordinary, quotidian life," she writes,

> profoundly shape moral attitudes, moral self-understanding, and what prospects we enjoy for robust moral community. Philosophically addressing these exchanges and experiences is, nonetheless, a significant challenge, for much of what transpires in them operates outside of conscious intentions, deliberate choices, and reflective consideration—those territories most well traversed in Western moral philosophy.

(423–4)

The area she describes "outside of conscious intentions, deliberate choices, and reflective consideration" is the ideological "spaces of meaning" informing habits of thought for a particular historical community.

In his neurological analysis of what he argues is a key source of the power of music, namely "the psychology of expectation" I examined in

Chapter 3, David Huron offers an analysis of emotions—he nicely calls it an understanding of "the dynamics of emotion" (1)—that are impersonal in the ways, following Yeats and Olberding, I am describing without being "noncognitive" and outside the ordinary notion of "experience." In analyzing music, Huron describes evolutionarily developed emotional responses occasioned by danger. He describes three experiential responses:

- the "thrills and chills" of frisson (in which "the first order of business is to produce an aggressive display" [33]);
- the odd "panting" of laughter (which "is a response to an apparent or momentary danger" [32]); and
- the "gasp" of awe (which "is a response to a sustained danger" [32]).

These three responses to danger, which are both affective and physiological, are related to what Huron describes as neurologically determined tension, reaction, and appraisal responses to danger (see Exhibit 5.4).

Exhibit 5.4: Feeling and Emotion

When I assert that these responses are "both affective and physiological," I want to recall Antonio Damasio's observation distinguishing between "feeling" and emotion," which I cite in Chapter 2. "The world of emotion," he says, "is largely one of action carried out in our bodies" while "feelings" are "composite *perceptions* of what happens in our body and mind when we are emoting" (*Self* 109). In the opposition between emotion and feeling, Damasio is reiterating the opposition between "noncognitive" affect and impersonal "experience" I describe here.

As we have seen, these feelings, Huron argues, are "strikingly similar" to what "physiologists have identified [as] three classic responses to danger: the *fight, flight,* and *freeze* responses" (35). Moreover, they correspond to three of the six primary emotions psychologists have identified: anger, fear, and awe-inspiring surprise.

Perhaps the equation of laughter and flight seems the least intuitive of Huron's identifications. In a note he emphasizes that "further support for the idea that laughter is linked to the flight response is evident in the rough-and-tumble play that is often associated with laughter in humans and other primates"—we have encountered this in Francis Steen's analysis of narrative in connection to rhesus playfighting—in which "a submissive animal [is] chased by a more dominant playmate, with the submissive animal laughing" (Huron 384). This qualification is important since I focus in this chapter on the fearful comedy of irony as well as the blunt melodrama of anger and the blank awe of tragedy. Huron's catalogue of emotional responses to life-threatening danger seems to skip one of the narrative genres I have catalogued, namely comedy. I return to the comic feeling of happiness toward the end of this chapter, as well I should.

I argued early in this book that the function of aesthetic phenomena in human cultures (e.g., "art narratives") is to take up evolutionarily adaptive behaviors (e.g., "everyday narratives") and re-deploy them to so-called *aesthetic* ends. Such redeployment, I noted, can be understood in relation to the evolutionary category of homology, where similar biological structures—I mentioned the physiology of the bat wing and the human hand—are taken up to different ends. As I suggested earlier in this chapter, Frow describes this as the "regrounding" of aesthetic experience. Thus, in analyzing the stimuli that give rise to "surprising events," Huron notes that "whether the stimulus is visual or auditory in origin," nevertheless response to that stimuli follow the same neurological pathways. Although Huron doesn't mention "discursive" as well as "visual or auditory" stimuli here, nevertheless, he does list "imagination response" as the first of his catalogue of "five response systems [which] arise from five functionally distinct neurophysiological systems" that answer life-threatening danger: "*imagining* an outcome," he notes, "allows us to feel some vicarious pleasure (or displeasure)—as though the outcome has already happened" (17, 8); and he speculates that "the imagination response is probably the most recent evolutionary addition" to these five systems of evolutionarily adaptive responses to life-threatening danger (17). Let me simply reproduce his table ("Table 1.1" on p. 16, reproduced here as Table 5.1 below) of five neurological systems—which are, in fact, physiological manifestations of neurological schemas (schemas, I am suggesting, which "structure" experience)—that, in his analysis, respond to life-threatening danger. By "outcome" in this table, Huron is describing the surprising life-threatening event for which these "functionally distinct neurophysiological systems" evolved rapid responses (see Table 5.1).

I am suggesting with Table 5.1, then, that we can understand literary genres as the re-deployments of the powerful discipline of evolutionary adaptive systematic responses to the environment: the discipline of "anticipating events," "deferred gratification," creating expected "accuracies," that map somewhat onto the catalogue of disciplines, which I set forth in Chapter 3. As I noted, Brian Boyd, in his evolutionary analysis of storytelling, argues that the adaptive function of discursive narrative is to promote the articulation of social/communal goals within a human community to ends of promoting collaborative action—such as the rhythmic and communal cries of lyric poetry Stephen Dedalus describes—to achieve those goals (see Boyd 42–50). Moreover, one can similarly argue for the adaptive function of music—notable work-songs or cadenced voicing in the synchronized drilling of fighting units—as creating social/communal goals and promoting collaborative action to achieve those goals. And, additionally, one could also argue that visual stimuli in social life—religious architecture, iconic representations, clothing design—serve the parallel adaptive functions of promoting shared action. I argued earlier that the formal aesthetics of discourse, music, and the plastic arts aims, not at promoting social cohesion and social action—the creation of social bonds, the anthropologist Robin Dunbar has argued, is the adaptive function of "the origin of language"—but rather at expanding the horizons of sensibility, affect, and cognition. Thus, everyday narrative, as Boyd argues in his study of narrative in the context of evolutionary biology, functions to get the listener or listeners to behave

Table 5.1

Response system	Epoch	Biological function
imagination response	pre-outcome	future-oriented behavioral motivation; enables deferred gratification
tension response	pre-outcome	optimum arousal and attention in preparation for anticipated events
prediction response	post-outcome	negative/positive reinforcement to encourage the formation of accurate expectations
reaction response	post-outcome	neurologically fast responses that assume a worst-case assessment of the outcome
appraisal response	post-outcome	neurological complex assessment of the final outcome that results in negative/positive reinforcements

in a certain way by creating a framework for communal action as well as a framework for communal understanding. To this end, the attention that literary narrative creates encourages the discernment of what Jim Phelan calls the "cognitive, emotive, and ethical responses" that narrative provokes and the discernment of "the complexity of the relationship between facts, hypotheses, and theories" (14, 15) that art narratives set forth. I should add that, in addition, aesthetic attention, focused upon in what one musicologist calls the "museum art" of concert performances (Hamilton 325) and, of course, the museum art of plastic-arts museums themselves, is designed to isolate so-called *aesthetic* experience from the social action of the musical, plastic, and discursive arts (see Exhibit 5.5).

Exhibit 5.5: Kantian Aesthetic Disinterestedness

In his discussion of *The Critique of Judgment* in his history of the term "experience," Martin Jay notes that "attentive listening, as James Johnson has shown, was an acquired skill in the eighteenth century based on the suppression of the kinesthetic body and the concentration of faculties on a single sensory input. The experience of passive listening was carefully segregated from that of dancing or communal singing as the ear was educated to have contemplative aesthetic experiences. The public concert hall, as we have noted, worked like the museum to deracinate works that had their origins in the church or aristocratic chamber and turn them into stimuli for pure aesthetic experiences. In literature as well, the habit of looking for actual personal references in concocted narrative had to be lost and what Catherine Gallagher has called 'nobody's story,' the realization of acknowledged fictionality, put in its place before the novel could come into its own" (144–5). Jay discusses an alternative to such Kantian disinterestedness in his analysis of the pragmatic aesthetics of John Dewey. "The segregation of 'fine' or 'high' art in museums and galleries, abetted by the rise of capitalism," he argues, "Dewey thus saw as largely pernicious: 'Objects that were in the past valid and significant because of their place in the life of a community now function in isolation from the conditions of their origin. By that fact they are also set apart from common experience, and serve as insignia of taste and certificates of special culture'" (163; Jay is citing Dewey's *Art as Experience*).

Here, then, in my argument, is the nature of genre: literary or aesthetic genres are not defined *in the first instance*, as Frow argues, "by the *actions* they are used to accomplish"; they are not in the first instance, as he notes Carolyn Miller argues, "typified rhetorical actions based in recurrent situations" (Frow, *Genre* 14; Miller 31). Rather, *in the first instance* we can understand aesthetic genre as a means of increasing "affective comprehension" in engagements with others and with experience in general. That is—again, I have to emphasize, *in the first instance*—literary genre takes up evolutionarily adaptive responses to life-threatening events in order to focus and develop the affective and cognitive potentials of those responses to the end of widening *experience* rather than promoting action. This is the object of study in the discipline of literary genres; and this is the object of study when literary narrative is deployed in the health humanities.

Thus, following Huron, I want to examine genre as allowing us to more fully *experience* the following phenomena. (By "more fully" I mean: with larger and more self-conscious intensity, with greater nuance, with wider fellow-feeling, with a greater sense of their "second instance" work in delineating the field of individual and social action.)

- the fear and laughter embedded in a flight response to danger;
- the anger and frisson embedded in a fight response to danger; and
- the passive suffering and awe embedded in a freeze response to danger.

I have described the distinction between the goals and strategies of the deployments of everyday discursive/narrative events and the deployments of aesthetic discursive/narrative events as the difference between "everyday" narrative and "art" narrative. This distinction is discernable in clinical medicine as well as in semiotic and literary studies. Patients bring "everyday" narratives to their healthcare providers, and the goal of the deployment of these narratives is to promote action in the world. But training in the "affective comprehension," stimulated by "art" narrative, allows healthcare providers to engage their patients more fully, to recognize and act upon the (usually) implicit goals in their patients' storytelling, and to combine—or at least to entertain—the importance of care as well as cure in their work with people who are often fearful, angry, or suffering with their plight. In the rest of this chapter, I pursue the practical wisdom of this enterprise in relation to the disciplined genres of literary studies.

Facing Death in Narrative Genres

Fearful Irony. In the rest of this chapter, I briefly analyze the affective comprehension of literary genres. To do so, I focus on discursive/narrative events that respond to and "reground" fear, anger, and awe in the face of death. The texts I have chosen to examine are literary works that my colleagues and I have repeatedly chosen in team-teaching a course in "Literature and Medicine" organized by myself and practicing physicians. As such, these literary ("art") narratives also function as "everyday" narratives as befits the double task embodied in such interdisciplinary courses. Grounding this chapter that is focused on literary form and death on texts chosen for our classes is not simply arbitrary. We talk in our "Literature and Medicine" classes of how the work in achieving an MD is no more arduous than the work in achieving a literary PhD, with one exception: training in healthcare, unlike disciplined literary study (and unlike as well the disciplines of the nomological and social sciences, which I discussed earlier) necessarily involves the confrontation with human suffering and death on a daily basis. The experience of this confrontation with death, in fact, constitutes the affective base of the texts I examine here: in the laughter of Shem's *House of God*, in the resistance to death in complicated lyrics of Donne and Thomas, and in the awe that death inspires in Edson's terrifying drama *Wit*.

I begin with the fearful laughter of irony in Samuel Shem's novel *The House of God*. *The House of God* is a novel that traces the first year of medical interns in a large metropolitan hospital in the United States. Young mostly male physicians encounter death and dying on a daily basis, but the novel is filled with cynicism, with sexuality (real and fantasized) in the midst of death and dying, and above all with strange laughter. The narrator and main character, Dr. Roy Basch, faces the worst week of the year coming up, "the one between Christmas and New Year's," which his partner tells him is "a week of death. Be careful, get ready. It's going to be terrible." "A Holocaust," Roy says; "Exactly. Savage," Berry replies. But afterwards Roy says "I started to laugh, Berry started to laugh, and soon the bed, the room, the world itself was one gigantic mouth and tongue and tooth engaged in one ellipsoid laugh" (199). In his neurological analysis of laughter-responses to music, Huron isolates one musical strategy (among others), namely "drifting tonality," which can help us understand the comic humor in response to the fear of death in *The House of God*. Of "drifting tonality" he notes that "when shifts of key occur frequently, the sense of tonality itself is lost or ambiguous" (285). Throughout *The House of God,* Shem continually creates such tonal/semantic shifts, as he does here, not only in juxtaposing the Holocaust and laughter, but even in the odd qualitative description of "ellipsoid" laugh, that joins mouth and mirth, so to speak, and may silently remember (i.e., allude to) Joyce's "ellipsoidal [billiard] balls," one of the jokes from *The Portrait* (192). As I note later, the "mouth-gesture" of laughter described here takes its place with mouth-gestures articulated in melodramatic and tragic affective responses to life-threatening situations. The "tonal drift" Huron mentions—and "mouth-gestures" more generally—drift between the bodily life of mouth (including the body's susceptibility to death itself) and the semiotic/"spiritual" life of gesture, the scandal of the speaking body.

Later, after breaking up with Berry at a New Year's party, Roy gets drunk and, watching nurses dance with one another, he thinks of "'The Follies' at Treblinka." Then he says:

> And then I thought about the pictures of the camps, taken by the Allies at liberation. The pictures showed emaciated men peering through the barbed wire, all eyes. Those eyes, those eyes. Hard blank disks. My eyes had become hard blank disks. Yet there was something in back of them, and, yes, that was the worst. The worst was that I had to live with what was in back of them, what I had to live with, the rest of the world must never see, for it separated me from them, as it had just done with my former best friends and with my one long love, Berry. There was rage and rage and rage, coating all like crude oil coating gulls. They had hurt me, bad. For now, I had no faith in the others of the world. And the delivery of medical care? Farce. My first patient of the New Year was a five-year-old found in a clothes dryer, face bloodied. She had been hit by her pregnant mother, hit over and over with a bludgeon of pantyhose stuffed with shards of broken glass.
>
> (213–14)

Despite a small number of passages like this—filled with pathos, anger, and debilitating fear—*House of God* remains a very funny book. Its comic laughter works in the way that Huron's musical laughter works and the way that the fearful irony I describe here works: they function by violating expectations. "Most of these violations," Huron writes, "involve schematic expectations .... But all of the laughter-evoking moments can be traced to violations of listener expectations." Moreover, he adds, "laughter-inducing passages are much more surprising than frisson-inducing or awe-inducing passages" (287). In this, the fearful laughter of ironic comedy, unlike the satisfactions of romantic comedy, calls attention to and emphasizes the affective comprehension of genre. Romantic comedy—like generic aesthetics more generally—promises a species of unalloyed pleasure, if not happiness itself.

The ambiguous comedy of *The House of God*, however, laughing in the face of death, instantiates ironic comedy where the Opponent, death itself, seems all there is. Early in his study, Huron catalogues "types of laughter": *nervous laughter*, in the face of threat; *slapstick laughter*, answering physical awkwardness; *sadistic laughter*, responding to the misfortunes of enemies; *surprise laughter*, confronted with safe surprises, like the bursting of a balloon; *social laughter*, that participates in social groups; and *humor laughter*, which is staged in joke-telling, as genres are staged—systems of discipline—as a form of entertainment (28). The ironic comedy of *The House of God* calls upon and provokes all these types of laughter, and in doing so, it creates its own affective comprehension of irony's laughing response to the terrible facticity of death itself.

Blunt Melodrama. If laughter, as Huron argues, is a social response to fear (27–31), fear also provokes a different type of "physiological reaction" in the almost anti-social aggressive display of narrative melodrama. "In the fight response," Huron writes, "the first order of business is to produce an aggressive display. By signaling one's readiness to fight, it is possible that the threatening individual might back down, and so an actual fight can be avoided. Aggressive displays can include the displaying of teeth, making eye contact with the other animal, and generating low-pitched vocalizations" (33). Such self-aggrandizing is anti-social insofar as it doesn't suggest social activities—as in the laughing/fearful playfighting I mentioned earlier— but rather suggests the assertion of self against the world. Furthermore, "the physiological reaction" Huron describes is *literally* aggrandizing: in this "fight" response to danger and death, he says, "there are a series of behaviors that are all intended to make the individual appear bigger—and so more intimidating" (33). Moreover, we can notice such self-assertion in melodramatic responses to death. This is surely Dylan Thomas's generic assertion in his powerful villanelle, "Do Not Go Gentle into that Good Night," when the open vowels of /ā/ and /ē/—"rave," "rage," "deeds," "green bay," "grieved," "grave," "blaze"—literally bare our teeth in recitation, even while softer vowels—"gentle," "good night," "dying," "near death," "fierce tears, I pray"—approximate the low-pitched vocalizations that Huron describes.

In analyzing the gestures of literary modernism in "Modernism as Gesture," I have described such phenomena as "mouth-gestures" (95). My description was tutored by a neuro-physiological analysis by Kiyoski Honda and his colleagues entitled "Physiology of the Lips and Modeling of Lip Gestures." I note that Honda and his colleagues describe and analyze stark gesticulations of the mouth by isolating

> three canonical patterns of lip and tongue gestures: the vowel /a/ for dynamic expression of various emotional signs, the vowel [/ū/] for sucking and demands, and the vowel [/ē/] for teeth display in grimace or laughter. In these elementary gestures, the lips and the tongue are tightly coupled with each other in the same manner as used for sucking, chewing or swallowing. These dynamic actions which are used for typical speech gestures are often explained by the neuromotor function for automatic pattern generation.
>
> (Honda et al. 244)

I sum up their findings by noting that "language takes up these neuromotor functions in order to create 'dynamic expression'" ("Gesture" 89); and I go on to add in a note that "these three gestures offer an uncanny parallel to the awe, frisson, and laughter that Huron traces in his neurological analysis of music" (96). I find in the physiological study of Honda and his colleagues a stark example of my contention of the way that art narrative—and, more generally, aesthetics (in Huron the aesthetics of music)—"take up" evolutionary-developed strategies for other ends.

In the present chapter, though, I want to emphasize the "mouth-gesture" in relation to the literary genre of melodrama. To this end, let us look briefly at John Donne's holy sonnet, "Death, Be Not Proud," which complements Thomas's villanelle insofar as the disciplined formality of these poetic genres—villanelle and sonnet—offer their own self-assertion again the world of ordinary discourse in their displays of discursive mastery. In his wonderfully accomplished history of the sonnet—a history organized as repeated "close readings"—Stephen Regan describes in Donne the disciplined complexity of literary texts (or "art narratives") I am setting forth throughout this book. "Donne's legacy for later sonnet writers," he notes,

> —for soldier poets such as Wilfred Owen, as much as for religious authors such as Gerard Manley Hopkins—has much to do with the subtle rhetorical contrivance by which he controls and contains the

most extreme anxieties and fears .... What seems at first to be a chiding, declamatory voice [in "Death, Be Not Proud"] takes on great tonal complexity, by turns chastising and confiding, steadily accumulating conviction through the simple, repeated conjunction 'And', and through the curt rhetorical question, 'why swell'st thou then?'

(60)

In focusing on the "tone" of the literary text, Regan touches upon the "aspects" of experience that Ludwig Wittgenstein addresses—how "when I read a poem or narrative with feeling, ... the sentences have a different *ring*"—which I have described as the *force* and *purport* of language beyond skimming "the lines for information" (§264). In his analysis, Regan unpacks the disciplined deployments of language to achieve these effects.

Here is Donne's sonnet.

Holy Sonnet VI: Death, Be Not Proud

Death, be not proud, though some have callèd thee
Mighty and dreadful, for thou art not so,
For those whom thou think'st thou dost overthrow,
Die not, poor death, nor yet canst thou kill me;
From rest and sleep, which but thy pictures be,
Much pleasure, then from thee much more must flow;
And soonest our best men with thee do go,
Rest of their bones, and soul's delivery.
Thou'art slave to Fate, chance, kings, and desperate men,
And dost with poison, war, and sickness dwell,
And poppy or charms can make us sleep as well
And better than thy stroke; why swell'st thou then?
One short sleep past, we wake eternally
And death shall be no more, Death, thou shalt die.

(Donne)

In his sonnet, the speaker—again, *literally*—aims at "deflating" his adversary death by likening death to small things: false dreadfulness, weakness, pleasure, less than poppy or charms, when death wants to provoke fear with its altogether false "swelling." Even the repetitious long /ē/ in the penultimate line—"sleep," "eternally"—repeats the phonemic mouth-gestures we find in Thomas. Like Thomas, in this poem Donne "stands up" to death, switches places with death to take on, in the poem's triumphant melodramatic ending, the very swelling and destruction of death the poem asserts. Such an ending creates what Huron calls the "abrupt modulation" (34) that gives rise to frisson in music and, I am arguing here, in the narrative genre of melodrama. Frisson, Huron writes, "is strongly correlated with marked violations of expectation—in particular, with dynamic, metric, and harmonic violations .... Frisson experiences are also reported when a high dynamic level is followed unexpectedly by a dramatic reduction in loudness" (283). The dynamics of Donne's sonnet are marked: this, after all, in the poem's work of deflation and self-aggrandizement.

Blank Tragedy. The awe of tragedy arises in its constant confrontation with death, a confrontation that does not dissolve the fear of death either in momentary laughter or in momentary self-assertion. "The feeling of awe," Huron notes,

> is a distinctive emotion in which fear and wonder are intermingled. A sense of awe might be evoked by a fearful reverence inspired by something sacred or mysterious. Awe can also represent a submissive fear in the presence of some great authority or power. In short, awe might be defined as a sort of "sublime fear." "Awe" combines mystery, wonder, and reverence with a touch of dread ....
>
> Five physiological indicators are associated with the experience of awe: (1) gasping, (2) breath-holding, (3) lowered chin with the mouth slightly opened, (4) immobility or stillness, and (5) reduced blinking. Gasping and breath-holding are especially tell-tale indicators.
>
> (288)

Here, as in the ellipsoid-laughter in Shem and the phonemic-gestures in Thomas and Donne, so too a mouth-gesture—"lowered chin with the mouth slightly opened"—marks the bodily-affect response of awe in face of life-threatening situations. To conclude, then, my small catalogue of literary genres understood in relation to affective responses to life-threatening situations—to death itself—I take up Margaret Edson's one-act drama, *Wit*, to complement the novel and the poems I have already discussed.

Wit is a one-act play that describes the last year in the life of a middle-aged woman, Vivian Bearing, who is a Professor of literature—focused, as it happens, on the poetry of John Donne—and suffering from stage-four metastatic ovarian cancer. Also, as it happens, the play begins with her thinking about her condition in relation to literary genres in the style of "fearful irony" I discussed in relation to Shem's novel. "*Irony* is a literary device," she says, that will necessarily be deployed to great effect.

I ardently wish this were not so. I would prefer that a play about me be cast in the mythic-heroic-pastoral mode; but the facts, most notably stage-four metastatic ovarian cancer, conspire against that. *The Faerie Queene* this is not.

And I was dismayed to discover that the play would contain elements of ... *humor*. (6)

Very soon after this opening, the play offers a flashback to Vivian's study of "Donne's Holy Sonnets, which," she says, "explore mortality in greater depth than any other body of work in the English language" (12). Her professor, E. M. Ashford, tells her that "the sonnet begins with a valiant struggle with death, calling on all the forces of intellect and drama to vanquish the enemy. But it is ultimately about overcoming the seemingly insuperable barriers separating life, death, and eternal life" (14). She notes that the proper punctuation of the final line of the poem is not the semi-colon and exclamation point of the edition Vivian uses in her paper, but simply a comma (in Donne's text I cited earlier). "Nothing but a breath—a comma—", Professor Ashford says, "separates life from life everlasting. It is very simple really. With the original punctuation restored, death is no longer something to act out on stage, with exclamation points. It's a comma, a pause" (14–15).

This is indeed awe-inspiring: fearful, reverential, mysterious, as is Donne's sonnet. But I want to conclude with another scene from this small tragedy, which distinguishes its tragedy from Donne's melodrama, a flashback when Vivian remembers a student—in a vivid "scene of instruction"—who asks: "Why does Donne make everything so *complicated*? ... I think," the student goes on, "it's like he's hiding. I think he's really confused, I don't know, maybe he's scared, so he hides behind all this complicated stuff, hides behind this *wit* .... Perhaps he is suspicious of simplicity" (60–1). Toward the very end of the play, Vivian is comforted when she eats a popsicle with her nurse, Susie, and she thinks: "Now is a time for simplicity. Now is a time for, dare I say it, kindness" (69). The simplicity of kindness Vivian calls for, like the tragic play itself, combines reverence and mystery. And Susie, the Helper in this tragedy of facing death (along with Vivian's students, who also function as the Helper-actant)—without nervous or slapstick laughter, without aggrandizing heroics—is left with the Wished-For Good, the uncomplicated love and community which, awe-inspiringly, both resists and succumbs to death. Tragedy, unlike the staged heroics of melodrama, plays out the social and communal nature of genre altogether.

The Discipline of Genres

What are we to make of all this? After all, we are all a lot like Professor Vivian Bearing, who makes wit and intellectualizing and Donne-like *complications* the work of her life, so that intellectually, we might study here, as I am doing in this chapter, the "circulations" of genre—its "re-groundings" and "un-groundings"—across language, sociology, morality, and nature, all the while, perhaps, avoiding the brute fact of death. To start to answer this question, "what are we to make of all this?", which perhaps means what are we to make of the aesthetics and genres of literature, let me turn to the juxtaposition of two stanzas from Wallace Stevens's enigmatic poem "The Pleasures of Merely Circulating," in which the laughter and wit of the circulation of generic intellectual heroics are ungrounded, so to speak, in the face of death.

> The garden flew round with the angel,
> The angel flew round with the clouds,
> And the clouds flew round and the clouds flew round
> And the clouds flew round with the clouds.
>
> Is there any secret in skulls,
> The cattle skulls in the woods?
> Do the drummers in black hoods
> Rumble anything out of their drums? (149–50)

Death calls up the affective comprehension of laughter, frisson, awe and allows us one way of thinking about the discipline of literary study in terms of affective responses to threats that are embodied in skulls and drummers and enacted in the abrupt modulation of the second stanza I am citing. Such threats seem re-grounded in the beauty and happiness—the anticipated well-being—of genres, the "keyings of the real" that John Frow describes.

But death—and the aesthetic "modulation" from angels and clouds to skulls and rumbling drums—also gives rise to "un-groundings" of brute facts and "rumbling" events: to simple but awful sadness, one of the primary emotions I haven't examined in this chapter (or, for that matter, throughout this book). Stevens, again, focuses on such a feeling in a poem entitled "The Plain Sense of Things":

> It is difficult even to choose the adjective
> For this blank cold, this sadness without cause.

The great structure has become a minor house.
No turban walks across the lessened floors. (502)

It might be there is no narrative genre for such sadness, such existential pathos that leaves us ungrounded, in "blank cold," futureless (see Schleifer, *Rhetoric and Death* 223–9). But beauty, as we have seen in Stendhal's comprehension, is simply "nothing other than the promise of happiness" (66), and in the quest for beauty, literary genres—notably, in comedy, which is a narrative genre I have not focused upon in this chapter—literary genres, I say, even in the face of death, like music, surprise us with laughter, heroics, and awe: they surprise us *into* laughter, heroics, and awe. In such surprises, if only momentarily, we may discover the intellectual discipline of re-grounding (as in Frye's analysis of disciplines) and the improvising discipline of play (as in Aristotle's practical wisdom) in the face of death.

The Affect of Aesthetics

Is there something "off" about this conclusion, which offers a backhand consolation for death, a promise of happiness is the face of death, particularly as it is figured in the breathtaking metonym of "turban" to answer the "blank cold" of "the plain sense of things," the blank of seeming positive (and positivist) fact without value? Does Stevens's poem, or my insertion of it near the end of this chapter on death and literature, give rise to an "experience of fraudulence" (312), which Sianne Ngai focuses upon in her analysis of the aesthetic category of "gimmick," but which she almost suggests might be an element in aesthetic experience altogether? Is the value-laden metaphorical language of literature a gimmick? Think of that moment in Yeats's poem "Easter 1916," where far more romantically than Stevens he precedes (rather than follows, as Stevens does) the plain sense of death with figurative language: "What is it but nightfall? / No, no, not night but death; / Was it needless death after all?" (Norton 1924). If death brings a kind of discipline to the apprehension of generic wholes, then the fine-grained aesthetics/experience of literary genres—the sadness, existential pathos, heroics, and awe I just mentioned—perhaps allows us to imagine situating blank cold, fear, and dread in relation to systems of feeling, structures of experience. Such situating—which is to say, such a "rescue" of value and affect from the abyss of death—might seem simply a gimmick, a phenomenon that seems to devalue what Ngai takes to be the source of value altogether, namely human labor and more generally (particularly in the context of meditating on death) human life itself. Ngai seems to suggest that the gimmick offers a model of aesthetics in general: "grounded in feeling," she notes,

> activated by appearance, as opposed to in concepts, rules, or laws, aesthetic judgment is by definition neither cognitive nor practical. Yet such judgments are crucially elicited in [the] immediate aftermath [of "feeling," or of experience more generally]. In the gimmick, specifically, our spontaneously affective, explicitly aesthetic appraisal of an object's form as unsatisfyingly compromised triggers and comes to overlap with economic and ethical evaluations of it as cheap and fraudulent.
>
> (3)

The gimmick, she notes, registers "an uncertainty about labor—its deficiency or excess—that is also an uncertainty about value and time" (1). But what she says about the aesthetics of the gimmick might be—in fact, has been— said about the aesthetic short-cuts to the practical wisdom of Aristotle's *phronesis*. In reading and discussing *Wit* with healthcare professionals and students—or *The House of God* or John Donne's sonnets—one seems to cheat suffering with vicarious suffering, to cheat experience with make-believe experience.

But can the "keyings of the real" Frow describes (50) be better described as an *aesthetic* structure of intergenerational caretaking rather than the devaluation of labor and life that Ngai asserts? This might be a "caretaking" theory of value rather than a labor theory of value. As I note more explicitly in Chapter 6, Sam Harris suggests a theory of value something like this under the category of "well-being" (24; see Exhibit 5.6).

Exhibit 5.6: A Well-Being Theory of Value

Central to classical economics—in Adam Smith, David Ricardo, and Karl Marx, stemming in large part from John Locke—is the labor theory of value. But, as I have argued (see *Political Economy* 70–9), the labor theory of value is organized around the strict necessity of subsistence: in the labor theory of value, value is measured against "going without"; one goes barefoot unless one labors to fashion shoes. In a consumerist economics, value is measured in relation to desire and fulfillment rather than subsistence-necessity; under these circumstances, value is measured in terms of "well-being," and the great difficulty—a difficulty absent in a world of the positivism of subsistence-necessities—is to figure out the nature and breadth of well-being itself. This is why, I suspect, that Sianne Ngai can so persuasively demonstrate the "cheap" gimmickry of much of the pleasures of consumerist capitalism. But a full-blown notion of "well-being"—such as the ancient Chinese notion of le (乐), which describes "feelings of joy, happiness, optimism and well-being" in relation to "the well-being gained when recovering from illness and when finally healing" (Yang and Zhou 182)—allows us a worldly and materialist notion of value, such as Sam Harris suggests in his study of materialist "human values," outlined in my concluding chapter, Chapter 6. In part, this is why in Chapter 6 I end these chapters—this "lectures-book"—by comparing the Chinese notion of le and Aristotle's notion of *eudaimonia* in relation to the worldly work of literature and healthcare (see Exhibit 6.12: Well-Being, Health, Aesthetics). Among other things, well-being as a measure of value entails the significant difficulties of analogy, homology, similitudes, aspects, likenesses, constellations, which govern the exposition of this lectures-book I described in Chapter 1.

Walter Benjamin offers a fine sense of such intergenerational caretaking in his essay "Little History of Photography." In that essay—as in Roland Barthes's *Camera Lucida*, in which Barthes explicitly narrates the manner in which death erupts in the contemplation of a photograph—Benjamin notes that

> no matter how artful the photographer, no matter how carefully posed his subject, the beholder feels an irresistible urge to search such a picture for the tiny spark of contingency, of the here and now, with which reality has (so to speak) seared the subject, to find the inconspicuous spot where in the immediacy of that long-forgotten moment the future nests so eloquently that we, looking back, may rediscover it.

(cited in Jay 338)

In engaging with this photograph, Benjamin describes an aesthetic moment in which "the future nests." In this, he describes an aesthetic "moment," which, like the generic "keyings" I have described, entwines itself with other times, with what Benjamin calls elsewhere the "secret agreement between past generations and the present one," which allows him to assert "our coming was expected on earth" (*Illuminations* 254). That expectation was the faith that those who came before us had that they would be understood, that their best intentions—even those only recoverable later— would be acknowledged and fulfilled, that by luck or by skill (the work of "keyings"), they would be able to so prepare us with their experience and wisdom that we would collaborate with them to create what Benjamin calls "the chain of tradition which passes a happening on from generation to generation" (*Illuminations* 98). In this, past events exist also within the context of their future history, their *purport*; they exist in the context of human life as a species phenomenon. This allows, for Benjamin, the possibility of "redemption," even in the face of death: "the true conception of historical time," he writes, "is wholly based on the image of redemption" (*Illuminations* 71; see also Schleifer *Modernism and Time* 60–2 for an earlier version of this argument). The "keyings" of intergenerational caretaking— like the intergenerational caretaking that characterizes healthcare—might well be the value of literary aesthetics even—perhaps, *particularly*—in the face of death.

Benjamin's focus on the aesthetic experience of the photograph is eerily similar to a seeming extra-aesthetic moment when Roland Barthes finds himself "in front of the photograph of my mother as a child" and tells himself "she is going to die: I shudder, like Winnicott's psychotic patient, *over a catastrophe which has already occurred.* Whether or not the subject is already dead," Barthes notes, "every photograph is this catastrophe" (cited in Jay 390). Jay situates his discussion of Barthes in relation to the fact that "Barthes, who had no children of his own ... therefore could not participate in the grand narrative of procreation that supposedly gives the individual's death a meaningful place in the story of our species" so that, in Barthes's words, "I could [do] no more than await my total, undialectical death" (Jay 389). Doing so, Jay argues, Barthes pursued "experiential intensities that refuse to be contained in narratives of closure and completion. What Barthes famously calls the *punctum*, the uncoded detail that eludes the unitary image he dubbed the photo's *studium*, could disrupt the totalizing potential in specularity" (390). Still, Barthes's *punctum* is, I believe, a small subset of the larger *purport* of literary aesthetics I discuss throughout this book in order to find, as does Benjamin, the experiential immediacy of the long-forgotten moment, in which the future "eloquently" nests. Ngai notes that the aesthetic category of "gimmick is ... the bad twin of Roland Barthes's melancholic, critically hallowed *punctum*, in a way underscored by its contrastingly intimate relation to comedy" (201; see also 202). But the purport of intergenerational solidarity, nesting in the aesthetic or extra-aesthetic experience of *punctum*, might be something more than simply a gimmick. Enacted comedies—particularly the communal laughter of jokes and their punchlines, but most notably Benjamin's comedy of redemption—are particularly clear examples of the narrative performances of purport, which perhaps in a strange manner combine gimmick and a promise of well-being.

Aesthetic Purport and the Promise of Happiness

After all, the generic "keying" structures I repeatedly return to in the present chapter—like the structures of experience conditioning aesthetic experience—are, after all, the creation of relationship, analogy, even homology, which give rise to the *values* of experience (its qualities) by provoking and conditioning the affective emotions I have described throughout this chapter. In his extended meditation on Shklovsky's notion of defamiliarization, which seeks to recover one's first "active absorption" of experience, at one point Michael Clune focuses on George Orwell's *1984*. He ends his discussion of the manner in which Orwell works "to endow the surface of the world with its never-fading vividness" (92). "Perhaps," he adds, "instead of worrying about losing the *knowledge* that grass is green, Orwell is concerned about losing the *sensation* of the greenness of grass" (100)—or one might say the "sensation" of the Welsh *glas/gwyrdd* of grass. Clune ends his discussion of *1984* by citing Winston Smith's assertion to his partner Julia that "so long as human beings stay human, death and life are the same thing." Julia answers (in a manner similar to Regina Barreca's assertion, with which I began) "rubbish! ... Don't you enjoy being alive? Don't you like feeling?" (cited in Clune 113). It is with a similar motive to Julia's exclamation that I so quickly turned from death to Stendhal's promise of happiness a moment ago, since experience—particularly experience under the category of aesthetics—is a locus of what I called in Chapter 1 prefacing these chapter-lectures as *meaningful value* (as opposed, perhaps, to the plain sense of things, which might well indicate a positivist conception of phenomena without value or meaning).

But there is more to say about Stendhal's promise of happiness. Clune nicely describes the nature of the pleasure aesthetics give rise to, in a register very different from that of aesthetic "gimmick" Ngai examines. His description nicely substantiates my argument that the experience of meaning—of *purport*—is tied up with its future orientation. "The aesthetic object," he writes,

> awakens me to vivid perceptual life, and, through its structure, defeats the tendency of that vividness to fade. As [Henry] Allison argues [in his analysis of Kant's *Critique of Judgment*], when I praise an image as beautiful, I praise the feeling that contemplation of the image gives me. But this feeling is a very strange thing. Unlike happiness or sadness, aesthetic pleasure is not a state that I simply detect in myself. Aesthetic pleasure extends into the future, beyond my present capacity to feel. But in the object, I perceive a guarantee of that extension.
>
> (40–1)

This is, indeed, a *promise* of happiness, the nest of the future, and as such it is performative rather than constative: constrained by social conventions and habits, essentially interpersonal rather than context-free signification, and, in its evaluation as successful or unsuccessful, felicitous or infelicitous, it exists in the performative *social* activity of judgment rather than in the once-and-for-all finality of truth-value. In its future orientation, it also suggests—perhaps a small consolation—that my earlier conclusion, which described the way in which the fleeting image of a turbaned person walking in a sound house with upright floors might surprise us into laughter, heroics, and awe as at least a momentary antidote to the plain sense of death. Here, then, I am reminded of Stanley Cavell's concise description of aesthetic experiences: "they provide pleasure, ... they compose unity, and ... they break off a line of thought" (209).

In the present chapter, I have repeatedly noted moments when I break off a line of thought—usually the thought of death. At the end of *Literature and Medicine*, as often at the end of the class I teach with the same name, we discuss a wonderful poem by Derek Mahon, "Everything is Going to Be All Right," where the speaker breaks off the line of thought leading to death when it states "There will be dying, there will be dying, / but there is no need to go into that." Instead, Mahon notes that "poems flow from the hand unbidden" and concludes:

> I lie here in a riot of sunlight
> watching the day break and the clouds flying.
> Everything is going to be all right. (240)

By way of commentary, in *Literature and Medicine* we cite an interview with the poet-physician Dr. John Stone, who notes that "one of the great functions of the physician is to say those few words ['everything is going to be all right'] to the patient from time to time" (240). This indeed, like Mahon's poem, is a promise of happiness, even if the poem—like the novel, poems, and play I discuss in this chapter—is honest enough to acknowledge that "There will be dying, there will be dying." Both this repetition-statement and the double-take on literature and death I pursue in this chapter set forth the uneasy relationship between what I've called the "abyss" of death and ongoing, intergenerational life and caretaking: a promise of happiness in the face of death.

CHAPTER 6
DISCIPLINED VICARIOUS EXPERIENCE: ACTION AND ETHICS IN LITERARY STUDIES

The Disciplined Experience of *Phronesis*

My final chapter focuses on practical wisdom occasioned by the disciplined study of literature and the most far-reaching ways in which literature helps condition habits of thought and the space of meaning at a particular time and place—which I want to emphasize is *our* time and, perhaps fantastically, the places of China and the United States brought together in the lectures from which this book takes its source. Before I begin—or maybe by way of beginning—let me recapitulate an argument I made several years ago (see Schleifer "Modalities") focused on the ways the practices of healthcare can help us understand *phronesis* and what Joseph North calls a "materialist aesthetics." Most scholars who study the nature of *phronesis* argue or assume that the practical wisdom Aristotle describes under this term is only obtainable through long-term first-hand experience. The goal of *phronesis* is to be able to discern what *counts* as the "ends" or goals that practical wisdom pursues. That is, practical reasoning does not simply find the best strategies to pursue the end of an action by some form of instrumental reason. Rather, procedures of practical reasoning are determined by discovering—by means of long experience, the traditional argument runs—what *counts* as an "end" in a particular situation. Martha Nussbaum, for instance, argues that *phronesis* focuses on "what is to count as the end" of action (61, n15).

In my argument, however, I suggest the special case of healthcare allows the creation of particular procedures to achieve the "ends" or goals of healthcare by means of vicarious experience, and in so doing it clarifies the worldly work of literature as well. The special case of healthcare is the fact that the *values* healthcare pursues are not abstract notions of good and evil—or good and bad, or better or worse—that lie at the base of the "idealist" aesthetics that North decries throughout his history of literary criticism. (For all his advocacy of the aesthetics of an "insipiently materialist practice of close reading" [cf. 27 and *passim*], North never offers a practical example of what such a practice might be. In part, Chapter 5 attempts to set forth a "materialist practices" of close reading and intergenerational caring in relation to the abysmal materialism of death.) That is, the widely accepted values of healthcare organize themselves in relation to *worldly* notions of good and evil that instantiate material rather than ideal values, the very materialist practice of close reading North seeks. As Edmund Pellegrino has argued, in medicine the "ends" of action constitute a well-defined tradition that can more readily than in a general morality offer agreement "on a *telos*—i.e., an end and a good"—namely "a healing relationship between a healthcare professional and a patient, [in which] most would agree that the primary end must be the good of the patient" (266). Specifically, as I argue in the present chapter, a materialist aesthetics focuses on "narrative knowledge"—explicitly, the ways that narrative comprehension informs and recognizes (cognitively and affectively) the double sense of the "end" of any narrative, its conclusion and its purpose. Moreover, a materialist aesthetics achieves this focus by means of the close reading of engagements with discursive art with the goal of shaping and enlarging the interpersonal— and often intergenerational—work of healthcare. If this is correct, then the discipline of literary studies, tutored by the practical wisdom of healthcare, aims to understand and promote the ways that a practical materialist aesthetics can instill strategies of engagement and caretaking (i.e., the promotion of well-being). Part of Albert Einstein's breakthrough in understanding was his development of a notational mathematic system unavailable to physicists before him (Newton did the same thing with the calculus); and part of Darwin's breakthrough in understanding was the development of questioning the self-evidently true (e.g., "why are there so many species?"). In a similar fashion, the discipline of literary studies creates "terms of art" (e.g., philological philosophy, semiotic analyses, and generic comprehensions) and disciplined engagements with "experience" that allow people to discern and take up practical wisdom by means of vicarious literary experience. The *values and goals* of that discernment and action are particularly clear in the clinic.

"Traditional" Disciplines

To begin my argument, then, let me touch upon late twentieth-century transformations of "traditional disciplines"—whose "traditions," as we have seen, date back to around 1870 in Western Europe and America. (For a thoughtful overview of recent "change and critical transition" in a host of intellectual disciplines impinging on the human sciences, see Waugh and Botha and, in fact, the whole volume they introduce.) The transformations I am describing—particularly in literary studies—were occasioned by new attention to historicist, interdisciplinary, and aesthetic/philosophical work since the time of Northrop Frye's essay in the mid-twentieth century, with which I began. Speaking particularly of literary studies, Frye wrote in 1949 that "if criticism is a science, it is clearly a social science, which means that it should waste no time in trying to assimilate its methods to those of the natural sciences. Like psychology, it is directly concerned with the human mind—[but] will only confuse itself with statistical methodologies" (43). The interdisciplinary work I pursue in the present chapter, then—unlike Frye's archetypal understanding of literature—pursues the imbrication of literary studies and moral philosophy to the ends, as I said, of provoking the practical wisdom of *phronesis. Phronesis,* I hope has become clear, is the practical material science of experience.

As I suggested in the preceding chapters, certain revolutionary protocols developed in Enlightenment Modernity or what is also called the Early Modern Period in Western Europe (Italy, Poland, France, Germany, Britain, the Netherlands, Sweden, etc.) in the sixteenth and seventeenth centuries. This revolution was based upon a new sense of what constituted knowledge itself, a new sense of the contours of human experience and the imagined possibilities of human experience, and the nature of "goods" produced by human labor, and it also included significant re-thinking of the nature of social and political life. The political implications of "early modern" culture, which can and should be contrasted with "traditional" pre-Enlightenment cultures, burst forth politically in the wake of the Thirty Years' War (1618–48)—that catastrophic war, one of the most destructive in human history, which was part of the social and political transformations I just mentioned. The political/social implications of that catastrophic European war manifested themselves in nation-states as we know them, a developing sense of individualism, a powerful sense of human agency in the world (as opposed to supernatural agency), which included "modern" understandings of freedom, fulfillment, and the re-thinking and re-appropriation of classical Greek notions of happiness, goodness, truth, and reason. It also resulted in what Hillis Miller calls "literature in our modern sense" (1). Enlightenment Modernity eventually manifested itself within what Adam Smith called the "commercial society" of the capitalist market system.

Many scholars since Frye have traced the fulfillments of Enlightenment Modernity and its transformation in early twentieth-century cultural modernism, say 1880 to 1930. Many people who lived through this period of cultural modernism—or whose grandparents or great-grandparents lived through this period—think of it as revolutionary: politically, intellectually, existentially. Such revolutionary modernism manifests itself in the human sciences as well. One thing transformed in this period is the received sense—what seems to us to be the self-evident sense—of the intellectual disciplines as we know them. Yet as I observed in Chapter 3, it is a notable fact that most of the seeming clear and distinct intellectual disciplines I have been focusing on in this book—the nomological sciences, the social sciences, the human sciences—are of relatively recent origin. Louis Hjelmslev and Northrop Frye make this clear when they talk about the *lack* of intellectual discipline in literary studies as late as 1943 and 1949, but even Joseph North suggests as much when he begins his concise history of "literary criticism" in the early 1920s. The professionalization of higher education, with its scholarly guilds, its delimited disciplines, its well-financed organizations, is little more than a century and a half old. The first graduate programs in the United States, for instance, were instituted with the establishment of the Johns Hopkins University in 1876, and while Hopkins—and soon after the University of Chicago—took its model from the seminar system of German universities, the thorough professionalization of disciplines in higher education coincided with the Second Industrial Revolution in the United States and Western Europe in the second half of the nineteenth century (see Schleifer *Political Economy* 54–7). In this concluding chapter, I want to revisit this "modernist" revolution by examining the ways that the discipline of literary studies and the human sciences in which it participates are transforming, in the twenty-first century, disciplines of knowledge that were the fulfillments of Enlightenment positivism by supplementing the "purity" of positive science with a sense of the values and ethics implicit within any analysis of experience, including the complexity of what I call at the end of this chapter "negative science" implicit in organizing a discipline around purport and value rather than positive "facts."

To begin, then, I want to describe the transformations of traditional disciplines in our own time, say the last two generations, perhaps beginning with Frye's *Anatomy of Criticism* in 1957, transformations I begin to catalogue in the "contexts" set forth with my thesis in Chapter 1. In this analysis, I hope to emphasize the manner of rethinking of disciplines in our time has led to "reordering and redescribing" (Felski 102) literary studies themselves. As I noted earlier in this book, in his attempt to articulate a scientific study of language, Hjelmslev argued that the traditional received notion of literary studies was purportedly not systematic because, as he said, "humanistic, as opposed to natural, phenomena are non-recurrent and for that very reason cannot, like natural phenomena, be subject to exact and generalizing treatment." As such, he goes on, traditional practices of the humanities pursue "mere description, which would be nearer to poetry than to exact science" (8). In contrast to this, as we have seen, Hjelmslev shares an advocacy of the systematic study of language and literature with Northrop Frye, whose masterful systematic analysis of literature in *Anatomy of Criticism* literally renovated the study of literature in north America. As I mentioned earlier, *Anatomy of Criticism* allowed advocates of the humanities to convince the US government that the humanities could help train Americans to compete with the Soviet Union, which had recently launched the first artificial satellite in 1957.

Traditional Literary Studies

Still, Hjelmslev's phrase "mere description" doesn't do justice to some remarkable achievements in historical study, whether it be literary history, history itself, or evolutionary biology. This is clear in Stephen Jay Gould's account of the achievements of evolutionary biology, which he describes as "the triumph of homology." He points out that historical sciences such as evolutionary biology—but also traditional literary history, which he does not mention—have been denigrated (as we see in Hjelmslev) as "something beneath science, something merely 'descriptive'" so that "they become, ... the 'soft' (as opposed to 'hard') sciences, the 'merely descriptive'" ("Triumph" 64). He argues, however, that "if the primacy of history is evolution's lesson for other sciences, then we should explore the consequences of valuing history as a source of law and similarity, rather than dismissing it as narrative unworthy of the name science" (68). Law and similarity—as I have suggested throughout this book in terms of "homology," "aspects," "analogy," "habits of thought," "semiotics," and "inference to the best explanation"—maintain discipline even as they offer alternatives, rather than all-out replacements, for the seeming self-evidence of Enlightenment canons of "positive" truth.

The achievement of law and similarity in history, Gould argues, is discernable in "historical reconstruction," which is achieved by means of inference. The "inferential nature of perception," I suggested earlier (see Moore 1110), is an alternative to self-evident positivism. In tracing the historical "methodology" in Darwin, Gould describes three principles of inferential thinking. The first is apprehending "large-scale results" (62), which approximates the "meaningful whole" of meaning and purport I have described throughout this book. Second is to document different "categories of results and [to] seek relationships among them" (62), which is the work of interdisciplinary and homological parallels I have also pursued throughout this book. The third, he says, is to "infer history from single objects" (63), such as "in the immediacy of that long-forgotten moment [in which] the future nests," which Walter Benjamin notices in an element of a particular photograph (cited in Jay 338), or the general "immediate" experience of the *punctum*, which Roland Barthes notices in photographs in general. Such "moments" of experience, Gould suggests, are the phenomena of recognized imperfection. That is, Gould argues that the inference of "history from single objects" was first achieved—or at least first most notably achieved— when Darwin assumed as his guide the "principle of imperfection" (63). His example is "the highly inefficient, but serviceable, false thumb of the panda, fashioned from the wrist's radial sesamoid bone because the true anatomical first digit had irrevocably evolved, in carnivorous ancestors of the herbivorous panda, to limited motility in running and clawing" (63). Gould describes this principle of imperfection—it is a *worldly* principle—as the transformation of function (e.g., from the flight accomplished by the bat's wing to the toolmaking accomplished by the human hand) in response to the austere discipline of evolutionary survival; the transformation of function of similar structures is, he says, the triumph of homology. Toward the end of this final chapter, I describe this principle of imperfection as a "negative science" as opposed to the self-evident "positivism" of positive science. Negation exists *outside* of positive science, *outside* of positive facts; it exists as solely inferential reasoning in the worldly contexts of systems of meaning and value, which promote worldly life and well-being.

Now, though, let me focus on law and similarity. Throughout this book, I have tried to articulate the relationship between law and similarity, including the family of meanings associated with "similarity": "analogy," "homology," "aspects," "similes," "metaphors," "literary/speech genres," "semantic depth." Thus, in these four chapter-lectures I have noted the relationship between law and similarity:

- in the similarities and differences of notions of "discipline" and, of course, the similarities and differences of "homological" intellectual disciplines (Chapter 3);

- in the similarities and differences of Wittgenstein's "aspects" and the value embedded in the appraisals discerned by speech-act theory (Chapter 4);

- in the similarities and differences of both speech genres and literary genres in relation to seeming "instances" of generic forms and aesthetics writ large (Chapter 5); and

- in the similarities and differences of action and ethics in literary studies (Chapter 6).

In describing historical science as pursuing "law and similarity," Gould posits that the simple "law" of survival—namely, that functional efficiency in life and procreation conditions species survival—can conjoin itself with the re-purposing of similarities. Thus, he ends "Evolution and the Triumph of Homology," a lecture he gave celebrating *Sigma Xi, The Scientific Research Honor Society*, with an observation similar to those of Wittgenstein, Austin, and Felski, when they notice that in our experience, as Rita Felski says of literature, that "we rediscover things as we know them to be, yet reordered and redescribed, shimmering in a transformed light" (102), a reordering and redescription, which I have described as the "double-take" of literary studies throughout this book. Gould ends by noting (again with a literary reference-allusion) that "I have presented nothing really new, only a plea for appreciating something so basic that we often fail to sense its value. With a bow to that overquoted line from T. S. Eliot, I only ask you to return to a place well known and see it for the first time" (69).

I have advocated throughout that the discipline of literary studies explicitly and implicitly pursues law and similarity as they manifest themselves in homology, aspect, and the *force* and *dynamism* of literary discourse. I have tried to do so explicitly, but such a pursuit, I believe, is also implicit in the traditional humanities Hjelmslev contrasts with the nomological sciences. Recently, my friend Stephen Regan published a masterful book on *The Sonnet*, which I already called upon in discussing John Donne's "Holy Sonnet." In this book, Regan offers powerful close readings of hundreds of sonnets in tracing the history of the genre. Unlike my analysis of the systematic nature of genre in Chapter 5, however, Regan deploys the sonnet genre as the framework of his study rather than the "system" through which one might analyze the nature of what seems to be the self-evident "facts" or "events" of experience itself. Still, he implicitly pursues the law and similarity Gould describes in history. He begins his book with a description of the "special qualities peculiar to the genre: brevity, musicality, and intimacy" while at the same time noting that the sonnet accommodates "the rhythms and stresses of the speaking voice" (2–3). He then almost immediately offers a close reading of Keats's poem, "When I have fears that I may cease to be." "Like many sonnets including those of Shakespeare," Regan notes, Keats's poem

> reveals a strong preoccupation not just with love and death, but with writing and reading, and with the value of poetry itself in a world overshadowed by ultimate 'nothingness'. At the same time we ... can also note the stylistic flourishes that are peculiarly Keats's own, including the strong caesura in line 12 and the fluent enjambment that follows, both of which allow for a subtle modulation of rhythm in the closing lines, and so avoid too neat a concluding statement in the couplet.
>
> (5)

Even as the first sentence of this quotation offers a plaintive paraphrase of the work I have been doing in these chapter-lectures, Regan's longer reading does indeed, as Hjelmslev says, approach the condition "nearer to poetry than to exact science," and his method does seem to be a more or less unrestricted "discursive form." Yet his focus on a literary genre, as I hope I might have indicated in Chapter 5, creates frameworks of both "law" (the sonnet's strict poetic form) and similarity (the various forces of different but related sonnets) for his accomplished close readings. Still, the overall purport of Regan's study is realized in his careful readings of so many sonnets, which allow his readers the intimacy and musicality of engagements with unique poems in our literary history. I will have occasion to return to Regan's detailed reading when I turn to Yeats's sonnet "Leda and the Swan" later in this chapter. But now I want to underscore that Gould's understanding of the law and similarity embedded in historical study emphasizes what I described at the end of Chapter 2 as "the essential character of the accidental" (cited in Bradbury and McFarlane 48), which, as you might remember, I went on to say is the character of experience itself.

Acts and Events

In this chapter, I pursue a different tack from Stephen Regan. Here, I want to examine the ways that we can understand how homological engagements with other disciplines allow the human sciences to widen its own work and that of other disciplines. This examination focuses on the ethics and the moral education implicit in the so-called vicarious experience that literature provokes and the discipline of literary studies investigates. To do this, I should return for a moment to J. L. Austin before turning to the vicarious experience provoked by Yeats's great sonnet "Leda and the Swan." In "A Plea for Excuses"—an essay that appeared almost at the same exact time of his radio lecture "Performative Utterances" (1956)—Austin carefully articulates a concept of action and most particularly the *event* of an action as essentially (socially) conventional rather than (individually) volitional. "Before we consider what actions are good or bad, right or wrong," Austin notes,

> it is proper to consider first what is meant by, and what not, and what is included under, and what not, the expression "doing an action" or "doing something". These are expressions still too little examined on their own account and merits, just as the general notion of "saying something" is still too lightly passed over in logic. There is indeed a vague and comforting idea in the background that, after all, in the last analysis, doing an action must come down to the making of physical movements with parts of the body; but this is about as true as that saying something must, in the last analysis, come down to making movements of the tongue.
>
> (*Papers* 178)

Later in this essay, Austin wonders "how far ... are motives, intentions and conventions to be part of the description of actions?" and suggests that "we can generally split up what might be named as one action in several distinct ways, into different *stretches* or *phases* or *stages*" (201). Austin defines these aspects of an action quite nicely: the *stages* of a so-called action describe the "machinery of the act," such as "the planning, the decision, and the execution" of an act; the *phases* of an action describe different ways of apprehending an action so that "we can say that he painted a picture ... or else we can say that first he laid on this stroke of paint and then that"; and the *stretches* of an action describe it in a single term so that the description of what is done "may be made to cover either a smaller or larger stretch of events" with the result that a person's "act" can be judged to be accidental or purposeful, "*either* as turning on the hot tap, which he did by mistake, with the result that Watkins was scalded, *or* as scalding Watkins, which he did *not* do by mistake" (201).

All three of these ways of describing what is meant by an action—of creating accounts that are "designed to pick out features of the world of indefinite complexity" (Platts cited by Moore 1145)—offer us significant frameworks for understanding what is meant by the general notions— the ordinary-language signification—of "events" and "wholeness." The unanalyzed notion of "action," Austin notes, is "a stand-in for a verb with a personal subject," and conceiving action on this level of abstraction implies that "all 'actions' are ... equal, composing a quarrel with striking a match, winning a war with sneezing" (*Papers* 178, 179). In this, Austin describes various actions as "commensurable" with one and other. Such an unanalyzed notion of "action" and its concomitant notion of "event" govern the seeming self-evidence of an event in the world such as a sneeze or as winning a war. Such a notion erases judgment from observation; it likewise erases ethics from experience. Yet as English speakers we make such a judgment even in the simple question (of experience) of whether a pair of pants is blue rather than gray. This question of color is an argument I have had with my wife, which I mentioned earlier; had we lived in Wales, as we have seen in Hjelmslev's delineation of colors in English and in Welsh in Chapter 4, there would be no need of making a conscious judgment at all and no need of our conjugal dispute. Our Welsh language, I noted earlier, would have made that judgment for us in shaping our experience of the world. In this we can see that simple "observations"—perhaps a species of Hjelmslev's "mere description," certainly the comprehension of "self-evident" and "self-contained" truths of positivism—are almost always also involved with judgments of value, force, and consequently felicity or infelicity.

Events as Wholeness and Well-Being

In fact, Sam Harris in his neurological analysis of ethics makes the global claim that "consciousness"—and by this he means "conscious experience"— "is the only intelligible domain of value. What is the alternative?", he asks. "I invite you to try to think of a source of value that has absolutely nothing to do with the (actual or potential) experience of conscious beings" (49–50). The ethically affirmative experience he describes throughout his analysis—the bedrock of his "materialist" argument for ethics, which I might note offers an alternative to Ricardo's and Marx's "labor theory of value," by which Sianne Ngai measures value in her aesthetics (see Exhibit 5.6: A Well-Being Theory of Value)—is the experience of "well-being" for conscious creatures, human and nonhuman; and throughout his neurological analysis of morality he repeatedly likens well-being to health—an act of similitude which captures one sense of the "figurative" language of literature Hillis Miller describes (41–4). "Many readers," Harris notes, "might wonder how can we base our values on something as difficult to define as 'well-being'? It seems to me, however, that the concept of well-being is like the concept of physical health: it resists precise definition, and yet it is indispensable" (24). As we have seen, A. J. Greimas makes a similar argument about the "very vague but necessary concept of the meaningful whole" set forth by discourse. In fact, "well-being" *is* a meaningful whole and as such conditions the evaluative judgment involved in grasping something as a whole (see Exhibit 6.1).

Exhibit 6.1: On Wholeness and Well-Being

In *Complexification,* his analysis of complex systems, John Casti argues that "meaning is bound up with the whole process of communication and doesn't reside in just one or another aspect of it. As a result, the complexity of a political structure, a national economy or an immune system cannot be regarded as simply a property of that system taken in isolation. Rather, whatever complexity such systems have is a joint property of the system and its interaction with another system" (269; remember the observation that the linguist Emile Benveniste noted in Exhibit 1.4: Scientific Realism, when he asserted that "phenomena belonging to the interhuman milieu ... have the characteristic that they can never be taken as simple data or defined in the order of their own nature but must always be understood as double from the fact that they are connected to something else, wherever their 'referent' may be. A fact of culture is such only insofar as it refers to something else" [38–9]). Along with politics, economics, health physiology, Casti could have included semiotics and literary studies more generally in his catalogue of disciplines focused on complexity and the complex wholeness of well-being. I am thinking particularly about the notion of the "meaningful whole" of discourse propounded by A. J. Greimas.

Alvin Goldman summarizes the work in cognitive science concerning "object representation," which is closely related to the seeming self-evident phenomenon of "wholeness." Such "wholeness" includes the notion of self-contained "event" I am talking about in this chapter. "According to the dominant theory, due primarily to Elizabeth Spelke," he writes, "the concept of a whole object is the concept of a connected and bounded region of matter that maintains its connectedness and boundaries when in motion .... Whole objects so characterized are not the only things the human mind recognizes as 'things' or 'entities,' but people have a strong representational bias or preference for whole objects" (178). Goldman goes on to note that "very young children have a bias toward interpreting new words they hear as whole-object names, such as names for rabbits rather than rabbit ears .... If asked to count the number of 'objects' in a (fairly empty) room, people would not be stupefied, because counting by Spelke-object criteria makes it manageable" (178). Complementing his discussion of things with actions ("events"), Goldman also gives evidence for the fact that "infants in their second half-year of life are obsessed with the success and failure of their plans. They mark self-failures with special labels [e.g. 'uh-oh']" (195). Still, while presenting this information, Goldman fails to note that judgments of success or failure—of *plans* as such—focus on activities grasped as a whole (and a "meaningful whole" at that). Goldman also notes that psychology takes up "central coherence" as an object of disciplinary study. "Central coherence," he notes, "is a tendency to focus on the large picture of things rather than the bits and pieces that make it up. Once a jigsaw puzzle has been assembled, one sees the picture as a whole and even has a hard time seeing the pieces as individual pieces" (204).

In his discussion of perception and aesthetics, Michael Clune offers what I might call a functional description of wholeness. Given the fact that "99 percent of what we do goes perfectly well without our being aware of it," he asks "why are we conscious of anything at all." He turns to neuroscience and suggests "the answer ... lies in the fact that much of the brain's activity is carried out by bundles of neurons working in isolation from each other. We become conscious of something," he speculates, "when all the different parts of the brain need access to the same bit of information. A new or unexpected situation, for example, for which the brain lacks an automated response [such as provided by David Huron's "five response systems" arising from "five functionally distinct neurophysiological systems" (180)], calls for consciousness in a way that a familiar one does not. When the spotlight of attention falls on that unfamiliar action, event, or perception, the information becomes available for all the brain's capacities" (82). Later he notes, "description that defamiliarizes, description that attempts to represent a thing as if it had never been seen before, recovers a distinctness, a completeness, a wholeness for the thing at the price of distancing it from the world" (119). Thus, he argues that habit, conditioned by the evolutionary advantage of "efficiency," saves energy: "once the brain has learned to recognize [an] image, it no longer requires the high 'metabolic costs' of intense sensory engagement." In this, he concludes, "we are subject to an incessant erasure of perceptual life .... The familiar object has become a cognitive whole practically sealed off from direct perceptual contact" (3).

But if cognition itself is experiential as well as ideational—as I have argued, tutored by literary study, from the beginning of this book (see Exhibit 1.1: The Experience of Meaning)—then the notion of "a cognitive whole" is subject to the very complexification that Casti describes. That is, the distance "from the world" provoked by aesthetic defamiliarization is not a species of unworldliness. Rather, it emphasizes the *value* of wholeness—the "meaningful whole" Greimas, semiotics, and literary studies more generally focus upon—in-forming experience itself. Like the notions of wholeness in Casti and Goldman, it reinforces the relationship between wholeness and well-being I am setting forth here. Still, the "price" of distancing distinctive wholeness from the world is the tendency, apparent in Kant, to separate aesthetics and experience from the "pure" reasoning of the nomological and social sciences; it is the tendency to replace worldliness with idealism.

In Exhibit 3.3: Commodity Fetishism and Intellectual Disciplines, I touch upon the manner in which the labor theory of value is organized around "positive" subsistence, a matter I discuss at length in *A Political Economy of Modernism* (70–9). In doing so I distinguish between "need"—the motor of subsistence—which can be "satisfied," and "pleasure," which can be "experienced" or "fulfilled." In doing so I cite Colin Campbell, who argues that "objects possess utility or the capacity to provide satisfaction" while "it is only necessary to employ one's senses in order to experience pleasure, and, what is more, whereas an object's utility is dependent upon what it is, an object's pleasurable significance is a function of what it can be taken to be" (cited in *Political Economy* 96). In this, the labor theory of value—included Marx's crucial notion of "surplus value"—focuses on the *fragmentation* of phenomena, how subsistence is a one-by-one affair, while a "well-being" theory of value, like *health* itself—which is etymologically related to the word *wholeness*—focuses on the *wholeness* of phenomena, well-being beyond the plain sense of ("positivist") subsistence. That is, the "wholeness" of pleasure—manifest in Aristotle's *eudaimonia* or "happiness"—results from the provisional wholenesses promised by both improvisation and the pursuit of "vague" categories like "health," "meaningful whole," "purport," "well-being" itself. Remember Stanley Cavell's observation: "A passionate utterance is an invitation to improvisation in the disorders of desire" (185).

"Science," Harris says later, "cannot tell us why, *scientifically*, we should value health. But once we admit that health is the proper concern of medicine, we can then study and promote it through science" (55). (Here he is describing sufficient but not necessary criteria for judgment, which I attributed to the social sciences.) Later he notes the relationship between "morality" and the experience of "well-being": "To say morality is arbitrary (or culturally constructed, or merely personal) because we must first assume that the [experiential] well-being of conscious creatures is good, is like saying that science is arbitrary (or culturally constructed, or merely personal) because we must first assume that a rational understanding of the universe is good" (261). In this, although he does not use Said's term, Harris argues that morality is and *has to be* "worldly," based, as it is, on worldly experience, on the wholeness of worldly well-being.

The Experience of Events

But we can account more precisely how value-judgment figures into the experience of an event grasped as whole and singular. For instance, what is the "event" of winning the War of 1812 (to return to Austin's example of the event of "winning a war" as opposed to sneezing), whose seeming final battle, the Battle of New Orleans, took place *after* the peace treaty was finalized in Ghent? Is the Battle of New Orleans "part" of the event of the war? Is it a "phase" of the event/action of the War of 1812 or somehow a distinct event in itself? Does it present necessary and sufficient criteria to *be judged* to be such an event? It is clearly not a necessary part of the war, which was concluded before the battle took place, but it was, in fact, sufficient to get Andrew Jackson elected President of the United States, whose presidency itself—its participation in the terrible racism of chattel slavery, its destruction of native American tribes, its resistance to judicial lawfulness—seems to call for judgment. Does the Battle of New Orleans "stretch" the event of the war to include Andrew Jackson's "heroism," that led to his subsequent election as President even though, strictly speaking, he was hardly a "war hero" since the war had already concluded. In all this, the apprehension of a seeming self-contained "fact" is a judgment of value, the "measure" of an act or event.

In a similar fashion, the philosopher Donald Davidson suggests that the concept of event presents indefinite complexity precisely because it can be analyzed globally (e.g., the queen killed the king) or in stages, phases, and/or stretches (e.g., the queen deliberated, moved her hand, poured the poison, and the poison killed the king a week later by affecting his nervous system in such and such a way) (57–61). By understanding an "event" as a complex phenomenon, I am suggesting that an "event" or an "action" is not a simple positive and self-evident fact "sealed off" from experience, but a complex phenomenon that is realized—embodied and *enacted*—by a more-or-less social value-judgment, a habit of thought, which participates in experience. Such a judgment is what Austin calls the staged machinery of an action. And it allows us to imagine that a community of subjects, rather than a single "hero," governs the *stages* of an "act" or of an "event."

In fact, all three of Austin's categories of action suggest larger contexts of understanding and comprehension:

- in the social "machinery" of action, where different actors accomplish the *stages* of an event/action (The Duke of Wellington, who argued for the cessation of the War of 1812; Andrew Jackson, who fought its superfluous battle);

- in the descriptive contours of different events (The Treaty of Ghent [December 1814], the Battle of New Orleans [January 1815]), which set forth the *phases* of an event/action, rather than the single uncomplicated notion of either war or peace; and

- in a grasped evaluative whole, whether the judgment made by United States voters in the presidential election of 1828, which elected Jackson; or in the contested previous election of 1824, in which Jackson won a plurality of electoral votes, but John Quincy Adams was elected by the House of Representative (and not US voters); or even in the implicit and explicit evaluations of later historians, all of whom apprehend the social worth of the so-called War of 1812 battle in the *stretches* of its consequences.

The judgments resulting from elaborate analyses of a seemingly self-contained event now might be understood as the "purport" of the event, as I set forth the notion of "purport" in Chapter 3. As such, "purport" includes the *force*—and implicit value—of meaning as well as propositional information. Here is how Austin puts it: "Once we realize that what we have to study is *not* the sentence but the issuing of an utterance in a speech situation, there can hardly be any longer a possibility of not seeing that stating is performing an act" (*Words* 138), in which "the issuing of an utterance in a speech situation" always also enacts and embodies a judgment of quality.

In Chapter 2, I set forth a thesis about the discipline of literary studies. Let me repeat it here:

Literary studies in a disciplined and systematic fashion—even when that discipline remains implicit in its practice rather than explicitly pursued—analyzes the mediating systems that govern seeming immediate felt "experience."

Now let me complicate my thesis:

Conceiving deployments of language as *actions in the world* pursuing the wholeness—and the alliterative "happiness"—of well-being allows us to engage the so-called acts or events of language and literature in such a way as to frame an analysis of the actions of language in relation to conventions, habits of thought, and prevailing more-or-less conscious value judgments rather than as simple self-evident meaning. It also complicates the seeming simple distinction between "real" experience and "vicarious" experience (and, perhaps, the distinction between "the real and the construed," with which I began).

The complication here is the "unpacking" of the "mediating systems" of the early thesis. The focus on conventions, habits of thought, and value judgments—all species of inferential thinking—is a focus on what I described as the "institutional facts of value in-forming (which is to say *constituting*) experience" at the end of Chapter 4. In-forming value creates the possibility of worldly aesthetics, "experiences" of wholeness and well-being that, as Henry Allison notes, extend "into the future, beyond my present capacity to feel" (cited in Clune 41). Well-being itself—Aristotle's *eudaimonia*—entails such a future orientation, the answer to the question, as Ian Johnson notes, "What sort of a life would we most wish for our children?" (cited in Schleifer and Vannatta *Chief Concern* 63).

So-Called Vicarious Experience

One significant motor of the manner in which institutional facts inform experience is, as recent studies in cognitive science, rhetoric, neurology, economics, and other disciplines have argued, the work of *vicarious* experience. Throughout this book I have used the term "so-called vicarious experience," and I have done so because the opposition between "actual" experience and "vicarious" experience is not at all clear once one thinks of experience in relation to mediating structures. Sometimes I ask my medical students to explain the difference between an "imagined" headache and a "real" headache. While they often turn to the distinction between headache-sensations occasioned by measurable physiological conditions and headache-sensations, which cannot be linked to measurable conditions, it is also clear to them that the phenomenology of a headache—the qualities of sensation/"experience" associated with a headache—does not regularly and simply associate itself with measurable physiological conditions. A hypnotically induced headache is hardly distinguishable from a chemically induced headache. This is why Alvin Goldman's comprehensive survey of the phenomenological *simulation* of experience that gives rise to what he calls "mindreading" or "mentalizing" (10) is particularly useful in examining "experiences" that are provoked and represented in literary narratives. Such experiences are often (and traditionally) called "vicarious" (see Exhibit 6.2).

Exhibit 6.2: Vicarious Literary Experience

In his study of the provocation of "experience" in literature, Clune describes three "particularly salient" differences between "experiences" provoke by literary texts and "experiences" of "actual images." "First," he notes, "the experience of a novelistic description of a thunderstorm, compared with the experience of an actual thunderstorm, requires a different kind of interpretation. The reader draws on various linguistic and cultural competences and assumptions," many of which have been discussed in this book. "The second obvious difference between real and literary experiences," he goes on, "is that the latter do not typically entail the same kinds of actions as the former." And finally, he notes, "the third difference between life and literature [is that] literary images are less vivid than actual images" (1–2). None of these differences, however, significantly affects the practical work of moral education I describe in this chapter, which takes up experience provoked by everyday and art narrative as a starting point for understanding, judging, and, perhaps most importantly from the vantage of moral behavior, planning or anticipating feelings and actions.

In his psychological and neurological survey, which catalogues considerable psychological data and neurological organizations (i.e., "structures," although he rarely uses this term), Goldman focuses upon the larger category of "simulated" experience, of which the vicarious experiences provoked by narrative form a subset. He claims that "simulation" allows us to "replicate" the experience of others in order to achieve "mindreading"— the ability to "attribute" mental states to others. Such mindreading, he argues, "is a key concept not only for philosophy of mind and the science of social cognition but also for any systematic attempt to grasp the elements of human sociality" (302). He further notes that "the term *replication* ... avoids connotations associated with computer simulation" (35): computer simulation, he suggests, creates models of behavior (e.g., the simulated activity of a hurricane) while replicated simulation allows us to know—to "grasp" and "experience"—what another's feelings, emotions, knowledge ("attitudes") are *like* (295), to "feel" the *qualities* of their experience. He argues that "mindreading" should replace the more technical term "Theory of Mind" (ToM) from the discipline of psychology because ToM is ambiguous insofar as it designates the human ability—and perhaps the ability for other primates and, perhaps, certain birds—to attribute mental states to conspecific individuals and even individuals of other species, while at the same time it designates such a human ability solely on the basis of inferential reasoning rather than what I might call the "experiential reasoning" occasioned by the automatic and volitional "simulation" of experiences themselves (see Exhibit 6.3).

Exhibit 6.3: Theory of Mind in Literary Studies

Jonathan Kramnick offers a detailed analysis of studies of the way "elements of the world .... that dwell inside other people's minds" are represented. "Much of the research on such representation," he goes on, "has fallen under the rubric of what cognitive science calls 'theory of mind' because it asks how one mind forms a theory of another. And much of the past decade's interdisciplinary work between cognitive science and literary studies—work by Alan Richardson, Ellen Spolsky, Balkey Vermeule, and Lisa Zunshine, for example—has brought theory of mind research to consideration of the novel, with its formal repertoire for the representation of mental states" (7–8; and Ch. 5 for his general analysis; note that the work of these scholars can be found in Works Cited below). The "formal repertoire" of the discourses of literary narrative he describes—and nicely sets forth in his study of the benefits and limitations of interdisciplinary work—is an instructive version of structures of (vicarious) experience.

Goldman argues that ToM, in its restricted sense of inferential reasoning, which is to say the "mental states" focused upon "propositional attitudes," is often understood in relation to "folk psychology." Although he does not say so, such "folk psychology" is nicely akin to "habits of thought" I have mentioned throughout this book. "A comprehensive account of mindreading, however," he contends, "should equally deal with other kinds of mental states: sensations, like feelings and pain, and emotions, like disgust and anger" (20). And he argues that such mental states take place when an observer *simulates* them—simulates feelings, emotions, and attitudes—in order to attribute them to others.

Let me add an observation about simulation, ToM, and vicarious experience in relation to evolutionary adaptation. Just as I mentioned in Chapter 5 that we can understand literary genres as the re-deployments of the powerful discipline of evolutionary adaptive responses to the environment on another *level*—in another discipline—of understanding and explanation, so we can understand literary narratives as the re-deployment of strategies of simulation, which serve adaptive ends, in a similar fashion. Goldman describes "low level" automatic simulation as "contagion," which is to say "a resonance or mirroring system" (222) such that we automatically imitate or replicate emotions in social intercourse (e.g., anger that gives rise to reciprocal anger, the imitation of facial or motor gestures, laughter participating in group laughter, mirror neurons that replicate observed motor-neuron activity). He further notes "the adaptive value of contagion, and how contagion could be transmuted into certain kinds of mindreading routines, namely *simulation* routines" (217). "Once emotion contagion mechanisms are in place," he concludes,

> how might this lead to mindreading? It is common for natural selection to build new capacities from existing ones. Traits that originally evolved for other uses and are subsequently co-opted for a new purpose are called *exaptations* [a term he cites from Stephen Jay Gould and Elizabeth Vrba]. If a contagion mechanism for a given emotion state is already in place, this mechanism might be co-opted for a new purpose, that of mindreading.
>
> (219)

And such homological re-purposing can be co-opted—by means of cultural, artificial selection rather than natural selection—to the ends of literary art and even, as I argue here, for healthcare education.

Vicarious Experience and Literature

It is my argument—although Goldman takes it up momentarily in the conclusion of his survey—that literary narrative both provokes and represents the phenomena of *simulated experience*, which can be understood as the *vicarious experience*, to which art narrative gives rise. As we have seen, David Huron includes "imagination response" as the first of his catalogue of "five response systems [which] arise from *five functionally distinct neurophysiological systems*" (17; italics added). In this—which seems a version of Goldman's more general category of Enactment-imagination—Huron is particularly interested in feelings and emotions, the primary emotions examined in Chapter 5, as they relate to everyday and aesthetic experiences: fearful laughter, aggressive self-assertions, awe. Scott Stroud, in a rhetorical analysis following the work of psychologist Albert Bandura, elaborates on vicarious experience in terms of the ways that emotions and feelings are imbricated with cognition. He notes that "given the limited experiences one has with the world and other people, ... 'vicarious' or 'observational' learning must be what accounts for the wide range of thinking and behavioral strategies that humans possess" (35). In his neurological analysis of morality (rather than the neurological analysis of aesthetics Huron pursues), Sam Harris argues in *The Moral Landscape* that it is not the fiction-making of aspect of language that constitutes its power or force, but rather it is its ability to create vicarious experience, which in turn provokes belief. "There is no question," he writes,

> that syntactic language lies at the root of our ability to understand the universe, to communicate ideas, to cooperate with one another in complex societies, and to build (one hopes) a sustainable, global civilization. But why has language made such a difference? How has the ability to speak (and to read and write of late) given modern humans a greater purchase on the world?... I hope it will not seem philistine of me to suggest that our ability to create *fiction* has not been the driving force here. The power of language surely results from the fact that it allows mere words to substitute for direct experience and mere thoughts to simulate possible states of the world. Utterances like, 'I saw some very scary guys in front of that cave yesterday,' would have come in quite handy 50,000 years ago. The brain's capacity to accept such propositions as *true*—as valid guides to behavior and emotion, as predictive of future outcomes, etc.—explains the transformative power of words. There is a common term we use for this type of acceptance; we call it "belief."

(150)

Hillis Miller reinforces Harris's description of the power of vicarious experience in more literary terms: he argues that "the first side" of what I might call in the context of my larger argument the two "aspects" of the double-take of literature is "an innocent, childlike abandonment to the act of reading, without suspicion, reservation, or interrogation. Such a reading," he concludes, "makes a willing suspension of disbelief, in Coleridge's famous phrase" (119). Miller's second aspect is the more disciplined "slow reading" of linguistic or cultural (ideological) analysis, which, in "suspicious" engagements with texts, interrogates their purport. For both Harris and Miller—and, in fact, in more general experiences of focused engagements with language—the power of experience provoked by language is that it approximates and simulates lived experience because it is rich in cognitive understanding (of facts), emotional responses (to events), and imagined futures (of purport, which "come in quite handy," as Harris says, in future behavior).

The experience that language provokes, then, contributes to the "practical" discipline of action and work in the world—the practical wisdom of *phronesis*. Still, so-called vicarious experience, which is usually understood as different-in-kind from "direct" experience, should be—perhaps already has been—redescribed and reimagined (see Exhibit 6.4).

Exhibit 6.4: Redescribing Vicarious Experience

Goldman makes clear throughout his survey that the difference-in-kind between enacted and simulated/vicarious experience is that fact that the simulated experiences attributed to others do not function as an occasion for action (or decision-making) in the observer, as they do in the "direct" experience of the observed cohort. Rather, their function is to allow the observer to anticipate (to use Huron's term) the decisions and behaviors of others. For aesthetics, however—particularly when we remember that "aesthetics" is "experience" focused upon in a particular way—the anticipation associated with simulated experience *enlarges* feeling, emotion, and understanding *as skills-set of interaction with a world of indefinite complexity* rather than as motivations for particular decisions or actions. This is particularly notable in healthcare, where healthcare professionals can come to "grasp" more about the feelings, emotions, and understanding of their patients in their work in order to achieve "the primary end" of healthcare, namely "a healing relationship between a healthcare professional and a patient" (Pellegrino 266). Still, it is my contention in this book that if experience itself can be apprehended as "mediated"—

through sensory systems designed for evolutionary adaptation rather than truth-discovery, through complex information systems, through the inferential nature of perception rather than through positive self-evident perception—then the notion of "direct" experience is much more complicated than it appears on first glance.

In an important gesture in redescribing vicarious experience—which, implicitly, redescribes the practical wisdom of *phronesis* as well—psychology in the last thirty years has investigated vicarious experience in the model of Social Learning Theory, which offers an alternative to the extreme stimulus-response positivism of Behavioral Psychology. Stroud notes that "one of the prime features of [the Social Learning Theory of Albert Bandura] is that humans can and do learn through observation and consequent modeling" (35). And I should add that "observation and modelling"—like the "keyings" of mammals and of literary genres—are not absolutely different-in-kind from "direct" experiences insofar as experiences themselves are reflected upon in a double-take or are even turned into an unreflected-upon "second nature" by means of habit. That is, insofar as "direct" experience is meaningful, like vicarious experience it is mediated through semiotic systems, as I noted in relation to Hjelmslev's formal disciplinary language of *purport* and the very transformation of experience Huron describes in his formal neurological account of affective engagements with music. Even when "experience"—feelings, emotions, cognition—contributes to decision-making and action, even seeming "direct" experience is mediated through "a continuous reciprocal inter-action between people and institutions. That connection occurs by vicarious, reinforcing, and symbolic processes" (Almeida 840, citing Bandura). Such connections, which we might think of as "structures" as Raymond Williams does, organize feelings/emotions/felt-understandings, as in Williams, but they also organize value, the (ethically) measured qualities of experience, "blue" or "gray," "felicitous" or "infelicitous," the measured worth of attention and expectation, or the subtle difference between labor and well-being as the touchstone of value. All such structures results in, as the title of this chapter has it, the disciplined structures of vicarious experience.

The Provoked Experience of Poetry. In this context, let me examine the ways that poetry gives rise to conscious experience. Here I want to follow the description of conscious experience in David Chalmers (among others) as correlating "well with what we might call 'awareness': the process by which information in the brain is made globally available to motor processes such as speech and bodily action" ("Puzzle" 84; see also Kramnick for a wide array of analyses of "experience" and "consciousness"). In this examination, we might get a better handle of what literature *does*. What literature does—what it accomplishes—is the creation or provocation of performative experiences of awareness: of objects of cognition, emotional affect, and the dynamism of the *force* of meanings, the attitudes, emotions, and feelings that Goldman traces in simulating experience. We can discern this work through the development and study of semiotic and discursive structures or features I have touched upon in this book, and which we can now see in Yeats's poetry as well. If one encounters Yeats's sonnet "Leda and the Swan" in *The Norton Anthology of English Literature* (the same is true in many other anthologies), there is a long footnote explaining the narrative myth of Leda's rape by Zeus in the form of a swan. The note in the *Norton Anthology* cites a passage from Yeats's book *A Vision* describing how the event of the poem is a "phase" (this is Austin's terms, but Yeats uses the term as well long before Austin does) of the "annunciation" of Greek civilization in grand historical terms; and it also cites a second passage by Yeats from the first publication of the poem describing how he was requested to write a poem by the editor of a political review, but by the time he wrote and revised the poem, Yeats himself notes that "bird and lady took such possession of the scene that all politics went out of it" (*Norton* 1929). Here is the poem.

Leda and the Swan

A sudden blow: the great wings beating still
Above the staggering girl, her thighs caressed
By the dark webs, her nape caught in his bill,
He holds her helpless breast upon his breast.

How can those terrified vague fingers push
The feathered glory from her loosening thighs?
And how can body, laid in that white rush,
But feel the strange heart beating where it lies?

A shudder in the loins engenders there
The broken wall, the burning roof and tower
And Agamemnon dead.

> Being so caught up,
> So mastered by the brute blood of the air,
> Did she put on his knowledge with his power
> Before the indifferent beak could let her drop? (*Norton* 1929)

I am fascinated by the ways that literary critics engage this poem, whether it be the simple historical context the *Norton* note seems to describe or more complex engagements. Paul de Man has meditated on the manner in which rhetorical questions at the conclusion of so many poems by Yeats give rise to uncertainty about their literal or figurative meaning, and more particularly about how they seem to provoke what he calls "vertiginous possibilities of referential aberration" (30) caught up with the "suspended uncertainty" (33) between understanding the question as literal or understanding it as figurative. (One can only wonder at the force of de Man's rhetoric, how "dizzying" [i.e., "vertiginous"] so oddly modifies possibilities even as "aberration" dryly characterizes the bottomlessness—"vertiginous" bottomlessness itself—of the erasure of reference to things in the world. You might remember I used the word *vertiginous* to modify the "plain sense" of death in Chapter 5.) De Man is making the distinction between a "real" question, which demands an answer, and a "rhetorical" question, which presents a propositional statement in the form of a question. In discussing this "suspended uncertainty," de Man focuses on Yeats's "Among School Children"—another iconic modernist poem—where the problem of reference has to do explicitly with aesthetic experience, "How can we know the dancer from the dance?" (30).

But "Leda and the Swan" focuses on the value and morality of violent action, not aesthetic apprehension, and its representation of seeming mindless violence—the brute fact of sexual violence that so upsets my students and seems often ignored in literary-critical accounts of the poem (see Exhibit 4.10: The Dismissal of Experience in Literary Studies)— leads to a vertiginous experience far beyond de Man's feelings on the connections between truth and falsity, knowledge and power, which we heard Austin thinking about in the previous chapter. Let us return to that. As you remember, Austin wonders about the function of evaluation in the arrangements of truth and falsity, which nicely maps onto the opposition between the figurative (evaluations of *force*, the "felicity" of actions) and the literal (simple truth-value). In de Man, the inability to absolutely distinguish between the performative and the constative deployments of language— this structural inability is one of the conclusions of Austin's analysis—gives rise to possibilities that language is not, after all, clearly and self-evidently referential. In a passage I noted in Chapter 4, Austin argues that:

> The more you think about truth and falsity the more you find that very few statements that we ever utter are just true or just false. Usually there is the question are they fair or are they not fair, are they adequate or not adequate, are they exaggerated or not exaggerated? Are they too rough, or are they perfectly precise, accurate, and so on? "True" and "false" are just general labels for a whole dimension of different appraisals which have something or other to do with the relation between what we say and the facts.
>
> (*Papers* 250–1)

In his argument, unlike that of de Man, Austin isn't worried about the slippage of the referential work of language, but rather he focuses on what Shoshana Felman describes as how "the referential knowledge of language" *engages* with "facts," how language "*has to do with reality*, that acts within reality" (51). Such action—such an "event"—allows us to more fully focus on the *force* of poetry, particularly the force provoked by disciplined vicarious experience, and, in relation to that force, the particular *truth-value* of an event. In the final unanswered question of "Leda and the Swan" Yeats meditates on this relationship between power and knowledge, he meditates on, as I just said, the measured qualities and the measured worth of force and truth: the value built into any experience at all, including the seeming "empty" experience of boredom I mentioned in Chapter 4. (Is it safe to bring up boredom once again?)

But let me get back on track: in this sonnet Yeats is asking us to wonder whether Leda can understand the historical meaning of the felt experience of seeming meaningless violence that overwhelms her. But the poem itself does something else: it allows us to engage the experience of violence itself, not in "*stretches* or *phases* or *stages*," in Austin's analysis of what constitutes an act, but as an overall vicarious experience, the "meaningful whole" of Greimas's semantics and the "overall meaning" that Jerry Vannatta and I borrowed from Greimas to designate a final "feature" of literary narrative in *Literature and Medicine*. As I mentioned earlier, Greimas more formally calls this "the still very vague, yet necessary concept of the meaningful whole [*totalité de signification*] set forth by a message" (59). In our book, Jerry and I catalogue thirteen "features" of literary narrative—we develop what Mark Platts calls the "semantic depth" of meaningful phenomena in a somewhat simple philological exercise of "close reading," which aims at investigating and experiencing "the features of the real world" (cited in Moore 1145)—in order, in our case, to help faculty teaching students committed to careers in healthcare by setting forth practical "road posts" of reading to organize and direct attention and expectation. Medical faculty teaching healthcare usually have little or no training in the discipline of literary studies, yet it is our belief, borne of our own experience, that even a rudimentary disciplined sense of engagement with literary texts in our students can widen their experience and understanding within their subsequent careers in healthcare (see Exhibit 6.5).

Exhibit 6.5: Vicarious Experience and Professional Training

The purpose of our classes and workshops—and of our book *Literature and Medicine*, as well—is to widen the *experience* of healthcare workers by means of the vicarious experience provoked by everyday narratives (vignettes from actual events in the clinic) and literary narratives. As I mentioned in Chapter 3 and at the beginning of the present chapter, such widening of experience is a source of the practical wisdom of *phronesis*. Toward the end of this chapter, I examine in greater detail the force of vicarious experience, which is reflected upon in "professionalization" workshops for practicing healthcare workers. In *Literature and Medicine* we include "Leda and the Swan" in the chapter devoted to the violence of domestic and sexual abuse, a vicarious experience of terrible sexual violence that many of our students engage with and discuss *as experience* for the first times in their lives. Sexual violence is a terrible fact that most healthcare professionals encounter, and thus "experience," in their professional work. Moreover, it takes its place with the more general violence, which is "baked into" the work of healthcare, as noted below. Our course bringing together literature and medicine, which Dr. Vannatta and I team-taught for two decades, forms the basis of our book *Literature and Medicine*, in which we try to replicate, for students, simulation of long-term experiences in the shorter course of one semester (and sometimes the shorter timeframe of a two-week medical-school course). The practical and pedagogical goal of the course is to render practical wisdom from vicarious experience. (See Shakir et al. for a systematic follow-up study, by means of a qualitative analysis, which traces the effects of our course on the subsequent medical careers of a number of our students.)

The manner in which Yeats's poem provokes the experience and contemplation of seeming meaningless violence allows students to vicariously experience violence, an aspect of healthcare, which is "baked into" its practical operations even though such violence is rarely addressed in systematic biomedical training. The violence "baked into" healthcare includes

- the violence that brings patients *to* the clinic—whether it be accidental or interpersonal violence or the felt-sense of violation enacted by illness and disease;
- the violence that takes place *in* the clinic in the sanctioned physical force of surgery, injections, and many other clinical procedures; and
- the violence that *inhabits* the unequal distribution and quality of medical care for different groups of people in many, if not most, societies.

In fact, in his close reading of Yeats's sonnet Stephen Regan offers a detailed analysis of the "features" that condition the vicarious experience of violence, which Yeats's poem provokes, even if he does not systematically set them forth. Regan notes

the powerful chiastic plosives [the phonemes /b/, /t/, /p/]—"sudden blow" and "beating still"—are played out in a mesmerizing series of strongly physical descriptions—"bill" and "breast" and "body", "broken wall" and "burning roof", and "brute blood of the air"—until the terrifying "drop" at the end of the poem[, which doesn't quite rhyme with "up"]. The strange ambivalent image of "great wings beating still" captures the wild, energetic movement of the swan's wings as it steadies itself above her, while also conveying the transfixed vision of Leda herself.

(165)

This passage (and, had I time to present it, Regan's close reading of the poem as a whole) enacts many of the features of narrative Jerry and I describe in *Literature and Medicine*. In that book, we catalogue thirteen "features" of literary narrative in order, as I have said, to help faculty teaching students committed to careers in healthcare. The point of these features—it is the point of disciplined intellectual work altogether, whether it be rudimentary or elaborately sophisticated—is worldly and thoroughly materialist: it allows people, as Platts suggests, to see and engage with phenomena that they might not have noticed before. (This is as true in the disciplined formulas of physics and the disciplined statistical analyses of sociology as it is in the disciplined features of narrative I recount here insofar as those disciplines—and intellectual disciplines in general—are "worldly," which is to say are "used by human beings who exist in history" [Said *Humanism* 61].) In other words, the seeming "simple" catalogue of features of narrative takes its place with Hjelmslev's systematic analysis of how the semantics of the language we are born into, such as the semantics of color I have brought up throughout this book, conditions our attention and expectation, conditions *experience and understanding* (the law that will govern the future). I won't discuss all our features we discuss in *Literature and Medicine* here, but simply mention a few in relation to Yeats's poem and Regan's analysis (see Exhibit 6.6).

Exhibit 6.6: Features of Narrative

Although I do not catalogue the thirteen features of narrative as part of my argument in this chapter, let me list them here as an aside. It should be clear that this is not an exhaustive catalogue but features of literary narrative that we have discovered through experience are particularly useful in the context of healthcare.

#1, The Dynamic of Form and Content

#2, Twice Told Stories

#3,4,5, Repetitions of Sound, Events, Themes

#6, The Unsaid

#7, Relational "Facts"

#8, Genres

#9, Narrative Agents and Concern

#10, The Witness Who Learns

#11, Defamiliarization and Style

#12, Narrative as Moral Education

#13, Overall Meaning

As I mentioned, this is not an exhaustive catalogue, and each feature does not demand terribly sophisticated analyses of the experience and schemas of literature. We hope, however—and we have found among our students and colleagues—that they do accomplish the goal of presenting, as I noted toward the beginning of this book, practical *transferable skills*, namely strategies of attention and expectation and the concomitant skill of inferential thinking, that can be shared and developed.

As I have noted, in his study of simulation theory—in which he equates "simulation" and "empathy" (11)—Goldman distinguishes between "low level" and "high level" simulation, which he maps onto "automatic" and "controlled" empathy. In doing so, he presents empirical and theoretical studies of "simulation," which offer a rational for our isolation of features of narrative for healthcare professionals. He notes that in one such study, Sara Hodges and Daniel Wegner distinguish automatic and controlled empathy by means of the following metaphors: they "characterize automatic empathy [e.g., the automatic smile in response to a smiling person] as having the inertia of running or tumbling downhill, whereas controlled empathy is as effortful as climbing a mountain. In attempts to reach the mountain peak, we search for grips, holds, and trails to help us on our way. Similarly, in trying to achieve empathy, we seek out aids to help us" (208). The "features" of narrative Vannatta and I isolate in literary texts, we have found, provide healthcare workers "grips, holds, and trails" in engagement with stories and patients who provide them with stories. Goldman more generally defines empathy (following Eisenberg and Strayer) as "vicarious sharing of affect," and notes that "empathy can be achieved in at least two ways: by 'catching' another's affect via emotional contagion or by adopting the other's perspective (using E-imagination [i.e., "controlled" empathy])" (291).

The Features of Vicarious Experience. The first feature of literary narrative we describe is the organization of "the dynamic of form and content" (feature #1), and in Yeats's sonnet we can notice how the octave and sestet of the sonnet form—the first eight lines and the final six lines in the Petrarchan sonnet—offers what we call a "twice told story" (feature #2).

We call the first feature "dynamic" in that, dynamically, it is a complex feedback system, wherein—as in Hjelmslev's semantic color schema—the form affects experiential content and the content shapes the form. In Yeats's sonnet this is further complicated in that its syntactic articulation, with a paragraph break in the middle of the sestet, somewhat obscures its sonnet-nature in the way that Charles Taylor suggests that performances of language can upset the strict hierarchy between "structures of rules" and "events" or "particular cases" ("Discussion" 176). Thus, students often do not recognize Yeats's poem *as* a sonnet, and they *almost never* recognize what Regan calls the "concealed double sonnet" of Wilfred Owen's "Dulce et Decorum Est" (309). (I myself didn't notice it until I read Regan's book.) The feature of "twice told story"—a rendition of the "double-take" of literature, with which I began this book—is a striking explicit feature of many literary narratives, and it is implicit, I contend, in art-narrative altogether.

An archetypal example of this feature is the detective story, in which first the crime is presented and at the end the detective—Sherlock Holmes does this over and over—retells the crime-events in a final narrative. This structure nicely maps onto diagnostic work in healthcare, but the octave and sestet of a sonnet also perform this repetition of events and explanations of (or meditations on) the events. This is clear in the violent rape of Leda, which Regan powerfully analyzes in the passage I quoted a moment ago, and also in the meditation on that very violence in the sestet. Such repetition calls upon readers—and healthcare workers—to not only think about the "facts" a patient presents, but the "aspects" of force, emotion, and, in the clinic, "the unsaid" (feature #6) patients bring to the clinic. (In Yeats's sonnet, the "unsaid" is the mythological framework hinted at with the reference to Agamemnon and even the pun of "the broken wall." Puns, like detective narratives, organize themselves around twice-told stories. But the unsaid is also, as my students noted in class, the brute fact of sexual violence, which the poem—or at least some of its "mythological" interpretations— somewhat obscures.) Finally, in this truncated engagement with literary features, we can attend to the "repetitions of sounds" in the poem (feature #3), which Regan cites in analyzing the poem in order to get an "overall meaning" (feature #13)—the meaningful whole of vicarious brute violence, and, perhaps most impressively in Regan's close reading, the manner in which Yeats presents a "witness who learns" (feature #10). Thus, Regan notes the way the sonnet conveys Leda's own "transfixed vision" and wonders "if Leda (in that moment of being both 'caught' and 'caught up') 'put on' the intellectual power of Zeus, enabling her to see into the future" (165). In this,

Regan notices how the poem joins its readers in Leda's experience, even when Yeats makes it not altogether clear whether the violence she *necessarily* suffers (how she is "caught") may nevertheless be *sufficient* to allow her to be "caught up" in meaning as well as violation.

In *Literature and Medicine*, Jerry and I also address the meaningful whole of Yeats's poem. "The great question of the poem," we note,

> is that of its "overall meaning": what is Yeats striving for? Most commentators relate the poem to Yeats's cosmological thinking—his sense that there is a great cultural crisis in the twentieth century that will lead to a new cosmic "dispensation" of human life. But we are suggesting that it is much more closely related to the experience of Yeats's (and our) time, which is a time of seeming senseless violence wherever we turn. In any case, Yeats's poetic impulse can shed light on the impulse often felt in victims of violence [and their caretakers]... to explain it away as the better alternative than to confront it and figure out what kind of practical actions that confrontation demands. In other words, to try to answer Yeats's question ["Did she put on his knowledge with his power ...?"] by saying, "there is no knowledge that can justify brutal violence—no excuse (such as [Leda's] ... fantastic beauty), no rationalization (such as "she never resisted"), no convenience (such as "it's not my business").
>
> (157–8)

In fact, we conclude by asserting that trying to answer Yeats's question "becomes itself an occasion for moral education, for self-consciously articulating value in the face of [seeming 'brute'] experience" (158). In this, we touch upon feature #12, "narrative as moral education," which I turn to later in this chapter.

I am suggesting here, then, that engaging with more or less traditional literary history in relation to the interdisciplinary study of Austin's philosophy of language, of cognitive psychology's "transportation theory," or Veblen's "institutional facts" in economics in order to understand what is necessary and what is sufficient in language—in engaging with traditional literary history in relation to these things—allows us to see beyond Hjelmslev's and de Man's seeming self-evident categories of "reference," unsystematic "mere description," even "truth and falsity." That is, by bringing a disciplinary reading of a poem together with other disciplinary understandings, we can position ourselves to undergo a double-take of experience itself: to "see things differently," as Austin says, "yet perhaps we know no more and are no cleverer" (*Papers* 194); or, as Wittgenstein says, to "*see* that [the image of a face] has not changed; and yet I see it differently" (§113). Or finally to remember as I silently recalled Rita Felski's words at the very beginning of this book, that in literature "we rediscover things as we know them to be, yet reordered and redescribed, shimmering in a transformed light" (Felski 102). With this catalogue I am suggesting that the descriptive close reading that Hjelmslev so easily dismisses—just like the complications of referential meaning that so easily upsets de Man—might be renewed and transformed by attending to the *experience* of force and power—inferred measures of value and worth that constitute the "third thing"—we encounter in literary studies. That attention, as I have suggested throughout this book, is *disciplined*: it grows out of systematic formal structures or procedures—Gould's "law and similarity"—that inhabit even the "mere description" Hjelmslev contrasts with "exact and generalizing treatment." It is the work of these chapter-lectures, as it is, I believe, the work of literary studies, to make those procedures and these language-events explicit. (See Exhibit 6.7.)

Exhibit 6.7: Kramnick's Discipline

This conclusion comes close to the argument Jonathan Kramnick makes in *Paper Minds* about the discipline of literary studies. But the manner in which the "practical wisdom" of disciplinary knowledge forms the *material* backbone of my argument—along with the "worldly" argument Edward Said makes for philology—distinguish my overall sense of the discipline of literary studies from that of Kramnick. That is, Kramnick's contention that, at least on some level, disciplinary knowledge from one discipline is incommensurable with knowledge from another discipline is obviated in the practical project of *phronesis*. Thus, the fact that the discipline of literary studies *focuses* on experience—this is one of Kramnick's main points, as it is mine—is not simply a "neutral" difference among equally efficacious disciplines, which pick out features of the world to develop "knowledge." Rather, insofar as practical wisdom organizes itself around "experience" in order to achieve some sense of well-being (*eudaimonia*), insofar as we seek worldly knowledge, other disciplines can learn from literary studies. Joseph North makes the stronger historical argument about the centrality of "close reading" to literary criticism, and how such close reading is an "insipiently materialist practice" (27), but he does not make clear, as does the phronetic pedagogy necessary to healthcare education, exactly what the practical materialism of disciplinary knowledge might be. He does note, however, that "[I. A.] Richards and [William] Empson put together what might fairly be called an incipiently materialist practice of close reading, based in an instrumental or (loosely speaking) pragmatist aesthetics, directed toward an advanced utilitarian model of aesthetic and practical education" (27).

The Impressionism and Style of Vicarious Experience. Let me turn to a more explicit examination of the performance of vicarious experience in art narrative that *"has to do with reality,* that acts within reality" (Felman 51). Although I am focusing on art narrative, I hope that the continuity between everyday deployments of discourse and art narratives—the continuity between speech genres and aesthetic genres—is clear. In his study of modernist painting—particularly impressionism and post-impressionism— Daniel Herwitz offers an explicit description of the performance of engagement with artworks that should demonstrate in greater detail how literature provokes experience. Here again let me set forth more fully a passage I have cited in part earlier. "The impressionist painting," Herwitz writes,

> was a breakthrough in form insofar as it abandoned the distanced, hermetic image, composing instead out of tiny brush strokes that the viewer must visually and actively complete, and that place the viewer in a state of active absorption. The viewer must formulate a scene from the sketch, from the brush stroke, from the ambient play of light and color, a scene that seems evanescent even as it appears so intensely in its moment. Like all moments, or suspensions of time, the impressionist painting already contains its passing within it ....
>
> [Likewise, he notes, in post-impressionism] nothing recedes toward a vanishing point in Cézanne, but rather achieves stability, order, and venerable solidity through the interrelationships of elements that are working formally rather than representatively.
>
> (184, 186)

In this analysis, Herwitz nicely outlines the "active absorption" of engagement, which Hjelmslev took to be more-or-less passive description. The "activity" of absorption, as Herwitz notes here, is a *future* engagement with the artwork, anticipated, so to speak, by the artist. It is "a breakthrough in form," not simply for the visual arts, but the kind of "breakthrough" Austin and Felman discern and enact in speech-act theory and that in this book I have attempted to describe in developing the relationship between the necessary and sufficient elements that constitute knowledge and, in my argument, experience as well. Both Regan and *Literature and Medicine* aim to make explicit what is "sufficient" to provoke vicarious experience in engagement with Yeats's poem, even while Yeats's concluding question in "Leda and the Swan" directly addresses possibilities of sufficiency or insufficiency, what Austin describes as felicitous or infelicitous speech acts (see Exhibit 6.8).

Exhibit 6.8: Enactment Imagination

Alvin Goldman, in his philosophical-psychological-neurological analysis, describes what he calls the "enactments" of simulation in mindreading ("Theory of Mind"). These disciplines in which he situates his argument are far afield from the semantic philology of speech-act theory of Austin and the Lacanian psychoanalysis of Felman: the "philosophy" of mindreading he pursues never even touches on ordinary language philosophy. Nevertheless, in his work he offers an understanding of the "active absorption" Herwitz describes in terms of motor activity in simulation (which category [i.e., "simulation"] includes as a subset the vicarious experience discussed in this chapter), and in doing so he clarifies what Felman means by suggesting that vicarious experience "*has to do with reality.*" "To enactively imagine seeing something," he argues, "you must 'try' to *undergo* the seeing—or some aspects of the seeing—despite the fact that no appropriate visual stimulus is present. When this is clearly understood, a wary reader might be skeptical of any substantial similarity between seeing and E-imagined seeing. 'When one looks at an object attentively,' a reader might reflect, 'the experience of it is far from passive. The object is scanned or tracked with the eyes. Saccadic eye movements [rapid eye movements between fixation points] accompany and facilitate attentive seeing. Surely this doesn't happen when one merely visualizes an object. Visualizing does not consist in literally *enacting* the seeing in a full-blooded sense. So postulating something called "enactment imagination" is misleading at best and positive nonsense at worst." "Wrong, wrong, wrong," Goldman replies to his simulated interlocutor. "Studies indicate that visualizing is, precisely, attempted *enactment* of seeing. Saccadic eye movements do occur during visual imagination (even when the eyes are closed), movements that approximate the ocular movements for corresponding acts of visual perception" (151–2). He describes a number of experimental psychological studies demonstrating his point and concludes by noting the disciplined scientific evidence in psychology and neurology "confirms that visual imagination is very much an enactment (simulation) of seeing in behavioral as well as purely cognitive terms" (152).

The impressionism I am describing (by means of Herwitz and Goldman) is a particular example of the force and power of style in the arts. In her analysis of the relation of ethics and aesthetics in Wittgenstein, Katherin Stengel examines the function of style in discourse in a manner that is parallel to Herwitz's discussion of the style of impressionist painting. Thus, she argues that "style adds value to neutral propositions, a 'voice' to the text. Values, according to Wittgenstein, lie outside the world [of the true/false of propositions and 'facts'] but not outside language. Though they cannot be depicted *in* propositional language, they can be revealed *with and through* propositional language, and this is where style comes in" (617). In Wittgenstein both aesthetics and ethics, she argues, "exceed the limits of propositional language" (612). For Wittgenstein, she contends,

propositional language depicts the factual world, in which "everything is as it is and happens as it does happen." Value statements, however, offer perspectives on the world's facts; this goes much further than just depicting "what is the case." Value statements, on Wittgenstein's view, do not depict reality and are not subject to the rules of propositions. They do not generate truth or falsehood; rather, they pertain to the distinction between what Wittgenstein calls "sense," that is, logical truth, and "non-sense," that is, that which in and through language eludes logical propositionality.

(614–15)

Sam Harris and Michael Moore would disagree with Stengel's contention that value statements do not depict or engage the world but simply "offer perspectives"; I join them in this in my understanding that any sense of the meaning and any phenomenology of "experience" always entail an engagement with *value*, which is not simply a "perspective" but experience itself. But they would agree with her contention, as I do, that the manifestation of value in language shows itself in style: style, she writes, is "that aspect of propositional language that precisely exceeds the propositional .... Style touches us like the timbre of a voice, but it cannot be captured 'objectively' in referential terms" (616). It can, however, be captured in the "active absorption" provoked by impressionist painting, which exceeds the propositionality of the "hermetic image." It is also captured in the everyday automatic "contagions" of experience and in "enactment-imagination" by which Goldman defines simulation. And in addition it is captured in the odd stylistics of this lectures-book itself. Michael Clune ends his impassioned argument of the ways that literature "renews" experience with a meditation on the manner in which Geoffrey Hartman defends the discipline of literary studies by identifying those studies with literature itself, with literature conceived as style. "Literary scholars break free of their isolation," he writes, "and travel into the spheres of the disciplines surrounded and protected by the aura of style. Their extra-disciplinary sentences cannot be taken seriously. But they can, Hartman predicts, be taken—as writing" (142).

Ethics and Action

If value inheres in the stylistics of language use, then ethics inheres in decision-making and action. Speech-act theory, as Austin developed it, in important ways grew out of his concern for the value of action or the quality of action, which is to say it grew out of his concern for ethics. You might remember I cited Austin earlier in this chapter discussing "what is meant by, and what not, and what is intended under, and what not, the expression 'doing an action' or 'doing something.'" Austin pursued these considerations in the larger context of moral philosophy and begins the passage I cited earlier by noting "in ethics we study, I suppose, the good and the bad, the right and the wrong, and this must be for the most part in some connexion with conduct or the doing of actions" (*Papers* 178). This in large part is why he gives so much attention to adverbs in analyzing the ordinary language of everyday narratives (e.g., he analyzes narratives taken from actual court cases in the legal system). Austin doesn't address literature or "art" narratives directly, but the chapter-lectures I have been presenting—and many other studies of speech-act theory in relation to literature, such as Felman's examination of speech acts in relation to Moliere's *Don Juan*—do so. "The beginning of sense," Austin writes,

> not to say wisdom, is to realize that "doing an action", as used in philosophy, is a highly abstract expression—it is a stand-in used in the place of any (or almost any?) verb with a personal subject, in the same sort of way that "thing" is a stand-in for any (or when we remember, almost any) noun substantive, and "quality" a stand-in for the adjective. Nobody, to be sure, relies on such dummies quite implicitly quite indefinitely. Yet notoriously it is possible to arrive at, or to derive the idea for, an over-simplified metaphysics from the obsession with "things" and their "qualities" .... We scarcely notice even the most patent exceptions or difficulties ... any more than we fret ... as to whether flames are things or events.
>
> (*Papers* 178–9)

Later in "A Plea for Excuses," he goes on to make clear the "modifications" that adverbs bring to actions. "Working the dictionary," he says, "it is interesting to find that a high percentage of the terms connected with excuses prove to be *adverbs*, a type of word which has not enjoyed so large a share of the philosophical limelight as the noun, substantive or adjective, and the verb: this is natural because, as was said, the tenor of so many excuses is that I did it but only *in a way*, not just flatly like that—i.e. the verb needs modifying" (*Papers* 187).

Austin's example of the difficulty of classifying flames is illuminating. Its implicit similes—"fire is like a thing," "fire is like an event"—is positively literary. (Felman's extended meditation on humor in Austin's work, as I mentioned, is, in a similar fashion, "positively literary.") But what makes something "literary"? In *On Literature*, Hillis Miller offers a short catalogue of features of literature very different from the formal features of literary narrative Jerry Vannatta and I deploy in *Literature and Medicine*, which I touched upon in connection to Yeats's poem. He notes five features: that literature is unique and strange (in this, he is instantiating Louis Hjelmslev's account of traditional views of the humanities as engaged unique phenomena); that it is "performative" in the ways I have been tracing; that it possesses "secrets," which "witnesses" experience; that it deploys figurative language; and that it is ambiguous in that one cannot be certain whether it is either a revelation of a pre-existing "world" or the creation of a nonexistent world (the real or the construed) (*On Literature* 33–45; see Exhibit 6.9).

Exhibit 6.9: On Witnessing

Miller does not make the connection between secrets and witnessing altogether clear in *On Literature*. In her account of the relationship between aesthetics and ethics in Wittgenstein, Stengel contends that "Wittgenstein calls that which is 'beyond significant language' the 'inexpressible' and stresses that, while it cannot be logically framed as a theme or propositional content, it can nonetheless be witnessed: it '*shows* itself.' This suggests that ethics and aesthetics are, indeed, 'one' insofar as the mode of being of the ethical is 'showing itself,' that is, being inherently aesthetic. More importantly, however, it means … that the ethical and the aesthetic belong to a domain radically distinct from both the merely referential and the merely mental or cognitive" (615). When Stengel says that the inexpressible that Wittgenstein describes "*shows* itself," she means that its force, its dynamism, even its purport is *experienced*. In *On Literature* Miller makes no mention of Wittgenstein, but Jerry Vannatta and I have borrowed "The Witness who Learns" (feature #10) from Miller. "The minimal personages necessary for a narrative are three," he writes: "a protagonist, an antagonist, and a witness who learns" ("Narrative" 75). In asserting that "the ethical and aesthetic belong to a domain radically distinct from both the merely referential and the merely mental," Stengel is describing the "third thing," which Viktor Zuckerkandl finds in music.

All the features of "literature" Miller describes are illuminated by Austin's reference to flames: its strangeness in Austin's wondering about the category of flames, about which we scarcely fret; the fact that flames seem to come into existence by means of their "activity"; that they call upon us to "witness"—which is to say, to reflect upon and re-think in a kind of "double-take"—concepts we thought we already knew; that the term *flames* is deployed as a similitude to understand something else; and that the phenomenon of flames itself is essentially ambiguous.

Most pertinent, here, is Miller's fourth feature, the manner in which literature uses figurative language. Miller claims that "new births are performed by language," that figurative language "illustrate[s] the extraordinary power tropes have to bring an imaginary personage to life," and, perhaps in circular reasoning, that "the presence of tropes ... is a clue ... [that the reader] may be about to read something that would be defined in our culture as 'literature'" (42–3). In fact, all three of these explanations of figurative language seem to melt into one another. That is, what Miller leaves out of his close-reading ("philological") discussion is the manner in which figurative language, like the adverbs Austin discusses, imports (or recognizes) the provoked experience of qualities into discourses about things and events. Even Austin's question "as to whether flames are things or events" (*Papers* 179)—like the question of whether my pants are blue or gray—is a question of how we can judge and, as we do so, how we experience phenomena.

Vicarious Experience and Moral Education

I have been examining the vicarious experience provoked by literary texts, but it is also important to see the ways that such experiences affect value-laden action in the world, how they condition what I might call "habits of action" as well as "habits of thought." In *The Call of Stories: Teaching and the Moral Imagination*, Robert Coles begins to focus on the work of the provoked experience of literature. "Novels and stories are renderings of life," he says;

> they can not only keep us company, but admonish us, point us in new directions, or give us the courage to stay a given course. They can offer us kinsmen, kinswomen, comrades, advisers—offer us other

eyes through which we might see others, ears with which we might make soundings. Every medical student, law student, or business school student, every man or woman studying at a graduate school of education or learning to be an architect, will all too quickly be beyond schooling, will be out there making a living and, too, just plain living—that is, trying to find and offer others the affection and love that give purpose to our time spent here.

(159–60)

The "renderings of life" Coles describes—remember Melville's "renderings"—is the provoked experience to which literary narrative (including narratives explicit and implicit in lyric poetry) give rise, just as his "purpose" is linked to the force of "purport" in language and literature. Moreover, such vicarious experience is the source of the practical wisdom of *phronesis* in the pursuit of well-being, and it allows students—"every medical student, law student, or business school student, every man or woman studying at a graduate school of education or learning to be an architect"—to achieve *phronesis* and a moral education less arduously than through the trials and errors of so-called direct experience.

Goldman offers an account of this phenomenon in his psychological/ neurological survey. He does so by citing a study which appeared in *Organizational Behavior and Human Decision Processes* by D. T. Gilbert et al. "If we wish to predict how we would feel upon finding our spouse in bed with the letter carrier on New Year's Eve," they write,

we might imagine the event and then take note of how we react to the mental image. Because real and imagined events activate many of the same neural and psychological processes ... reactions to imaginary events can provide useful information about one's likely reactions to the events themselves.

(cited in Goldman 169)

Goldman reformulates this passage in the language of experimental psychology—noting that a person observes "the hypothetical event, feeds this imagined observation into an affect-generating mechanism, and lets it operate on the input to produce affective outputs" (169), and so on—but his conclusions can be taken up, homologically, in the disciplined study of literary narrative (see Exhibit 6.10).

Exhibit 6.10: Interdisciplinary Homologies

When I mention that conclusions in one discipline "can be taken up, homologically," in another discipline, I am offering an alternative Donald Davidson's contention, which I noted in Chapter 2, that "it is one thing for developments in one field to affect changes in a related field, and another thing for knowledge gained in one area to constitute knowledge of another" (247). Similarly, Jonathan Kramnick argues, with literary studies particularly in mind, that "the desire to overcome boundaries between disciplines of knowledge and to integrate fields of study ... rests on a mistake: namely, that the separate disciplines have a common object to which the can be reduced or oriented" (17 and *passim*). He goes on to argue that "clarifying this mistake would begin with the recognition that a pluralistic array of disciplines matches up with a pluralistic vision of the world: endocrine cells for the biologists, tectonic plates for the geologists, librettos for the musicologists, and so on" (17). What neither Davidson nor Kramnick seems to recognize is that a discipline can take up "knowledge" from another discipline to be "repurposed" in the manner of understanding homological structures in evolutionary biology, which I discussed in Chapter 3. This has been my experience working with colleagues and students trained in biomedicine and training for healthcare work. Thus, the features of literary narrative I have described in this chapter can be repurposed to contribute to strategies for enhancing empathy in healthcare; and the more-or-less self-evident value of the "primary end" of "healing relationship" in healthcare can be repurposed to contribute to the recognition of the centrality of value judgments in the human sciences and to the "primary end" of "well-being" as a theory of value. We can even "apply" philological concerns in engaging with psychology. Psychology has coined the term "transportation" to describe the psychological phenomenon of vicarious experience (though I must note, Goldman does not take up this figure of speech in his extensive psychological/neurological survey of simulation). In "Enhancing Physician Empathy," Dr. Casey Hester and I argue that "we find the spatial metaphor of 'transported' movement embedded in the description of a psychological experience a bit troubling precisely in the way that, by asserting a sense of being engulfed in a narrative, it precludes—or at least discourages—analysis of the mechanisms by which storytelling affects the experience of those encountering stories. But in any case," we note, "there is good empirical evidence that such experiences of 'losing' oneself in a story is an important aspect of narrative" (109–10). Hillis Miller, as we have seen, describes such "losing oneself" as *Schwärmerei* [*On Literature* 94, 118–22]). A focus on metaphors—"transportation," "losing oneself," even Goldman's taking up and then parsing the complicated meanings of "simulation" in computer science and psychology—is an example of the ways that "interdisciplinarily" one can "take up" strategies of one discipline for the practical understanding of another.

The penultimate feature of literary narrative we describe in *Literature and Medicine* is "Narrative as Moral Education" (feature #12). There we argue that this feature of narrative focuses on the border between everyday life and narrative knowledge in a manner that allows literary texts to lend themselves to moral education. This is a crucial aspect of what cognitive psychology calls the "transportation" to which literature gives rise insofar as literary narratives allow readers to test out their judgments and responses to experiences they haven't encountered in real life: the example of the New Year's Eve spousal betrayal narrated by Gilbert et al. and cited by Goldman offers an instance of such testing. As we have seen, Francis Steen suggests that such "testing out"—he describes it as the ability to "construe" possible outcomes of action in the world—is the evolutionary-adaptive function of narrative, and as we have also seen he argues that one can discern the structure of human narratives in the playfights of rhesus macaque monkeys. Finally, we have also seen, John Frow makes a homologous argument in contending that "aesthetic practices [are] ... *keyings* of the real" (50; italics added). Playfighting, keying, even the etiquette (as the translation of the Confucian notion of *li* [礼]), which I mention in citing Amy Olberding's study of "A Confucian Contribution to Moral Philosophy," all exhibit and rehearse predictable structures of experience and structures of action.

The focus on the future—we saw in David Huron's analysis of the aesthetics of music in Chapter 5—presents one way in which ethics and literary study are imbricated with one another. Like language and literature in my argument in this book, ethics in general—and Robert Coles's presentation of teaching the moral imagination more particularly—is future-oriented: it seeks to devise principles and, probably more significantly, habits of thought and action that will condition and govern future conduct. Since the literary arts take up language as their medium, they are, as we have seen, basically future-oriented. Thus, I noted earlier that Charles Sanders Peirce asserts the "symbol" (as opposed to "icon" or "index") is best understood as the "law that will govern the future" (I, 23). In addition—again, as we have seen—the future-oriented force of discourse is perhaps most readily apparent in the study of speech-act theory, which—in Austin's inaugural articulations (in "Performative Utterances" [*Papers*] and in *How to Do Things with Words*)— focuses on explicit and implicit promising. Promising, I want to suggest—and the promising power of discourse in general—is one of the defining features of human life and human experience. Thus, the well-known biologist E. O. Wilson, in his study of *Consilience*, argues that "contract formation is more than a cultural universal. It is a human trait as characteristic of our species as language and abstract thought, having been constructed from both instinct and high intelligence" (171). At another extreme, Felman begins her study of Austin and Lacanian psychoanalysis with a chapter entitled "The Promising Animal." And, needless to say, promising and the promising power of discourse in general are central constituent elements of ethics.

In a related fashion, Scott Stroud has suggested that the power of literary narrative is to create vicarious experience—or the "transportation" theory of cognitive psychology and the wider theory of Goldman's "simulated minds"— that can shape the future judgments and actions of its readers. Literary narrative, Stroud argues, provides the "subjects" of vicarious experience (i.e., readers and listeners) with a "type of knowledge ... gained by virtue of the literary narrative's aesthetic qualities, which result in a certain type of activity in the reader" including the reader's "identification with the values, beliefs, and/or behaviors of the simulated agent" (20). The "aesthetic qualities" he describes are precisely the result of the features of literary narrative and of literature more generally that I have outlined throughout this book and that the literary scholars I cite throughout this book—Miller, Hartman, Kramnick, North, Clune, Ngai, Regan, etc.—outline in different registers in their work. The features of literature and the "aesthetic qualities" they give rise to, as Stroud argues, create, as we have seen, a "simulation" of experience from which a reader can "construe" possible endings and concerns for fictional stories. Like Steen, Stroud sees literary works serving life beyond the particular knowledge, experiences, and emotions they provoke: serving healthcare and well-being in my defining examples. (Note my citation of Walt Whitman in the book's epigraph promising to be "good health" to his readers;

and in the *Encyclopedia Americana* article defining "literature," which I wrote, I mention that the "*Ayurveda*, the Indian science of medicine, believed that a perfectly structured couplet could clean the air and heal the sick" [22.559].) In Stroud's understanding, the reader uses "imagination to test the viability of certain values and goals in terms of what results they would have for one's life and its flourishing." "Powerful fiction," Stroud concludes, "is useful in getting one to possibly revise, strengthen, or change one's values. Literary narrative, therefore, holds important cognitive value in enabling readers to grow and develop morally" (26). The provoked experience that Stroud describes is a result of all the techniques of literary style—the "features" of literary narrative, which I have been outlining to demonstrate that the discipline of literary studies makes the seeming immediate sensations of experience the objects of analysis. The ability to grasp literary narrative as both aesthetic and extra-aesthetic, like the teaching of literature in the context of medicine, leads to a special kind of reading and attention, which the features and protocols of reading literary narrative help attain.

Beyond "Keying": The Programmed Discipline of Literature

Stroud's argument about the efficacy of literature as part of a moral education nicely complements John Frow's sense of literary genre as "keying" behavior in the world and Francis Steen's similar discernment of the work of "plot" structures in rhesus playfighting. Moreover, it allows us to understand more fully the ways that literature contributes to the education through experience that is at the heart of Aristotle's conception of *phronesis*. Central to Stroud's argument is his notion of "identification." His analysis of identification offers a re-description and re-purposing of Goldman's social-scientific "e-imagination." "What I mean by *identification*," he writes,

is the process by which a reader finds a character depicted in a novel to instantiate values and/or strategies of action (or belief) that are seen as worthy of acceptance by the reader. I do not mean this in merely a descriptive sense of noticing similarities; instead, the sense of identification used here is that in cases of persuasion and belief change. Thus, a judgment is made in such a case of identification about portrayed values and/or strategies that result in the reader changing, reinforcing, or modifying her own held values or strategies of action.

(33–4)

Stroud concludes that readers learn from the identifications provoked by literary narratives during reflection after engagement, what he calls the "*reflective afterlife*" of a literary narrative (36) and what I am calling the "double-take" of literature. (Notice the future orientation of this process.)

The "double-take" of the reflective afterlife of literature can be systematically organized to the ends of *phronesis*, both to particular strategies of "practical reasoning" and to the general end of "well-being" (*eudaimonia*). Moreover, such an organization can allow us to discern more precisely implicit features or aspects of literary texts. Thus, in one example, Dr. Casey Hester led a workshop on medical professionalism in pediatrics, in the organization of which Dr. Vannatta and I joined her. In our country, advanced medical students, residents, and practicing physicians in all specialties must demonstrate competency in professionalism. The Accreditation Council of Graduate Medical Education [ACGME], which administers the assessment of such competencies, designates "Milestones" for various medical specialties (e.g., pediatrics, internal medicine, radiology), which are "competency-based developmental outcomes" (Hester et al. 263). The achievement of these outcomes is mandatory in medical education for students and residents and a part of periodic re-certification of practicing healthcare workers. In pediatrics—Dr. Casey's specialty—six Milestones for competency in professionalism include (1) awareness of personal/professional boundaries, (2) empathy, (3) professional duty, (4) self-awareness, (5) sensitivity to ambiguity, (6) trustworthiness (Hester et al. 264). The goal of articulating Milestones aims at "eliminating the ambiguity of inconsistent definitions of professional objectives [and] assessment" (264). Each Milestone has a description of five levels of competency, from novice to master. Let me offer one example. The ACGME spells out level 1 ("novice") and level 5 ("master") in relation to "empathy," with three progressively accomplished levels in between. (The ACGMD has such descriptions for five levels of each of the six Milestones in pediatrics.)

Level 1. Sees the patients in a "we versus they" framework and is detached and not sensitive to the human needs of the patient and family.

* * *

Level 5. Is a proactive advocate on behalf of individual patients, families, and groups of children in need. (Hester et al. 274)

The job of our workshop was to supply these moral concepts with "semantic depth."

To this end, our workshop took a literary work—Dr. Richard Selzer's "Imelda," a short story that depicts a highly efficient but arrogant surgeon operating in a Central American "medical mission"—and asked participants to reflect upon the quality of various professional behaviors of the literary character of the surgeon. In the workshop, we helped the workshop participants

> to go through the process of seeing that in some areas the surgeon is highly professional, but in others he falls short. Being able to cite specific examples from the story allows participants to sort through the components of what professional behavior is and what it is not—in this case, defined by the six Professionalism Milestones for Pediatrics[, namely empathy, duty, boundaries, self-awareness, ambiguity, trustworthiness]. This helps participants gain clarity in the process of defining professionalism; and it also helps participants in realizing that professionalism is not a dichotomous concept (e.g., one that lends itself to complete disambiguation).
>
> (272)

In many ways, this exercise in developing criteria for discerning and evaluating behavior is very much like the "keying" that Frow and Steen describe in relation to literary genres and literary narratives. Participants are positioned to "construe" future behavior and future judgment. But they do so not by means of the engaged simulated experiences of keying and playfighting, but from the reflective afterlife of experience, a double-take that is beyond the enactments of keyings.

In the workshop, the reflective afterlife of experience is socially organized. Workshop participants are divided into working groups of three to six individuals, who read the Milestone levels together, then engage with Selzer's story in group discussion, and decide through consensus which level of the different professionalism categories best characterizes the behavior of the surgeon. Then, a group discussion of all participants is led by the facilitator, during which individuals and small groups attempt to justify and reconcile any disagreements on appraised Milestone levels. During this discussion, professionalism terms are disambiguated by the facilitator in an attempt to achieve group consensus on a single level (1 through 5) for each of the Milestones for the behaviors occurring in the literary narrative. Following the discussion and the reporting of all groups, the participants are asked to reflect upon how they may use literary narrative in their home institutions to help their own trainees and faculty more precisely understand and articulate the Milestones of medical professionalism by participating in a careful discussion of actions and their assessment of physicians in literary narrative (Hester et al. 270–1). The group- or social-nature of this reflective exercise is of the utmost importance in that it demonstrates to participants that value-judgments are not simple arbitrary and "subjective," but the outcome of shared belief systems, what I have called in this book "habits of thought" and what Mark Platts calls a shared sense of "semantic depth."

I am suggesting that Platts's notion of "semantic depth" arises by means of social reflection. This is clear in the fact that what Wittgenstein calls a "family of meaning" (§77) aggregates around certain semantic meanings, semantic "fields." As I mentioned in the first two chapters—and have occasionally returned to in each of these four chapter-lectures—Platts offers a detailed outline that suggests a systematic disciplinary understanding of "semantic depth." Let me repeat his contention one more time, which I hope, at the end of this book, might be discovered as reordered and redescribed, shimmering with new connotations. "Moral concepts," he notes,

> have a kind of semantic depth. Starting from our austere grasp upon these concepts, together perhaps with some practical grasp upon the conditions of their application, we can proceed to investigate, to experience, the features of the real world answering to these concepts. Precisely because of the realistic account given of these concepts and of our grasp upon them—precisely because they are designed to pick out features of the world of indefinite complexity in ways that transcend our practical understanding—this process of investigation through experience can, and should proceed without end.
>
> (cited by Moore 1145)

Our workshop begins with an "austere grasp" of the Milestones of Pediatric medicine, outlined in the ACGMD protocols, and our workshop participants begin "with some practical grasp upon the conditions of [the applications of these moral concepts]." But the reflective judgments of the represented behaviors of the surgeon allow us to "proceed to investigate, to experience, the features of the real world answering to these concepts." The work of the discipline of literary studies, then—measured in the "austere" protocols of behavior and the staged collective judging of those behaviors in the workshop—"picks out features of [a] world of indefinite complexity." Finally, this is a "process of investigation through experience," the work of the human sciences, which, like all disciplines, occasions social and collaborative reflection. In the human sciences—and in literary studies— such reflection works to develop a better sense of what well-being *is*, and in so doing conditions future worldly action. In other words, the workshop, like the disciplined study of literature, works to develop organizations of experience—structures of experience—in order to grasp with precision and commitment what counts as the ends of worldly action by means of practical wisdom (*phronesis*). In doing so, the workshop helps us understand how literature, like healthcare, works to articulate and deepen promises of human well-being.

Negative Science and Literary Studies

As this should suggest, the work of *phronesis*—like the work of the human sciences—is complex in the same way that "professionalism is not a dichotomous concept (e.g., one that lends itself to complete disambiguation)" (Hester et al. 272) and in the same way that well-being is complex. Moreover, the inability to achieve "complete disambiguation" participates in the "principle of imperfection" that Gould describes in Darwin ("Triumph" 63). In her study of speech-act theory I cited in earlier chapters, *The Scandal of the Speaking Body*, Shoshana Felman describes the opposition between the simplifications found in both positive science and propositional language (the simplicity of constative affirmation and, in fact, "complete disambiguation") and the complexity of performative language (the complex double-take of constative/performative, meaning/force, fact/ value, pure reason/practical reason, and the "scandalous" double-take of spiritual speech/material body, with which Felman names her study).

This opposition can help us understand more fully the ethical import of literary language implicit in literary style. In her study of Austin's work— and especially the "style" of Austin's deadpan humor—Felman writes about simplification. By "simplifications" she means the simplicity of positivism, the simple opposition of true and false in constative propositions, the simple self-evidence ("disambiguation") of the "certainty" of clear and distinct ideas, which Descartes pursues in mathematical physics. In "simplifications," she writes, "the negative has always been understood as what is reducible, what is to be eliminated, that is, as what by definition is opposed, is referred, is *subordinated* to the 'normal' or to the 'positive'" (101). In my catalogue of double-takes just now, simple disambiguation subordinates the second term to the first term (e.g., the performative is subordinated to the constative by the Logical Positivists, value is subordinated to fact in the *Wikipedia* definition of "fact" I cite in Chapter 4, the material body is subordinated to the transcendental truths of language in the dichotomy of Felman's title, *The Scandal of the Speaking Body*).

Against this "simple" definition of negation, Felman asserts a "radical negativity" that she finds in Austin and in speech-act theory more generally, and what the logical positivists describe as the so-called nonsense of literature. "Radical negativity (or 'saying no')," she writes,

> belongs neither to *negation,* nor to *opposition,* nor to *correction* ("normalization"), nor to *contradiction* (of positive and negative, normal and abnormal, "serious" and "unserious," "clarity" and "obscurity")—it belongs precisely to *scandal*: to the scandal of their nonopposition. This scandal [is]... *outside of the alternative,* [it is] a negativity that *is* neither negative nor positive.
>
> (104)

Felman is describing what might be called "negative science" as opposed [absolutely? rhetorically?] to the "positive sciences" of Enlightenment truth (see Schleifer *Intangible* xix). Such a "negative science" is the science of "play"—of Goldman's "make believe" and Cavell's improvisation—rather than the science of "truth" that seems to transcend worldliness in the manner that Errol Morris defines "reality," which I discuss in Chapter 1. And in the context of these four chapter-lectures, the opposition between constative propositional statements and performative statements constitutes the play between seriousness and playfulness, the play and laughter of keying. (Had I moment, I might discuss, philologically in a "close reading," the "semantic depth" of our English word *play* as a physical attribute [e.g., the "play" between ajoining structures (OED, I.5c: "in a joint, mechanism, etc.: freedom or room for movement; the space in or through which a thing can or does move")] and *play* as joyful recreation [e.g., the "play" of enjoyments (OED, II.6a: "exercise or activity engaged in for enjoyment or recreation rather than for a serious or practical purpose; amusement, entertainment, diversion")].) (Notice in this long and convoluted sentence the play of parentheses and square brackets.)

One striking example of Felman's "negativity that *is* neither negative nor positive" (104) is the number zero, which presents a phenomenon that is both part of (internal to) the system of numbers and contiguous with (external to) that system: it is a palpable material example of "double-take." In his rich scholarly history of the number zero, Robert Kaplan describes this "play"—this ambiguity—as "the uncomfortable gap between numbers, which stood for things, and zero, which didn't" (75). Brian Rotman clarifies this further. Zero, he argues, has a

> double aspect ..., as a sign inside the number system and as a meta-sign, a sign-about-signs outside it [a sign, that is, signifying the absence of numerical signs], that has allowed zero to serve as the site of an ambiguity between an empty character (whose covert mysterious quality survives in the connection between "ciphers" and secret codes), and a character for emptiness, a symbol that signifies nothing.
>
> (13)

Such ambiguity, Rotman takes pains to explain, should "be seen not as an error, a confusion to be clarified, but as the inevitable result of a systematic linguistic process" (3; see Exhibit 6.11).

Exhibit 6.11: Systematic Ambiguity

In *Structural Semantics* as we have seen, Greimas describes the way that ambiguity is a constituent feature of "systematic linguist process[es]" rather than a confusion to be clarified. He argues that the "edifice" of language "appears like a construction without plan or clear aim, like a confusion of floors and landings [*paliers*]: derivatives take charge of classes of roots; syntactic 'functions' transform grammatical cases by making them play roles for which they are not appropriate; entire propositions are reduced and described as if they behaved like simple adverbs" (133). Greimas summarizes this situation by asserting that "discourse, conceived as a hierarchy of units of communication fitting into one another, contains in itself the negation of that hierarchy by the fact that the units of communication with different dimensions can be at the same time recognized as equivalent" (82; see Schleifer *Intangible* 52–8 for an elaboration of "the semiotics of negation"). The situation, which Greimas describes, *calls for* the double-take with which I began.

The "systematic linguistic process," which Rotman describes, is the undecidability—the existence "*outside of the alternative*" Felman designates (104)—which is built into systematic linguistic processes themselves, about whether any particular utterance is constative or performative, whether it renews or transforms the work of language, whether it is a meaning or a purported force, whether it is a "direct" or a "simulated"/"vicarious" experience. It is the undecidability of whether the experience a literary work provokes is true or false. "Like zero" in the course of the development of mathematics, Kaplan writes in *The Natural History of Zero*, "numbers were becoming invisible: no longer descriptive of objects but objects—rarefied objects—themselves. 'Three' was once like 'small': it could modify shoes and ships or sealing wax. Now it had detached itself so far from the rabble of things that instead those ephemera participated briefly in its permanence" (75). What is most striking in Kaplan's account in the context of my discussion of the place of modifiers in speech-act theory—and particularly adverbs—is the transformation of numbers functioning like modifiers ("like 'small'") into numbers possessing "positive" constative existence as nouns. Equally striking, I think, is its erasure of both worldliness and experience from knowledge.

This might be clearer if I return to the notion of "nonsense" found in Wittgenstein and the logical positivists. In her study of the relation between aesthetics and ethics in Wittgenstein, Stengel clarifies the use of the term "non-sense" by the logical positivists and by Wittgenstein himself. Thus, she notes that

> the notions of "sense" and "non-sense" are at the core of [Wittgenstein's] *Tractatus* .... It is crucial to keep in mind that the opposite of "sense [Sinn]," according to Wittgenstein, is not "non-sense [Unsinn]" (as is often wrongly suggested) but, rather, "senseless(ness) [sinnlos]"; "senseless" are those propositions that are simply false in logical terms, that depict a fact or state of affairs falsely. Nonsensical sentences, however, can never depict a fact since they do not refer to facts—in the Wittgensteinian sense—at all. Thus, the ethical and the aesthetic fall within the purview of the "nonsensical" dimension of language.
>
> (615)

Thus, the rejection of "nonsense" by the logical positivists, like the rejection of analyses outside of the nomological sciences by many in biomedicine (i.e., the rejection of non-quantifiable sciences such as Gould's homological evolutionary biology, Freud [and Felman's] psychoanalysis, or aesthetics in art and philosophy), is a gesture of dismissal rather than engagement; it is a dismissal of value ("the ethical and the aesthetic"). Moreover, "nonsense," in Stengel's argument, is a version of Felman's "radical negativity (or 'saying no')" (104), and the very fact that it is a worldly act—"saying no" to someone, to some state of affairs—situates it *as* a speech-act, which is always also a worldly act of ethical appraisal.

In addition—although she does not say so—the "scandal" Felman refers to is the scandal of the engagements of the human sciences with the arts, studying:

- fiction, for instance, that is neither true nor not true;
- poetry, such as Yeats's poem, that creates the "impersonal feeling" I described earlier that nevertheless feels overwhelming;
- music, that is a "third thing," as Viktor Zuckerkandl notes, that is neither physical nor psychological;
- impressionist paintings, whose impressions seem created neither by artist nor by viewer; and
- the very "institutional fact" of literature—and of literary and speech genres more specifically and experience and aesthetics discussed in Chapter 5—that, as Felman says elsewhere in her book, "is no longer simply a preexisting *substance*, but an *act*, that is a dynamic movement of modification of reality" (51).

The "reality" that is modified is the reality of institutional facts, habits of thought, spaces of meaning, habits of action: it is the "reality" of value. In this way, then, the discipline of literary studies can engage and interact with acts, which as worldly events are taken up to systematically describe the complexity of human experience and the complexity of well-being.

Some Final Double-Takes

Needless to say, as Northrop Frye argued many years ago, disciplinary language is never "simple" precisely because it seeks to look beyond everyday intuitions of experience (including the "intuition" that experience itself is "immediate") to encounter "reality"—even if it is wise not to forget, as I suggested in Chapter 1, the practical wisdom of the "reluctant realism" Noam Chomsky articulated (see Exhibit 1.8: Reluctant Realism). And certainly the language of speech-act theory—in Felman, in Wittgenstein, in the obscurity of the "negative science" I am presenting in the present chapter—needs the work of discipline to achieve its insights. Remember the catalogue of the meanings of "discipline" with which I began Chapter 3, the "challenges of discipline" as I called them: how discipline builds bridges, resists instinct, creates freedom, institutes intellectual insight, professionalizes knowledge, and, although I did not include this in my original catalogue even as I have pursued it throughout this book, how it creates homological cross-disciplinary work.

But along with the "work" of the discipline of literary studies, there is the pleasures of literature as well, the transformations of experience I described earlier in this chapter, the pleasure of positioning ourselves:

- to "see things differently," as Austin says, "yet perhaps we know no more and are no cleverer"; or,

- as Wittgenstein says, to "*see* that [the image of a face] has not changed; and yet I see it differently"; or,

- as Gould says, quoting T. S. Eliot, "to return to a place well known and see it for the first time"; or finally

- as Rita Felski said, as noted at the beginning of this book, in literature "we rediscover things as we know them to be, yet reordered and redescribed, shimmering in a transformed light."

As I argued earlier, this catalogue of the work or results of encountering literature gives rise to *disciplined attention* that grows out of systematic formal procedures that implicitly inhabit even the "mere description," which Hjelmslev contrasts with "exact and generalizing treatment." It has been the work of these chapter-lectures to make explicit those procedures and the language-events, to which they give rise. I should finally add that this catalogue seems to indicate in addition to the knowledge that the discipline of literary studies creates, it also engages the power or force of its "promise of happiness"—often an *intergenerational* promise—I mentioned in Chapter 5.

Still, it is the possibility of knowledge along with power—the *possibility* of the constative about which I, like Felman (and even Austin), speak somewhat negatively—that inhabits disciplinary study. Let me return to Wallace Stevens's poem "The Plain Sense of Things," which we shared together in Chapter 5.

> It is difficult even to choose the adjective
> For this blank cold, this sadness without cause.
> The great structure has become a minor house.
> No turban walks across the lessened floors. (502)

Perhaps it is the formal elegance of Stevens's figure, "No turban walks across the lessened floors"—that element of "style," which, as Stengel notes, "adds value to neutral propositions, a 'voice' to the text" (617)—which marks the ways that literary texts respond momentarily to what Stephen Regan calls the "nothingness" that Keats faces in his poem: "turban" and "lessened floors," remind us of "the great structures"—like the structures of intellectual disciplines, like the structures of experience, like the complex structure of language Greimas describes—which we build to make our shared lives and our well-being better even so.

Conclusion: *Phronesis* and *Eudaimonia*

In conclusion to this book, I'd like to return to the interdisciplinarity of the health humanities, which had been a counterpoint to my arguments during my lecture series at the Harbin Institute of Technology on the cold winter days of 2020 and a counterpoint to the chapters of this book as well. After all, as I note in Chapter 1, it has been my engagement with healthcare workers and healthcare students that has made me aware of the need to articulate, as clearly as I can, the force and meaning of the human sciences, how they can homologically inflect, so to speak, knowledges in other disciplines. So, then, I end with a quotation from the book Jerry Vannatta and I wrote, *The Chief Concern of Medicine*. "The privileged narratives of literature," we wrote,

> like caring for people in ill health, are a central aspect of all organized human communities. In fact, there is a wealth of evidence in evolutionary cognition that narrative organizations of cognition are inherited strategies of understanding in human experience. People tell one another stories just as they care for the health and well-being of one another, and such storytelling, like practices of healing, is at times everywhere taken to be sacred, honorable, important, a special gift and grace that is part of our human inheritance. Like healing and health care, the power of storytelling is often taken to be mysterious. As Anatole Broyard says in his posthumous book, *Intoxicated by My Illness*, "all cures are partly talking cures. Every patient needs mouth-to-mouth resuscitation, for talk is the kiss of life." This description of "talking cures"—Broyard of course is using Sigmund Freud's early description of his medical practice—emphasizes the

fact that while medicine often aspires to the status of an exact and methodological science, it is at the same time engaged at the level of person-to-person encounter in a manner similar to the impression of a person-to-person encounter that narrative storytelling enacts and literature often provokes. This real-life engagement in medicine—like its representations in literature—entails the *honor, imagination,* and *value* that the humanities attempts to comprehend in the goal-oriented understanding of narrative.

(7)

Such "honor, imagination, and value" might allow us to more fully comprehend the vague—but as Sam Harris says "indispensable" (24)—notion of well-being (*eudaimonia*).

The Philosophical Physician. In his "intellectual biography" of Sigmund Freud, Joel Whitebook describes the "materialist and empiricist vein" of Freud's work as the quest of "philosophical anthropology ... pursued ... in a specific mode—namely, as what the French called a *médicin-philosoph*, a philosophical physician" (99). The example he sets forth is that of John Locke, "who was himself a physician"; "Locke ... argued," Whitebook notes, "that, instead of investigating formal logic, one ought to examine the workings of the empirical mind." People like Locke and Freud assumed that "these sciences"—and Whitebook explicitly calls them "the human sciences"—"were simultaneously scientific and philosophical .... They were philosophical in that the rejected scientism—that is, the claim that empirical science exhausts the domain of legitimate knowledge .... And they were scientific in that they rejected philosophy's pretensions at self-sufficiency." Thus, an Enlightenment figure like "Diderot believed, for example, that because the physician was on *intimate terms with our creaturely existence*, he possessed a privileged mode of access into the realm of human nature" (100–1). Freud found such a philosophical physician in his teacher, Jean-Martin Charcot. For Charcot, Freud wrote, "'the apparent chaos presented by the continual repetition of the same symptoms ... gave way to order,' and the 'nosological picture [i.e., the classification of diseases] emerged.' Like an Aristotelian *phronimos*, a man of practical reason, Charcot would perceive the universal—the 'type' as he called it—in the particular" (Whitebook 116–17).

As a "philosophical physician," uniting both creaturely materialism and a quest for a sense of human nature, Freud has become a significant figure in literary studies, as perhaps citations throughout this book from

Shoshana Felman's psychoanalytic/speech-act/literary study suggests. Rita Felski describes this combination of materialism and philosophy in her definition of literature more explicitly: "we are eternally enmeshed within semiotic and social networks of meaning that shape and sustain our being," she writes, and such "semiotic material is ... *configured* by the literary text, which refashions and restructures it, distancing it from its prior uses and remaking its meanings" (85, 102). Thus, it is no accident that Freud, as a philosophical physician, takes up a prominent role in the discipline of literary studies despite his shortcomings. In his biography, Whitebook offers a strong psychoanalytical critique of Freud's shortcomings, his sexist-patriarchal prejudices and "mistakes in his thinking[, which are] manifold and all-too-familiar" (170). The goal of re-examining Freud's life and culture, Whitebook argues, is to "critically reappropriate" Freud's ideas (170). Similarly, the goal of the work of the health humanities—which refashions received ideas of literary studies more generally—is to critically reappropriate the notions of health and wisdom (*eudaimonia* and *phronesis*)—the notion of well-being—in the active absorption of experience (see Exhibit 6.12).

Exhibit 6.12: Well-Being, Health, Aesthetics

Although my touchstone throughout has been Aristotle, one can find a sense of well-being in other cultures besides Western culture. In China, for instance, there is an ancient notion of *le. Le* (乐) "is a word carrying several different meanings [in Chinese]. Firstly, it expresses the feeling of joy, happiness, optimism and well-being. Secondly, it can describe the melody of music, the sound in harmony. Moreover, which is not well known by people, the original meaning of 'Le' in ancient times, is basically the well-being gained when recovering from illness and when finally healing. Gradually, 'Le' evolved into a general concept which not only expresses well-being from owning a healthy body, but extends to the meaning of well-being derived from material and spiritual wealth" (Yang and Zhou 182). In this term—perhaps more fully than in *eudaimonia*—"well-being" encompasses health and aesthetics, the worldly work of literature and healthcare.

* * *

I've named this concluding section with two terms from Aristotle, the "practical wisdom" of *phronesis* and the "happiness" or "well-being" of *eudaimonia*, even if in the end I supplemented them with *le* (乐). *Phronesis*, as I have suggested throughout this book, is surely an ethical enterprise: practical wisdom does work in the world, as Edward Said mentioned, and its wisdom seeks to discern and add value to the world. But the happiness of *eudaimonia*—and also of *le*—is also worldly: it includes the widening of sensibility, understanding, and affect, melody and harmony, that I have suggested is the work of aesthetics, the (speech-act) promise of happiness Stendhal asserts as the essence of the arts, and finally the well-being by which Sam Harris defines value and the intergenerational caring in which Walter Benjamin recovers value. It is not an easy happiness, as I hope my chapter-lecture on aesthetic genres in relation to death makes clear. But it is a happiness, like the happiness we often find in *phronesis*, that participates in Wittgenstein's "lighting up" (§118) of experience, knowledge, and action, which the discipline of literary studies allows us to discern and disseminate.

WORKS CITED

Almeida, Felipe. "Vicarious Learning and Institutional Economics." *Journal of Economic Issues*, vol. 45, 2011, pp. 839–55.

Altieri, Charles, "Why Pound's Imagist Poems Still Matter." In *Ezra Pound in the Present: Essays on Pound's Contemporaneity*, edited by Paul Stasi and Josephine Park. Bloomsbury Academic, 2017, pp. 3–20.

Austin, J. R. *How to Do Things with Words*. Harvard University Press, 1960.

Austin, J. R. *Philosophical Papers*. Oxford University Press, 1979.

Bachelard, Gaston. *The New Scientific Spirit*. Translated by Arthur Goldhammer. Becon Press, 1984.

Bakhtin, Mikhail. *Speech Genres and Other Later Essays*. Translated by Vern McGee. University of Texas Press, 1987.

Bandura, Albert. *Social Learning Theory*. Aldine Atherton, 1971.

Barreca, Regina. "Writing as Voodoo: Sorcery, Hysteria, and Art." In *Death and Representation*, edited by Sarah Webster Goodwin and Elisabeth Bronfen. Johns Hopkins University Press, 1993, pp. 175–90.

Barthes, Roland. *Elements of Semiology*. Translated by Annette Lavers and Colin Smith. Hill and Wang, 1967.

Benjamin, Walter. *Illuminations*. Translated by Harry Zohn. Schocken, 1969.

Benjamin, Walter. *One-Way Street*. In *Selected Writings, Volume 1 1913–1936*, edited by Marcus Bullock and Michael Jennings; translated by Edmund Jephocott and Kingley Shorter. Harvard University Press, 1996, pp. 444–88.

Benjamin, Walter. *The Arcades Project*. Edited by Rolf Tiedemann; translated by Howard Eiland and Kevin McLaughlin. Harvard University Press, 1999.

Berlant, Lauren. *Cruel Optimism*. Duke University Press, 2011.

Berlant, Lauren. "Structures of Unfeeling: 'Mysterious Skin.'" *International Journal of Politics, Culture, and Society*, vol. 28, no. 3, 2015, pp. 191–213.

Blanchot, Maurice. *The Writing of the Disaster*. Translated by Ann Smock. University of Nebraska Press, 1986.

Boyd, Brian. *On the Origin of Stories: Evolution, Cognition, and Fiction*. Harvard University Press, 2009.

Bradbury, Malcolm and James McFarlane. "The Name and Nature of Modernism." In *Modernism: 1890–1930*, edited by Malcolm Bradbury and James McFarlane. Penguin Books, 1976, pp. 19–55.

Brody, Howard. *Stories of Sickness*. Second edition. Oxford University Press, 2003.

Casti, John. *Complexification: Explaining a Paradoxical World through the Science of Surprise*. Harper Perennial, 1995.

Cavell, Stanley. *Philosophy the Day after Tomorrow*. Harvard University Press, 2005.

Works Cited

Chalmers, David. "The Puzzle of Conscious Experience." *Scientific American*, vol. 273, no. 6, 1995, pp. 80–6.

Chalmers, David. *The Conscious Mind: In Search of a Fundamental Theory*. Oxford University Press, 1996.

Charon, Rita and Maura Spiegel. "On Conveying Pain/On Conferring Form." *Literature and Medicine,* vol. 24, 2005, pp. vi–ix.

Clune, Michael. *Writing against Time*. Stanford University Press, 2013.

Coles, Robert. *The Call of Stories: Teaching and the Moral Imagination*. Houghton Mifflin Harcourt Publishing, 1989.

Comas, James. *Between Politics and Ethics: Toward a Vocative History of English Studies*. Southern Illinois University Press, 2006.

Culler, Jonathan. "Convention and Meaning; Derrida and Austin." In *Contemporary Literary Criticism: Literary and Cultural Studies*, fourth edition, edited by Robert Con Davis and Ronald Schleifer, Longman, 1998, pp. 331–43.

Currie, Mark. "Event." In *Future Theory: A Handbook to Critical Concepts*, edited by Patricia Waugh and Marc Botha. Bloomsbury Academic, 2021, pp. 225–36.

Damasio, Antonio. *The Feeling of What Happens: Body and Emotion in the Making of Consciousness*. Harcourt, 1999.

Damasio, Antonio. *Self Comes to Mind: Constructing the Conscious Brain*. Vintage, 2012.

Damrosch, David. "Foreword." In *Anatomy of Criticism*, edited by Northrop Frye. Princeton University Press, 2020, pp. ix–xviii.

Davidson, Donald. *Essays on Actions and Events*. Oxford University Press, 1980.

Davis, R. C. and Ronald Schleifer, editors. *Contemporary Literary Criticism: Literary and Cultural Studies*. Fourth edition. Longman, 1998.

De Man, Paul. "Semiology and Rhetoric." *Diacritics*, vol. 3, no. 3, 1973, pp. 27–33.

Derrida, Jacques. "Signature Event Context." *Glyph*, vol. 1, 1977, pp. 172–97.

Donald, Merlin. *Origins of the Modern Mind: Three Stages in the Evolution of Culture and Cognition*. Harvard University Press,1991.

Donne, John. "Death, Be Not Proud." https://www.poetryfoundation.org/poems/44107/holy-sonnets-death-be-not-proud. Accessed September 17, 2020. [I have modified the poem to its original punctuation while maintaining the modern English spellings of this version.]

Doyle, Roddy. *The Woman Who Walked into Doors*. Viking, 1996.

Dunbar, Robin. *Grooming, Gossip, and the Origin of Language*. Harvard University Press, 1996.

Edson, Margaret. *Wit*. Faber and Faber, 1999.

Emery, Nathan and David Amaral. "The Role of the Amygdala in Primate Social Cognition." In *Cognitive Neuroscience of Emotion*, edited by Richard Lane and Lynn Nadel. Oxford University Press, 2000, pp. 156–91.

"Fact." https://en.wikipedia.org/wiki/Fact. Accessed September 10, 2020.

Felman, Shoshana. *The Scandal of the Speaking Body: Don Juan with J. L. Austin, or Seduction in Two Languages*. Translated by Catherine Porter. Stanford University Press, 2003.

Felski, Rita. *Uses of Literature*. Blackwell, 2008.

Frow, John. "'Reproducibles, Rubrics, and Everything You Need': Genre Theory Today." PMLA, vol. 122, 2007, pp. 1626–34.

Frow, John. *Genre*. The New Critical Idiom Series. Routledge, 2015.

Frye, Northrop. "The Function of Criticism at the Present Time" (1949). In *Contemporary Literary Criticism: Literary and Cultural Studies*, fourth edition, edited by Robert Con Davis and Ronald Schleifer. Longman, 1998, pp. 39–56.

Gagnier, Regenia. *The Insatiability of Human Wants: Economics and Aesthetics in Market Society*. University of Chicago Press, 2000.

Gilbert, D. T., Gill M. J., and Wilson, T. D. "The Future is Now: Temporal Correction in Affective Forecasting." *Organizational Behavoir and Human Decision Processes*, vol. 88, 2002, pp. 430–44.

Goffman, Erving. *Frame Analysis: An Essay on the Organisation of Experience*. Basil Blackwell, 1974.

Goldman, Alvin. *Simulating Minds: The Philosophy, Psychology, and Neuroscience of Mindreading*. Oxford University Press, 2006.

Gould, Stephen Jay. "Evolution and the Triumph of Homology, or Why History Matters." *American Scientist*, vol. 74, no. 1, January–February 1986, pp. 60–9.

Gould, Stephen Jay. *Wonderful Life: The Burgess Shale and the Nature of History*. Norton, 1989.

Gould, Stephen Jay and Elizabeth Vrba. "Exaptation: A Missing Term in the Science of Form." *Paleobiology*, vol. 8, 1982, pp. 4–15.

Greimas, A. J. "La linguistique structural et la poétique." In *Du Sens*. Seuil, 1970. This essay does not appear in the English translation of *On Meaning*.

Greimas, A. J. *Structural Semantics: An Attempt at a Method*. Translated by Daniele McDowell, Ronald Schleifer and Alan Velie. University of Nebraska Press, 1983.

Hamilton, Andy. "The Aesthetics of Imperfection." *Philosophy*, vol. 65, 1990, pp. 323–40.

Hardcastle, Valerie Grey. *The Myth of Pain*. MIT Press, 1999.

Harman, Gilbert. "The Inference to the Best Explanation." *Philosophical Review*, vol. 74, 1965, pp. 88–95.

Harpham, Geoffrey. "Roots, Races, and the Return to Philology." *Representations*, vol. 106, 2009, pp. 34–62.

Harris, Sam. *The Moral Landscape: How Science Can Determine Human Values*. Transworld Publishers. 2010.

Hester, Casey and Ronald Schleifer. "Enhancing Physician Empathy: Optimizing Learner Potential for Narrative Transportation." *Enthymema*, vol. 16, 2016, pp. 105–18. This is a special issue, "Medicine and Narrative" edited by Elena Fratto.

Hester, Casey, Jerry Vannatta and Ronald Schleifer. "Medical Professionalism: Using Literary Narrative to Explore and Evaluate Medical Professionalism." In *New Directions in Literature and Medicine Studies*, edited by Stephanie Hilger. Reprinted in Schleifer and Vannatta, *Literature and Medicine*. Palgrave, 2019, pp. 263–78.

Herwitz, Daniel. "The New Spaces of Modernist Painting." In *The Cambridge History of Modernism*, edited by Vincent Sherry. Cambridge University Press, 2016, pp. 181–99.

Hjelmslev, Louis. *Prolegomena to a Theory of Language*. Translated by Francis Whitfield. University of Wisconsin Press, 1961.

Honda, Kiyoshi, Tomoyoshi Kurita, Yuki Kakita and Shinji Maeda. "Physiology of the Lips and Modeling of Lip Gestures." *Journal of Phonetics*, vol. 23, 1995, pp. 243–54.

Works Cited

Horkheimer, Max and Theodor Adorno. *Dialectics of Enlightenment.* Translated by Edmund Jephcott. Stanford University Press, 2002. [Earlier translation by John Cumming: Seabury Press, 1972].

Huron, David. *Sweet Anticipation: Music and the Psychology of Expectation.* MIT Press, 2008.

Jacobs, Courtney and Ronald Schleifer. "Literary Genre and Emotional Experience: The After-Effects of Intergenerational Trauma in the Neo-Slave Narrative of Toni Morrison's *Beloved.*" *Swiss Papers in English Language and Literature,* vol. 38, 2019, pp. 145–66.

Jay, Martin. *Songs of Experience: Modern American and European Variations on a Universal Theme.* University of California Press, 2005.

Joyce, James. *Ulysses.* Modern Library, 1961.

Joyce, James. *The Portrait of the Artist as a Young Man.* Viking, 1966.

Kaplan, Robert. *The Nothing That Is: A Natural History of Zero.* Oxford University Press, 1999.

Kramnick, Jonathan. *Paper Minds: Literature and the Ecology of Consciousness.* University of Chicago Press, 2018.

Kuhns, Richard. *Structures of Experience: Essays on the Affinity between Philosophy and Literature.* Basic Books, 1970.

Labatut, Benjamin. *When We Cease to Understand the World.* New York Review Books, 2021.

Larkin, Philip. "Aubade." *Poetry Foundation.* https://www.poetryfoundation.org/poems/48422/aubade-56d229a6e2f07. Accessed August 8, 2021.

Latour, Bruno. *We Have Never Been Modern.* Translated by Catherine Porter. Harvard University Press, 1993.

Leys, Ruth. "The Turn to Affect: A Critique." *Critical Inquiry,* vol. 37, 2011, pp. 434–72.

Locke, John. *Essay Concerning Human Understanding.* Clarendon Press, 1975.

Locke, John. *A Letter Concerning Toleration.* Edited by James Tully. Hackett Publishing, 1983.

Marx, Karl and Frederick Engels. *Manifesto of the Communist Party.* Translated by Samuel Moore. In Marx/Engels *Selected Works,* Vol. 1. Progress Publishers, 1969, pp. 98–137. https://www.marxists.org/archive/marx/works/download/pdf/Manifesto.pdf Accessed August 4, 2021.

Massumi, Brian. *Parables for the Virtual: Movement, Affect, Sensation.* Duke University Press, 2002.

Miller, Carolyn. "Genre as Social Action." In *Genre and the New Rhetoric,* edited by Aviva Freedman and Peter Medway. Taylor & Francis, 1994, pp. 23–42.

Miller, J. Hillis. "Presidential Address 1986. The Triumph of Theory, the Resistance to Reading, and the Question of the Material Base." *PMLA,* vol. 102, 1987, pp. 281–91.

Miller, J. Hillis. "Narrative." In *Critical Terms for Literary Study,* edited by Frank Lentricchia and Thomas McLaughlin. University of Chicago Press, 1995, pp. 66–79.

Miller, J. Hillis. *On Literature.* Routledge, 2002.

Moore, Michael. "Moral Reality." *Wisconsin Law Review*, vol. 1982, no. 6, 1982, pp. 1061–156.

Morris, David. *The Culture of Pain*. University of California Press, 1993.

Morris, Errol. *The Ashtray (Or the Man Who Denied Reality)*. University of Chicago Press, 2018.

Moscoso, Javier. *Pain: A Cultural History*. Translated by Sarah Thomas and Paul House. Palgrave, 2012.

Ngai, Sianne. *Theory of the Gimmick: Aesthetic Judgment and Capitalist Form*. Harvard University Press, 2020.

Nietzsche, Friedrich. *On the Genealogy of Morals*, in *On the Genealogy of Morals and Ecco Homo*. Translated by Walter Kaufmann. Vintage, 1967.

North, Douglas. "Institutions." *The Journal of Economic Perspectives*, vol. 5, 1991, pp. 97–112.

North, Joseph. *Literary Criticism: A Concise Political History*. Harvard University Press, 2017.

Norton Anthology of English Literature. Third edition, volume 2. Edited by M. H. Abrams, George Ford and David Daiches. Norton, 1974.

Nussbaum, Martha. *Love's Knowledge: Essays on Philosophy and Literature*. Oxford University Press, 1990.

Olberding, Amy. "Etiquette: A Confucian Contribution to Moral Philosophy." *Ethics*, vol. 126, 2016, pp. 422–46.

Peirce, Charles Sanders. *Collected Papers*. Vols. 1–6. Edited by C. Hartshorne and P. Weiss. Harvard University Press, 1931–1935.

Pellegrino, Edmund. "Toward a Virtue-Based Normative Ethics for the Health Professions." *Kennedy Institute of Ethics Journal*, vol. 5, 1995, pp. 253–77.

Phelan, James. *Narrative as Rhetoric: Techniques, Audiences, Ethics, Ideology*. Ohio State University Press, 1996.

Polkinghorne, Donald. *Practice and the Human Sciences: The Case for a Judgment-Based Practice of Care*. SUNY Press, 2004.

Putnam, Hilary. *Ethics without Ontology*. Kindle edition. Harvard University Press, 2004.

Qian, Yingyi, "How Reform Worked in China." In *In Search of Prosperity: Analytic Narratives on Economic Growth*, edited by Dan Rodrik. Princeton University Press, 2003, pp. 297–333.

Qian, Zhongshu, *Limited Views: Essays on Ideas and Letters*. Edited and translated by Ronald Egan. Harvard University Press, 1998.

Regan, Stephen. *The Sonnet*. Oxford University Press, 2019.

Richardson, Alan. *The Neural Sublime: Cognitive Theories, Romantic Texts*. Johns Hopkins University Press, 2010.

Rotman, Brian. *Signifying Nothing: The Semiotics of Zero*. Stanford University Press, 1987.

Russell, Bertrand. *Mysticism and Logic*. Doubleday Anchor, n.d. [1917].

Sacks, Oliver. *Seeing Voices: A Journey into the World of the Deaf*. University of California Press, 1989.

Sacks, Oliver. "The Case of the Colorblind Painter." In *An Anthropologist on Mars*. Vintage, 1996, pp. 3–41.

Works Cited

Sacks, Oliver. *Musicophilia: Tales of Music and the Brain.* Knopf, 2007.

Said, Edward. "The Politics of Knowledge." In *Contemporary Literary Criticism: Literary and Cultural Studies,* fourth edition, edited by Robert Con Davis and Ronald Schleifer, Longman, 1998, pp. 157–66.

Said, Edward. *Humanism and Democratic Criticism.* Columbia University Press, 2004.

Saussure, Ferdinand de. *Course in General Linguistics.* Translated by Roy Harris. Open Court Press, 1986.

Saussy, Haun. "The Prestige of Writing: *Wen,* Letter, Picture, Image, Ideography." In *Great Walls of Discourse and Other Adventures in Cultural China.* Harvard University Press, 2001, pp. 35–74.

Schleifer, Ronald. *A. J. Greimas and the Nature of Meaning: Linguistics, Semiotics, and Discourse Theory.* Routledge; University of Nebraska Press, 1987.

Schleifer, Ronald. *Rhetoric and Death: The Language of Modernism and Postmodern Discourse Theory.* University of Illinois Press, 1990.

Schleifer, Ronald. "Literature." *Encyclopedia Americana.* Fifteenth edition, vol. 22, 1998, pp. 559–60.

Schleifer, Ronald. *Analogical Thinking: Post-Enlightenment Understanding in Language, Collaboration, and Interpretation.* University of Michigan Press, 2000.

Schleifer, Ronald. *Modernism and Time: The Logic of Abundance in Literature, Science, and Culture, 1880–1930.* Cambridge University Press, 2000.

Schleifer, Ronald. *Intangible Materialism: The Body, Scientific Knowledge, and the Power of Language.* University of Minnesota Press, 2009.

Schleifer, Ronald. "Modalities of Science: Narrative, Phronesis, and the Practices of Medicine," *Danish Yearbook of Philosophy,* vol. 44, 2009, pp. 77–101.

Schleifer, Ronald. *Pain and Suffering.* Routledge, 2014.

Schleifer, Ronald. *A Political Economy of Modernism: Literature, Post-Classical Economics, and the Lower Middle-Class.* Cambridge University Press, 2018.

Schleifer, Ronald. "The Aesthetics of Pain: Semiotics and Affective Comprehension in Music, Literature, and Sensate Experience." *Configurations,* vol. 26, 2018, pp. 471–91.

Schleifer, Ronald. "Modernism as Gesture: The Experience of Music, Samuel Beckett, and Performed Bewilderment." *Criticism,* vol. 61, 2019, pp. 73–96.

Schleifer, Ronald. "The Role of Narrative Structures and Discursive Genres in Healthcare Education and Practice." In *Narrative Medicine in Education and Practice,* edited by Anders Juhl Rasmussen, Anne-Marie Mai, Helle Ploug Hansen. Gads Forlag, 2021, pp. 37–50.

Schleifer, Ronald and Jerry Vannatta. *The Chief Concern of Medicine: The Integration of the Medical Humanities and Narrative Knowledge into Medical Practices.* University of Michigan Press, 2013.

Schleifer, Ronald and Jerry Vannatta. *Literature and Medicine: A Practical and Pedagogical Guide.* Palgrave, 2019.

Schleifer, Ronald, Robert Con Davis and Nancy Mergler. *Culture and Cognition: The Boundaries of Literary and Scientific Inquiry.* Cornell University Press, 1992.

Searle, John. *Speech Acts.* Cambridge University Press, 1969.

Shakir, Mubeen, Jerry Vannatta and Ronald Schleifer. "Effect of College *Literature and Medicine* on the Practice of Medicine." *Journal of the Oklahoma State Medical Association*, vol. 110, 2017, pp. 593–600.

Shem, Samuel. *The House of God*. Berkley, 2010.

Shklovsky, Viktor, "Art as Technique." Translated by Lee T. Lemon and Marion J. Reis. In *Contemporary Literary Criticism: Literary and Cultural Studies*, fourth edition, edited by Robert Con Davis and Ronald Schleifer, Longman, 1998, pp. 54–66.

Shouse, Eric. "Feeling, Emotion, Affect." *M/C Journal*, vol. 8, December 2005. www.journal.media-culture.org.au/0512/03-shouse.php. Accessed September 14, 2020.

Spinks, Lee. "Thinking the Post-Human: Literature, Affect, and the Politics of Style." *Textual Practice*, vol. 15, no. 1, 2001, pp. 23–46.

Spolsky, Ellen. *The Contracts of Fiction: Cognition, Culture, Community*. Oxford University Press, 2015.

Stalling, Jonathan and Ronald Schleifer. "Unpacking the Mo Yan Archive: Actor-Network Translation Studies and the Chinese Literature Translation Archive." In *A Century of Chinese Literature in Translation (1919–2019): English Publication and Reception*, edited by Leah Gerber and Lintao Qi. Routledge, 2021, pp. 23–40.

Steen, Francis. "The Paradox of Narrative Thinking." *Journal of Cultural and Evolutionary Psychology*, vol. 3, 2005, pp. 87–105.

Stendhal. *On Love*. Translated by B. C. J. G. Knight. Penguin Books, 1975.

Stengel, Kathrin. "Ethics as Style: Wittgenstein's Aesthetic Ethics and Ethical Aesthetics." *Poetics Today*, vol. 25, 2004, pp. 609–25.

Stevens, Wallace. *Collected Poems*. Alfred Knopf, 1971.

Stroud, Scott. "Simulation, Subjective Knowledge, and the Cognitive Value of Literary Narrative." *Journal of Aesthetic Education*, vol. 42, 2008, pp. 19–41.

Sweet, Sam. "A Boy with No Birthday Turns Sixty: The Long and Tangled History of Alfred E. Neuman." *The Paris Review*, March 3, 2016. https://www.theparisreview.org/blog/2016/03/03/a-boy-with-no-birthday-turns-sixty/. Accessed January 21, 2022.

Taylor, Charles. *Sources of the Self: The Making of the Modern Identity*. Harvard University Press, 1989.

Taylor, Charles, David Carr and Paul Ricoeur. "Discussion: Ricoeur on Narrative." In *On Paul Ricoeur: Narrative and Interpretation*, edited by David Wood. Routledge, 1991, pp. 160–88. (Taylor's contribution appears on pp. 174–79.)

Trilling, Lionel. *The Liberal Imagination*. Viking, 1950.

Veblen, Thornstein. *Absentee Ownership and Business Enterprise in Recent Times* [1923]. Beacon Press, 1967.

Veblen, Thornstein. *The Place of Science in Modern Civilization and Other Essays* [1919]; published as *Veblen on Marx, Race, Science and Economics*. Capricorn Books, 1969.

Vermeule, Blakey. *Why Do We Care about Literary Characters?* Johns Hopkins University Press, 2010.

Wang, Tiao and Ronald Schleifer. *Modernist Poetics in China: Consumerist Economics and Chinese Literary Modernism.* Palgrave-Macmillan, 2022.

Warren, V. I. "Feminist Directions in Medical Ethics." *Hypatia*, vol. 4, 1989, pp. 73–87.

Waugh, Patricia. "Paradigm." In *Future Theory: A Handbook to Critical Concepts*, edited by Patricia Waugh and Marc Botha. Bloomsbury Academic, 2021, pp. 93–113.

Waugh, Patricia and Marc Botha. "Introduction." In *Future Theory: A Handbook to Critical Concepts*, edited by Patricia Waugh and Marc Botha. Bloomsbury Academic, 2021, pp. 1–38.

Weber, Samuel. *Institution and Interpretation.* University of Minnesota Press, 1987.

Weiner, Jonathan. *The Beak of the Finch.* Vintage, 1995.

Whitebook, Joel. *Freud: An Intellectual Biography.* Cambridge University Press, 2017.

Wiener, Norbert. *Cybernetics.* MIT Press, 1961.

Williams, Raymond. *Marxism and Literature.* Oxford University Press, 1977.

Wilson, E. O. *Consilience: The Unity of Knowledge.* Knopf, 1998.

Wittgenstein, Ludwig. *Philosophical Investigations.* Revised fourth edition. Translated by G. E. M. Anscombe, P. M. S. Hacker, and Joachim Schulte. Blackwell Publishing, 2009. https://edisciplinas.usp.br/pluginfile.php/4294631/mod_resource/content/0/Ludwig%20Wittgenstein%2C%20P.%20M.%20S.%20Hacker%2C%20Joachim%20Schulte.%20Philosophical%20Investigations.%20Wiley.pdf. Accessed September 19, 2020.

Woolf, Virginia. *Mrs. Dalloway.* Harvest Books, 1953.

Wu, Nicholas. "Trump Compares Pete Buttigieg to Alfred E. Neuman of MAD." *USA Today*, May 11, 2019. https://www.usatoday.com/story/news/politics/2019/05/11/trump-compares-buttigieg-alfred-e-neuman-mad-magazine-fame/1174608001/. Accessed September 12, 2020.

Yang, Defeng and Zhou Han. "The Comparison between Chinese and Western Well-Being." *Open Journal of Social Sciences*, vol. 5, no. 11, 2011, pp. 181–8. https://www.scirp.org/journal/apercitationdetails.aspx?paperid=80745&JournalID=2430. Accessed December 7, 2021.

Zahle, Julie, "Methodological Holism in the Social Sciences." *The Stanford Encyclopedia of Philosophy* (Summer 2016 Edition). Edward N. Zalta (ed.), URL = <https://plato.stanford.edu/archives/sum2016/entries/holism-social/>. Accessed August 7, 2021.

Zhu, Liya. "The Language and Vision of Qian Zhongsju: Introduction to 'Chinese Poetry and Chinese Painting,' 'On Happiness,' and 'A Prejudice.'" *Genre*, vol. 43, 2010, pp. 219–37.

Zuckerkandl, Victor. *Sound and Symbol: Music and the External World.* Translated by Willard Trask. Princeton University Press, 1969.

Zunshine, Lisa. *Why We Read Fiction: Theory of Mind and the Novel.* Ohio State University Press, 2006.

INDEX

Note. An open access version of this book is available at Bloomsbury Open Access. The pdf file is available for fine-tuned indexical searches.

Accreditation Council of Graduate Medical Education (ACGME) 238
  pediatrics, Milestone levels 238–40
  protocols 240
Adorno, Theodor 57, 106–7, 125
  Dialectics of Enlightenment 57, 107
aesthetics
  active absorption 7–8, 30, 64, 93, 105, 189, 226–7, 229, 249
  art narratives 25, 90–1, 148, 173, 175–7, 180, 210, 212, 223, 226, 230
  belletristic criticism 31
  Clune's perception 204
  cultural studies *vs.* 49–50
  of dance 217
  death 184
  defamiliarization 70
  definition 2, 161
  deployment experience 3, 7, 13
  disinterestedness 175
  Doyle's novel 52–6
  economic enterprises 87
  ethics and 231
  everyday narratives 25, 44, 174, 213
  Felski's metaphor 91
  forms of attention 139, 141, 148
  Frye's view 71
  Geistigkeit concept 73
  gimmicks 82–4, 185–7, 189–90
  healthcare 214, 249
  historicist recovery 40, 122
  human cultures 173
  interdisciplinary studies 120–1
  intergenerational notion 25, 164
  Kantian Enlightenment 90, 175
  keying structure 188–91, 235
  limit experience 155–8
  of literary studies 22–3, 34, 37, 59, 65–6, 69, 74, 81, 155, 162–3, 236–7
  of meaning 142
  of music 110, 129, 180
  nature of genre 176, 179, 184, 199, 245
  Ngai's theory 38–9, 83–5, 203
  North's definition 43, 193–5
  phenomenon of pain 52–3, 112, 140
  of well-being 250
  of wholeness 205
  Wittgenstein's 228, 231, 244
  worldly behavior 75–6, 82, 209
affective comprehension 55, 163–4, 169–72, 176–7, 179, 184
Almeida, Felipe 126, 138, 150, 215
Altieri, Charles 30, 56
Amaral, David 51
ambiguity 238–9, 243
  units of communication 243
American *Declaration of Independence* 2
Aristotle 59. *See also eudaimonia; phronesis* or practical wisdom
  theory of motion 103
Arnold, Matthew 11, 65, 81
attention and expectation 52, 101, 104, 139–41, 156, 160, 215, 219, 221–2
Atwood, Margaret
  The Handmaid's Tale or *The Penelopiad* 132
audience 22, 30–5, 52, 60, 66
Austin, J. L. 16, 20, 27, 29, 43, 77, 79–80, 93, 105, 118–20, 128, 147, 150, 152–3, 167, 199, 201–2, 206–8, 216–18, 224–5, 227, 229–30, 232, 241–2, 246
  "A Plea for Excuses" 151
  How to Do Things with Words 9

Index

Papers 21, 151, 202, 232
"Performative Utterances" 146, 201, 236

Bachelard, Gaston 19, 157
Bakhtin, Mikhail 151, 159, 164, 186
Bandura, Albert 213, 215
Barreca, Regina 157, 161–3, 189
Barthes, Roland 8, 92, 188–9, 198
    Camera Lucida 187
Benjamin, Walter 20, 26, 27, 67, 84, 92, 142,
    147, 187–9, 198, 250
    constellation 26
Berlant, Lauren 13, 48
biology 14, 23, 25, 56–7, 61
Blanchot, Maurice 159
boredom 147–8, 152, 218
Botha, Marc 195
Boyd, Brian 91, 174
    On the Origin of Stories: Evolution,
    Cognition, and Fiction 90
Bradbury, Malcolm 64, 200
Brody, Howard, *Stories of Sickness* 39

Casti, John 205
    Complexification: Explaining a
    Paradoxical World through the
    Science of Surprise 203
Cavell, Stanley 9–10, 12–13, 16, 20, 25, 44,
    51, 67, 79–80, 120, 146, 190, 206, 242
Chalmers, David 28, 47, 95, 152–3, 216
    The Conscious Mind 45–6
    dualism 45–6
Charon, Rita 8, 54
Chinese
    concept of happiness 2, 66
    culture and tradition 22, 67–8
    English language teachers 6
    literary and narrative arts 31–3
Chomsky, Noam 23–4, 245
close reading 8, 17, 19, 37–40, 65, 88–9,
    91, 139, 180, 194, 199–200, 219–20,
    225–6, 232, 242
Clune, Michael 4, 8, 18, 29, 36, 38, 40, 54,
    61, 67, 69–70, 74, 77, 79, 81–2,
    120–3, 134, 139–40, 156, 189–90,
    204, 209–10, 229, 236
    Writing against Time 70, 120
Coles, Robert 49, 232–3, 235
    Call of Stories: Teaching and the Moral
    Imagination 235
Comas, James 71

commensurability 11, 13–14, 106
commodity fetishism 82–3, 85, 103, 170,
    205
constellation 26, 42, 74, 187
construe 8, 11–13, 17, 21, 37, 93, 114–15,
    208, 231, 235–6, 239
consumerist capitalism 38, 80, 82–3, 86,
    122, 148, 187
Culler, Jonathan 18, 171
cultural studies 32, 46, 49–50, 89, 131,
    164
Currie, Mark 128

Damasio, Antonio 48, 50, 172
Damrosch, David, "Foreword" to *Anatomy*
    of Criticism 132
Davidson, Donald 62–3, 91, 111, 134, 234
    Essays on Actions and Events 61
Davis, Robert, *Contemporary Literary*
    Criticism: Literary and Cultural
    Studies 65–6
death
    aesthetic affects 185–9
    affective comprehension of 184–5
    blank tragedy 182–3
    and fearful laughter 177–9
    melodramatic responses 179–82
Declaration of Independence
    "pursuit of happiness" 2
Dedalus, Stephen 174
defamiliarization 8, 10, 70, 121–2, 140, 189,
    205, 221
    Clune's view 69–70
De Man, Paul 217–18, 225
Derrida, Jacques 128, 147, 170–1
disciplinary knowledge 11, 225–6
discipline
    action and work 214, 246
    of death 155, 157–8, 160, 164, 168–70,
    173–4, 176–7, 179–81
    deliberate 21
    different fields and culture 62
    experience analysis 108–10, 131, 138
    formal structure 26
    Geistigkeit 72–4
    of genres 184–5
    goal 5
    health humanities 87–98
    homology 108, 153, 234
    humanities 14, 24, 63
    of improvisation 9, 78–82

intellectual 5, 17, 74–5, 82–7, 102–4, 117, 148, 221, 247
keying behavior 237, 240–1
Kramnick's 225–6
literary studies 3, 6, 8, 12, 15–19, 22, 27–37, 56, 59–61, 153
literature and 41–3
nomological science 116
psychoanalysis 227, 249–50
of semiotics 114
social sciences 11
study of signification 112
three categories 67–72
traditional 194–7
vicarious experience 76–8, 193–7, 199, 201, 209, 215, 217–19
distinctive features 58, 131, 144, 159–60
Donne, John 149, 177, 181–4, 186
"Death Be Not-Proud" 180–2, 183, 199
double articulation 53, 56
aesthetic "experience" 55
language 51
double-take of literature
aesthetics 156–7, 159
Benjamin's citations 27
Classicism and Romanticism 4
deliberate discipline 21–2, 32, 50
Doyle's novel 53–6
flames 232
healthcare 3, 7–8
implicit features 238
knowledge and power 4, 7, 40
linguistic articulation 51
narrative genre 169, 171, 177, 191, 238
pain and happiness experience 53, 55
reflective afterlife 239
schematic elements 102–3, 108
scientific realism 14–15
simple opposition 241–3
structures of experience 5, 23, 24, 28–9, 49, 77, 122, 224
vicarious experience 213, 215
Wissenschaft and *Bildung* 41
Wordsworth's poetry 37
worldliness 20
Doyle, Roddy 54–6
description of pain 52–6
The Woman Who Walked into Doors 52–6, 89, 139
Dunbar, Robin 174

Edson, Margaret, *Wit* 163, 177, 182–3
Eliot, T. S. 14, 20, 199, 246
Emery, Nathan 51
Enlightenment 59, 73–4, 83, 90, 106–7, 117, 124–6, 195–7, 242, 248. *See also* post-Enlightenment
Enlightenment Modernity 57, 59, 106, 126, 195–6
ethics
action and 229–32
aesthetics and 231
neurological analysis 202–3, 206
eudaimonia 1–3, 58, 66, 187, 206, 209, 225, 238, 247–50
events
facts 10, 16, 43–5, 56–7, 105, 117, 120–31
purport 206, 208
whole and singular 206–7
experience
"action" and "acts" 58
aesthetic 3, 40, 44, 50–2, 58–9, 155–8
affective 25, 47–8, 55, 64
of color spectrum 142
conscious 46, 50
double-take 3–5, 7–9, 15, 20–3, 26–30, 32, 37, 40–1, 49–50, 53, 56
facts and events 43–5, 56–7
Geistigkeit concept 72–4
habits of thought 3, 13–14, 31–2, 34–5, 42, 47–8, 58, 62
hard problem 28–9
historicizing of 122
immediate sensations 11, 23, 45, 47, 57–8, 60
of meaning 3–4, 45, 92, 108–14, 142, 144–5, 152, 190, 205
Oxford English Dictionary definition 45
power of wealth 43
reading 8, 39
reality 14, 23
religious 110
representation 50–6
structures 10, 23, 48, 56, 116
undisciplined structure 26–7
vicarious 9, 25, 47, 49, 58–9
well-being 58

fear, social response 179
feedback 17, 32, 56, 92, 95, 97–8, 100–1, 124, 138, 223

Index

feeling 4
  affect and 12
  emotion and 50, 172–3, 210–11, 213–15
  experiences 29
  fear and awe 149, 182
  freedom 79
  impersonal 169–72, 245
  of joy 2, 66, 187, 249
  of life 121
  provocation 35, 111
  psychological theory 107
  readers 18, 145–6, 148, 181
  structures 9, 24, 35, 43–4, 47–8, 100,
    107, 114, 116, 140, 156, 161, 185–6
Felman, Shoshana 20, 30, 39, 105, 118–19,
  132, 148, 218, 226–7, 230, 236, 241,
  244–6, 249
  Scandal of the Speaking Body, The 147,
    242
Felski, Rita 9, 17, 50, 77, 80, 90–1, 98, 100,
  113, 126, 197, 199, 225, 246, 249
  Uses of Literature 50, 90, 98
Fenollosa, Ernest 133
  "The Chinese Written Character as a
    Medium for Poetry" 133
fiction 86, 90, 112, 213, 236–7, 245
  discursive arts 50
  fact and 7
  Kramnick's analyses 29
Flanagan, Owen 13, 48, 58, 107, 112, 126,
  142
Foucault, Michel 6, 9
Freud, Sigmund 73, 132, 152, 244, 247–9
  as "philosophical physician" 247–9
Frow, John 58, 161–5, 167–9, 173, 176, 184,
  186, 235, 237, 239
  Genre 58, 169, 176
Frye, Northrop 11, 23, 45, 47, 57–8, 65,
  70–5, 78, 90, 100, 112, 114, 116,
  131–2, 158–60, 164, 170, 185, 195–7,
  245

Gadamer, Hans-George 44, 56
Gagnier, Regenia 85
Geistigkeit 72–4
genre
  affective comprehension 169–76
  death narrative 177–83, 250
  diagnosis logic 160–1
  discipline 184–5

etiquette, language, and a natural fact
  164–9
first instances 176
irony 168
keying behavior 237, 239
keyings of reality 161–4
law and similarity 198–200
nature 158–60
speech 245
vicarious experience 215, 226
Godzich, Wlad 155–6
Goffman, Erving 161–2
Goldman, Alvin 18, 33, 39, 48, 89, 105, 115,
  227, 229, 233–7, 242
  *Simulating Minds: The Philosophy,
    Psychology, and Neuroscience of
    Mindreading* 18, 76, 90, 94, 107, 120,
    139, 162, 204–5, 209–14, 216, 222
Gould, Stephen Jay 91, 99, 103, 109, 134,
  197–200, 212, 225, 241, 244, 246
  "Evolution and the Triumph of
    Homology, or Why History Matters"
    199
  "Exaptation: A Missing Term in the
    Science of Form" 212
  *Wonderful Life: The Burgess Shale and
    the Nature of History* 99
Greimas, A. J. 51–2, 55, 63, 79, 89, 160, 167,
  203–5, 218, 243, 247
  *Structural Semantics: An Attempt at a
    Method* 63, 79, 243

habits of thought 3, 13–14, 31–2, 35, 42,
  47–8
  attention and expectation 139–40
  experience of meaning 58, 96, 100
  nature of value 119, 126–7, 131, 139–41,
    143, 150
  as primary emotions 156, 165–6, 171
  vicarious experience 193, 197, 208–9,
    211, 232, 236, 240, 245
Hamilton, Andy 25, 175
Han, Zhou 2, 66, 187, 249
Harbin Institute of Technology 7, 31, 63,
  65, 247
Harbin lectures
  bridge-building metaphor 67–9
  consumerist capitalism 80–7
  discipline as freedom 78–80
  discipline of literary studies 87–9

discussion of feedback 98–108
future-oriented nature of discipline 67
intellectual discipline 70–8
meaning and purport 92–8
objects of humanities 108–14
phronesis 89–92
resisting instinct 69–70
structures of experience 114–16
Hardcastle, Valerie Grey 48, 99, 101, 139
Myth of Pain, The 99
Harman, Gilbert
"The Inference to the Best Explanation"
143
Harpham, Geoffrey 22
Harris, Sam 48, 58, 75–6, 96, 104–5, 159,
186–7, 202–3, 206, 213–14, 229,
248, 250
*The Moral Landscape: How Science Can
Determine Human Values* 213
Hartman, Geoffrey 37–8, 229
healthcare
biomedical sciences 11
everyday narrative 39, 90, 166, 176
intergenerational caretaking 188
limit experience of death 156, 164, 177,
186
phronesis 7, 34, 193–4, 247
practices, goals and purpose 31, 34
primary end 214
professional education and practice 32–3
vicarious experience 219–23, 226, 234,
236, 238, 241
worldly work 3, 6
health humanities 3, 5–6, 11, 12, 19, 29–30,
39, 40, 48–9, 61, 63
Herwitz, Daniel 30, 93, 226–8
Hester, Casey 90, 234, 238, 240–1
"Enhancing Physician Empathy:
Optimizing Learner Potential for
Narrative Transportation" 234
higher education 41, 43, 61, 65, 82, 158, 196
imaginative writing in 41
Wissenschaft and *Bildung* 41
historicism 38, 40, 49, 164
Hjelmslev, Louis 12, 34, 55, 88–90, 92–4,
109, 112–14, 128, 139, 141–2, 144,
196–7, 199–200, 202, 215, 221–5,
227, 231, 246
Prolegomena to the Theory of Language
88, 92, 139, 141

homology 37, 87, 91, 95, 103, 120, 134, 162,
173, 187, 189, 197–9
interdisciplinary 234–5
Honda, Kiyoshi 180
Horkheimer, Max 57, 106, 125
Dialectics of Enlightenment 57
Huron, David 44, 48, 68–9, 91, 110–12,
114–15, 117, 139, 162–3, 172–3,
176–80, 182, 205, 212–13, 215, 235
*Sweet Anticipation: Music and the
Psychology of Expectation* 110, 163

images, philological "unpacking" 136–7
impressionism 30, 226–8
improvisation 9, 25, 64, 78–81, 140, 206, 242
incommensurability 11, 109
Industrial Revolution, second 60
inference to the best explanation 11, 62,
143, 161, 197
information 17, 33, 95, 107–8, 111, 119,
124, 145, 148, 152–3, 181, 204–5,
208, 211, 215–16, 233
instruction, scene of 10, 12–13, 30, 183
intellectual discipline 5, 17, 74–5, 82–7,
102–4, 117, 148, 221, 247
commodity fetishism 82–6
interdisciplinarity 22, 61, 247
interpretant 93
irony genre 168

Jacobs, Courtney 97, 169
Jay, Martin 6, 9, 25–7, 44, 56, 72, 74, 84, 91,
99, 103, 110, 142, 155–6, 175, 187–8
*Songs of Experience: Modern American
and European Variations on a
Universal Theme* 26, 84
Jefferson, Thomas 2
jokes 147–8, 178, 189
Joyce, James 18, 64, 178
Portrait of the Artist as a Young Man
159, 161, 166

Kant, Immanuel 49, 59, 76–7, 90, 156, 190,
205
aesthetic disinterestedness 175
Critique of Judgment, The 175
Kaplan, Robert 243–4
Keats 247
"When I have fears that I may cease to
be" 200

Index

keying 12, 55, 237–9, 242. *See also* construe
  genre and reality 161–4, 184, 186,
    188–9, 215, 235
Kramnick, Jonathan 15, 17–19, 21–2, 27–9,
    30, 33, 38, 44–5, 49, 54, 61, 74, 91,
    156, 211, 216, 225, 234, 236
  on disciplinary knowledge 225–6
  *Paper Minds: Literature and the Ecology
    of Consciousness* 70, 225
Kuhns, Richard 10, 25
  *Structures of Experience: Essays on the
    Affinity between Philosophy and
    Literature* 10
Kuhn, Thomas 9, 13–16, 19, 98, 102–4

language
  appraisals 145–53
  double articulation 51
  enactment of value 117–20
  examination of color 141–4
  facts and events 120–32
  forms of attention 139–41
  instincts and 69–70
  optical illusion 144–5
  systematic analysis 58
  Wittgenstein's "aspects" 132–9
Larkin, Philip 158
  "Aubade" 158
Latour, Bruno 9, 59
laughter 58, 110–11, 147–9, 163–4, 171–3,
    176–80, 182–5, 189–90, 212–13, 242
le (乐, Chinese for wellbeing) 2, 66, 187,
    249–50
Leys, Ruth 164, 169–71
literary studies
  aspects 56–9
  Chinese teachers 31
  critical revolution 1920 31
  cultural and aesthetic studies 49–50
  deliberateness 21
  discipline 21–2, 59–63
  dismissal of experience 149
  formalism 20, 33, 49, 164
  goal and purpose 5
  implicit values 31
  materialism 33, 34, 38, 46
  narrative genres 57
  negative science 241–7
  notion of *institution* 42
  politics of 33, 36

purport 22
reading 17–18
traditional 197–200
literature. *See also* literary studies
  concept and function 60
  discipline 41–3
  forms of 57–8
  healthcare, relationship with 2
  meaningfulness 4
  modern Western concept 41
  "practical wisdom" of *phronesis* 7
  worldly work 6
living well 1–2
Liya, Zhu 26
Locke, John 28, 83, 124, 131, 186, 248
  Essay Concerning Human Understanding 2
  A Letter Concerning Toleration 2
Lodge, David, *Small World* 132

MacPhee, Ross 103
Mahon, Derek 2
  "Everything is Going to Be All Right"
    190–1
Marxism
  Communist Manifesto 84
  literary scholars 82
  social analysis 38
  surplus value notion of 83, 186, 203, 206
Marx, Karl 81, 83–6, 125, 186
  Manifesto of the Communist Party 84
Massumi, Brian 169, 171
McFarlane, James 64, 200
meaning
  construing 115
  disciplined knowledge 67–8, 72, 76,
    91–100, 105
  events of sound 135
  experience of 4, 108–14, 126
  feeling 116
  force of 216–20, 247
  means of genre 163, 169, 171
  metaphor and simile 134
  and purport 136, 141–2, 149, 152, 160,
    244
  referential 224–5
  semantics 128–32, 240
  spaces 165, 193, 245
  surface 120
  temporality 144–7
  value 118, 150–1, 190, 198, 208

meaningful whole 160, 198, 203–6, 218, 223–4
Miller, Carolyn 176
Miller, Hillis 24, 41–3, 60, 66, 76–7, 92, 105, 126, 164, 176, 195, 203, 213–14, 230–2, 235–6
   On Literature 41, 60, 92, 126, 230–1, 235
   "Presidential Address 1986. The Triumph of Theory, the Resistance to Reading, and the Question of the Material Base" 105
Montaigne, Michel de, "Of Experience" 9, 26–7
Moore, George 33
Moore, Michael 24, 59, 62, 72, 74, 77, 108, 131, 141, 143, 149–50, 198, 202, 219, 229, 240
   Moral Reality 59, 62, 149
moral education 3, 35, 50, 58–9, 69, 98, 111, 201, 210, 222, 224, 235, 237
   vicarious experience 232–3
moral reality 59
Morris, David 51, 101
Morris, Errol 13–16, 19–21, 23, 51, 97–8, 101–3, 242
   The Ashtray (Or the Man Who Denied Reality) 13, 23, 102
Morrison, Toni 97
Moscoso, Javier 53
   Pain: A Cultural History 52
mouth gestures 178, 180–1

Nabokov, Vladimir 4, 82
narrative
   art 31, 90–1, 148, 175, 226
   clinical medicine 66
   death 155, 177–83, 188
   disciplinary rules 100–1
   discourses 3, 5, 8
   everyday 25, 90–1, 120, 219, 230, 235
   explicit and implicit forms 112
   features 17, 98, 110, 116, 122, 131, 160, 165, 173–4, 189, 194, 197, 216, 218, 221–4, 233–5, 237–8, 240, 247–8
   of feeling 145, 147
   film narrative 114–15
   genres 25, 57–9, 162–3, 167–9, 185
   health humanities 176
   historical instances 103
   literary 33, 50
   pain 52–3

personal reference 175
slave 97
unified 26
vicarious experience 209–12, 236
negative science 142, 196, 198, 246
   literary studies 241–3
New Criticism 19, 49, 88
Ngai, Sianne 23, 25, 33, 38–9, 48, 64, 82–6, 93, 141–2, 156, 170, 185–7, 189–90, 203, 236
   Theory of the Gimmick: Aesthetic Judgment and Capitalist Form 38
Nietzsche, Friedrich 17, 19–21, 91, 95, 97
   On the Genealogy of Morals, in *On the Genealogy of Morals and Ecco Homo* 95
nomological sciences
   biomedicine 34, 244
   commensurable phenomena 106
   definition 95
   facts and events 11, 16, 105, 117, 123–31, 135
   formulas 93, 116
   healthcare as 33
   homological transformation 92, 199
   human "experience" 11, 22, 24, 45
   humanities *vs.* 56
   intellectual framework 77, 88
   language model 96
   level of complication 17
   purity of 75, 205
   reading 18
   versus social and human sciences 98–102, 177, 196
   wisdom of *phronesis* 59
North, Douglas 42–3
North, Joseph 12–13, 19, 21, 31–3, 38, 48–9, 61, 65, 71, 74, 88, 156, 164, 193–4, 196, 225, 236
   Literary Criticism: A Concise Political History 31, 49, 65–6
Nussbaum, Martha 7, 20, 78, 193

Olberding, Amy 165–6, 171–2, 235
overtone 92, 106, 133, 135
Owen, Wilfred, "Dulce et Decorum Est" 223

pain
   affect experience 47, 55
   definition 46

Index

double articulation 56
historical and psychological evidence
     118–19
narrative recounting 52–3
non affective 48
notion of experience 45, 47, 50, 54
Routledge Series 46
vocal signal 51
Peirce, Charles Sanders 12–14, 36, 62, 68, 81,
     93, 112–14, 120, 124, 126, 140–3, 236
     logic of abduction 143
Pellegrino, Edmund 194, 214
Phelan, James 91, 175
philological philosophy 2, 6, 19–20, 134,
     137, 156, 194
philosophical physician 2, 6, 248–9
phoneme 51, 55, 58, 130–2, 139–40, 142,
     144, 159–60, 220
phronesis or practical wisdom 6, 7, 25, 30,
     34, 58–9, 66, 74, 78, 84, 89–90, 98,
     115, 186, 193, 195, 214–15, 219, 225,
     233, 237–8, 241, 247, 249–50
     disciplined experience 193–4
physics 11, 19, 23, 36, 57, 71–2, 74, 77, 79,
     81, 98, 114, 117, 125, 157, 170, 221,
     230, 241
poetry
     aesthetics 112
     definition 51, 67
     discursive arts 50
     genres 140
     Kramnick's analyses 29
     language of 147
     patterns or markings 68
     philosophy *versus* 10
     provoked experience 215–22
     semiotic description 51–2, 55
     structure of experience 56
     value 200
     Wordsworth's 37
Polkinghorne, Donald 67, 116
positive science 11, 14, 59, 196, 198, 241–2
positivism 15, 45–6, 57, 83, 106–7, 125–6,
     143, 150, 157–8, 170, 187, 196, 198,
     202, 215, 241
post-Enlightenment 125
Pound, Ezra 56, 91, 133
     in relation to "The Chinese Written
          Character as a Medium for Poetry"
          133

promise 26, 51–2, 55, 80, 116, 160, 167,
     179, 186, 189, 206, 241. *See also*
     Stendhal
     of happiness 2, 53, 69, 185, 189–91,
          246, 250
purport 9, 11, 22
     experience of meaning 75–6, 80, 92–8,
          104, 107, 109, 111–13, 115–16
     genre 160, 181
     Hjelmslev's view on 92–3
     keying structure 189–91
     literary studies 38, 51, 55
     nature of value 128, 136, 141, 145–6,
          149–50, 152–3
     neurological examination 94
     vicarious experience 196–8, 200, 206,
          208, 214–15, 231, 233, 244
Putnam, Hilary 57–8

Qian, Yingyi 85
Qian, Zhongshu, "Chinese Poetry and
     Chinese Painting" 26

reading (as a term of art) 17–18, 38–40,
     88–9, 199–200, 223–7, 232
     different ways of 102–4
Regan, Stephen 180–1, 199–201, 220–1,
     223–4, 227, 236, 247
     The Sonnet 199
reluctant realism 23–4
Richardson, Alan 211
Rotman, Brian 243–4
Russell, Bertrand 23, 157–8

Sacks, Oliver 93, 113–16, 139, 141, 157
     *Musicophilia: Tales of Music and the
          Brain* 93, 114, 116
     *Seeing Voices: A Journey into the World
          of the Deaf* 116, 157
Said, Edward 19, 58, 75–7, 106, 156, 206,
     221, 225, 250
Saussure, Ferdinand de 55, 62, 81, 88, 95,
     112, 114, 128, 142
Saussy, Haun 68
scene of instruction 10, 12–13, 30, 183
Schleifer, Ronald 2, 26
     *Analogical Thinking: Post-Enlightenment
          Understanding in Language,
          Collaboration, and Interpretation*
          106, 125, 134

Chief Concern of Medicine: The Integration of the Medical Humanities and Narrative Knowledge into Medical Practices 2, 40, 63, 66, 89, 91, 143, 149, 160–1, 167, 209, 247

Culture and Cognition: The Boundaries of Literary and Scientific Inquiry 167

Intangible Materialism: The Body, Scientific Knowledge, and the Power of Language 46, 79–80, 141

Literature and Medicine: A Practical and Pedagogical Guide 59, 89–91, 98, 109, 122, 141, 168, 177, 190–1, 218–19, 221, 224, 227, 231, 235

"Literature" for the *Encyclopedia Americana* 67, 237

Modernism and Time: The Logic of Abundance in Literature, Science, and Culture 188

"Modernism as Gesture: The Experience of Music, Samuel Beckett, and Performed Bewilderment" 180

Pain and Suffering 46–7, 64, 89, 100–1, 119, 140

A Political Economy of Modernism: Literature, Post-Classical Economics, and the Lower Middle-Class 26, 83, 87, 148, 165, 205

Rhetoric and Death: The Language of Modernism and Postmodern Discourse Theory 158, 185

"The Role of Narrative Structures and Discursive Genres in Healthcare Education and Practice" 59

scientific realism 14–16

Searle, John 57, 118–19, 125, 127–8
  Speech Acts 119, 127

semantic depth 72, 97, 155, 159, 198, 218, 239–40, 242

semiotics 20, 23, 34, 37, 50, 55, 62–3, 79, 81, 88, 91, 93, 112, 114, 121, 142, 148, 167, 170, 197, 203, 205, 243

Shakir, Mubeen 32, 58, 220

Shem, Samuel 182
  The House of God 163, 177–9

Shklovsky, Viktor 121, 189

Shouse, Eric 169

Smith, Adam 42

social construction 12–14, 55, 102

social institutions, definition 42

sound
  "brute-fact" nature 129
  quality of 133

speech-act theory 23, 25, 92, 105
  aesthetics 157, 167
  literary studies 56–7
  nature of value 116, 118–19, 127, 132, 147–8
  vicarious experience 199, 227, 229–30, 236, 241–2, 244–5

speech genres 121, 159, 164–6, 198–9, 226, 245. *See also* Bakhtin, Mikhail

Spiegel, Maura 8, 54

Spinks, Lee 169

Spolsky, Ellen 211

Stalling, Jonathan 95

Stendhal 2, 53, 69, 185, 189–90, 250

Stengel, Kathrin 228–9, 231, 244–5, 247

Stevens, Wallace 185, 247
  "The Plain Sense of Things" 184, 246
  "The Pleasures of Merely Circulating" 184

Stroud, Scott 213, 215, 236–8

Sweet, Sam 136–7
  "A Boy with No Birthday Turns Sixty: The Long and Tangled History of Alfred E. Neuman" 136

Taylor, Charles 13, 35–6, 42, 71, 76–7, 95–7, 101–2, 105, 118, 132, 165, 168, 223
  Sources of the Self: The Making of the Modern Identity 36, 42

theory of mind (ToM) 90, 107, 210–12, 227
  enactment of simulation 227–8
  literary studies and 211

theory of value 82–3, 103, 122, 186, 203, 205–6, 234

Trilling, Lionel 35, 39

value. *See also* theory of value
  habits of thought 119, 126–7, 131, 139–41, 143, 150
  meaningful value 5, 20, 46, 189
  purport 128, 136, 141, 145–6, 149–50, 152–3
  speech act theory 116, 118–19, 127, 132, 147–8
  surplus 83, 186, 203, 206

Index

Vannatta, Jerry 2, 40, 62–3, 66, 89–91, 122, 143, 160, 167, 209, 218–19, 222, 231, 238, 247
   Chief Concern of Medicine: The Integration of the Medical Humanities and Narrative Knowledge into Medical Practices 2, 40, 63, 66, 89, 91, 143, 149, 160–1, 167, 209, 247
Veblen, Thorstein 13, 31, 35, 36, 42–3, 47–8, 57, 62, 83, 87, 100, 118–19, 126–8, 138–9, 224
Vermeule, Blakey 211
vicarious experience. *See also* Theory of mind
   acts and events 201–2
   actual *vs.* 209
   as a discipline 76–8, 193–7, 199, 201, 209, 215, 217–19
   features 222–5
   habits of thought 193, 197, 208–9, 211, 232, 236, 240, 245
   healthcare 219–23, 226, 234, 236, 238, 241
   impressionism and style 226–9
   inferential reasoning 211
   in literature 210, 212–15
   moral education 232–6
   poetry 215–22
   professional training 219–20
   purport 196–8, 200, 206, 208, 214–15, 231, 233, 244
   real *vs.* literary 210
   redescription 214–15
   Social Learning Theory 215
   Speech-act theory 199, 227, 229–30, 236, 241–2, 244–5
violence 52, 76, 149, 160, 163, 217–20, 223–4

Wang, Tiao 20, 26, 31, 60, 63, 85, 126, 133–4, 148, 157
   Modernist Poetics in China: Consumerist Economics and Chinese Literary Modernism 31, 60, 148
Warren, V. I. "Feminist Directions in Medical Ethics" 39
Waugh, Patricia 9, 13, 15–17, 37, 102–3, 124, 195
Weber, Max 81
Weber, Samuel 78
Weiner, Jonathan 99

well-being
   Aristotle's view 58
   concept 1–3
   health and 7
   health aesthetics 249
   lived experience 58
   theory of value 186–7
   wholeness and 202–6
wen (文) 67–8, 113
Whitebook, Joel 6
   Freud: An Intellectual Biography 73, 248–9
wholeness 160, 202–6, 208–9. *See also* meaningful whole
Wiener, Norbert 152–3
Wikipedia 14, 29, 102, 123–5, 137–8, 148, 150, 242
Williams, Raymond 10, 24, 35, 47–50, 84, 100, 156, 215
   Marxism and Literature 47
   on "structures of experience" 10
Wittgenstein, Ludwig 4–5, 12–16, 18, 20–1, 37, 44, 47, 56, 62–3, 68, 77, 92, 109–10, 113, 118, 125, 144–7, 150–2, 181, 225, 231, 240, 250
   on aspects 132–9, 199
   ethics and aesthetics 228–9, 244–6
   Philosophical Investigations 132
Woolf, Virginia *Mrs. Dalloway* 162
word-instances, philological philosophy 20
Wu, Nicholas
   "Trump Compares Pete Buttigieg to Alfred E. Neuman of MAD" 138

Yang, Defeng 2, 66, 187, 249
Yeats, W. B. 33, 63, 150, 171, 182, 217, 220–4, 227, 231, 245
   "Among School Children" 217
   "Easter 1916" 185
   "Leda and the Swan" 1, 40, 76, 149, 200–1, 215–24
   Norton Anthology of English Literature, The 216–17
   A Vision 216

Zahle, Julie 99
Zhongshu, Qian 26
Zhu, Liya 26
Zuckerkandl, Victor 52, 55, 118, 124, 129–30, 132–3, 138, 153, 231, 245
   image of musical notion 129
Zunshine, Lisa 211